Jesus Christ *Fulfills* Messianic Prophecies

by

Victor Vadney

DESERT WILLOW PUBLISHING

Copyright © 2014

Jesus Christ *Fulfills* Messianic Prophecies

by Victor Vadney

Desert Willow Publishing. P.O. Box 7719, Abilene, TX 79608
http://www.desertwillowpublishingonline.com

Printing by Lightning Source, Inc.

Paperback ISBN 978-1-939838-10-0

E-book ISBN 978-1-939838-12-4

Cover by Desert Willow Publishing

Library of Congress Control Number: 2014904760

All rights reserved solely by the author. Except as provided in the Copyright Law of 2009, no part of this book may be reproduced without the prior written permission by Desert Willow Publishing.

Scripture quotations marked (NASB) are from the NEW AMERICAN STANDARD BIBLE, Copyright 1960, 1962, 1963, 1968, 1971, 1972, 1973, 1975, 1977, 1995 by The Lockman Foundation. Used by Permission.

Acknowledgments

First, I wish to thank God for His answers to my prayers. Although I have worked hard to write this book, I know that it is God who has given me the strength to finish this book, and I am sure that He has guided my way through it also.

Second, I wish to dedicate this material to Jesus Christ and His Church. I especially want to acknowledge and give thanks for Christ's rule over all His churches.

Third, I wish to thank all who read and made suggestions for my manuscript. Your efforts have vastly improved it.

Fourth, I wish to thank The Lockman Foundation for their permission for me to quote from the New American Standard Bible (NASB), including both the Old and New Testaments.

Fifth, I wish to thank you, my reader, for purchasing this book. After reading this book, I hope you will be able to rejoice with me that **Jesus Christ *Fulfills* Messianic Prophecies**.

TABLE OF CONTENTS

Acknowledgments 3
Preface 7
Introduction 9
    The Predictive Nature of Prophecy 9
    Prophets' Inspiration & Understanding 11
    The Old Testament 12
    Essential Historical Considerations 17
    The Controversy 18
    Messianic Prophecies Are Ancient 22
    Christ's Hermeneutics on Prophecies 25
    Implied Fulfillment 28
    The Critical Application & Fulfillment 29
    Context Is Very Important 30
Prophecies & Fulfillments 33
    Creation (Genesis 1:1) 33
    One Flesh (Genesis 2:24) 34
    The Woman's Seed (Genesis 3:15) 35
    All Nations Blessed (Genesis 22:18) 37
    Lion of Judah (Genesis 49:9-10) 38
    Star of the Messiah (Numbers 24:17) 39
    A Prophet Like Moses (Deuteronomy 18:15, 18) 41
    Hanged on The Tree (Deuteronomy 21:22-23) 50
    He Shall Be A Son To Me (2 Samuel 7:12-16) 51
    Against the LORD and His Christ (Psalm 2:1-3) 52
    Your Are My Son (Psalm 2:7) 55
    Out of the Mouths of Infants (Psalm 8:1-2) 55
    Not to Undergo Decay (Psalm 16:8-10) 57
    The Crucifixion of Christ (Psalm 22) 58
    They Hate Me Without A Cause (Psalm 35:19) 70
    Offerings Not Required (Psalm 40:6-8) 71
    He Who Eats My Bread (Psalm 41:9) 75
    Your Throne, O God (Psalm 45:6-7) 76
    A Word About Psalm 69 88
    Zeal And Reproach (Psalm 69:9) 89
    They Gave Me Gall & Vinegar (Psalm 69:21) 91
    Let His Homestead Be Desolate (Psalm 69:25) 92
    Jesus Spoke In Parables (Psalm 78:2) 94
    Angels Worship Him (Psalm 97:7) 96

You Founded The Earth (Psalm 102:25-27) 97
Let Another Take His Office (Psalm 109:8) 99
The LORD says to my Lord (Psalm 110:1) 100
A Priest Forever (Psalm 110:4) 101
The Rejected Stone (Psalm 118:22-23) 104
Blessed Is He Who Comes (Psalm 118:26) 106
The LORD Has Sworn To David (Psalm 132:11) 107
Isaiah Saw Christ's Glory (Isaiah 6:1-3) 108
Why Jesus Taught In Parables (Isaiah 6:8-10) 110
The Virgin & Her Son Immanuel (Isaiah 7:14) 112
The Rock of Offense (Isaiah 8:14) 117
I and the Children (Isaiah 8:16-18) 118
The Prince of Peace (Isaiah 9:1-7) 119
A Branch of Jesse (Isaiah 11) 129
The Sun Darkened (Isaiah 13:10) 133
Laying in Zion a Stone (Isaiah 28:16) 134
Healings & the Gospel (Isaiah 35:5-6) 136
Voice in the Wilderness (Isaiah 40:3-5) 138
Behold, My Servant (Isaiah 42:1-4) 140
Every Knee Bows (Isaiah 45:22-23) 146
Light for the Gentiles (Isaiah 49:1-13) 147
The Suffering Servant (Isaiah 52:13 through 53:12) 149
All Be Taught of God (Isaiah 54:13) 172
Covenant with David (Isaiah 55:3) 173
A House For All Nations (Isaiah 56:6-8) 174
A New Covenant (Jeremiah 31:31-34) 177
The Son of Man (Daniel 7:13-14) 179
70 Weeks & Messiah (Daniel 9:24-27) 181
Out of Egypt (Hosea 11:1) 185
3 Days & 3 Nights (Jonah 1:17) 186
Bethlehem Ephrathah (Micah 5:2) 187
Mounted on a Donkey (Zechariah 9:9) 188
Whom They Pierced (Zechariah 12:10) 189
Prepare Your Way (Malachi 3:1) 191
Turn Hearts of Fathers (Malachi 4:6) 193
Conclusion 195
Bibliography 197
Index of Biblical Passages 203

Preface

Although Messianic prophecies were well accepted by Christians prior to the emergence of liberal theology in the 18th century, these prophecies are now deemed controversial by many. The liberal, critical theologians contend that no Old Testament prophecy was fulfilled by our Lord Jesus Christ or His church. However, this denial is a marked departure from the understandings of the ancient rabbis who lived and wrote prior to the time of Christ. This is also a marked departure from the teachings of our Lord Jesus Christ as well as His apostles and prophets. Indeed, it was these men who were responsible for producing the New Testament books. Lastly, it is a marked departure from the understanding of the writings of the early church fathers.

This calls for a thorough study of the Scriptures, aided by the writings of the ancient rabbis and the apostolic fathers. Indeed, this approach will reveal that our Lord Jesus Christ fulfilled and continues to fulfill Old Testament Messianic prophecies in a manner impossible for any other human.

Fifty-eight Old Testament passages are analyzed with the emphasis on both their content and their relationships to the New Testament. In these we find examples of prophecies that only our Lord Jesus Christ could fulfill, prophecies that involve the Godhead, prophecies displaying typology, or prophecies that involve implied fulfillments.

The biblical text, used by permission from The Lockman Foundation, is the *New American Standard Bible* (NASB) in its most recent 1995 edition. This translation was purposely selected for this book because it explicitly reveals Old Testament quotations in the New Testament text. Once again, I thank The Lockman Foundation for giving me the permission to use the NASB in this book.

In regard to the NASB, the following should be noted:

1. <u>Italics</u> found in the NASB indicate words not found in the original languages but which are implied by them.
2. <u>Small Caps</u> in the NASB New Testament indicate Old Testament quotations or obvious references to Old Testament texts.
3. <u>Asterisks</u> in the NASB refer to verbs that are historical presents in the Greek text, but are translated with the English past tense in order to reflect modern usage.

A number of Old Testament versions in electronic format were used in this book to compare translations. Their abbreviations and names are found in the following list:

- ASV—American Standard Version
- CEV—Contemporary English Version
- DNT—Darby's New Translation
- DRB—Douay-Rheims
- ESV—English Standard Version
- GWT—God's Word
- HCSB—Holman Christian Standard Bible
- ICB—International Children's Bible
- KJV—King James Version
- NAB—New American Bible
- NASB—New American Standard Bible
- NCV—New Century Verison
- NIV—New International Version
- NKJV—New King James Version
- NLT—New Living Translation
- NRSV—New Revised Standard Version
- RSV—Revised Standard Version
- TEV—Good News Translation
- TLB—The Living Bible
- TMSG—The Message
- YLT—Young's Literal Translation

Introduction

The Predictive Nature of Prophecy

Liberal, critical theologians generally deny that prophecy is predictive. They will accept prophecy as being "ethical." But predictive prophecy is something they cannot accept, especially if it involves prophecy about our Lord Jesus Christ.

However, long ago God Himself revealed through His written word the predictive nature of prophecy. Moses' comments show that prophecy is predictive:

> [21]"You may say in your heart, 'How will we know the word which the LORD has not spoken?' [22]When a prophet speaks in the name of the LORD, if the thing does not come about or come true, that is the thing which the LORD has not spoken. The prophet has spoken it presumptuously; you shall not be afraid of him." Deuteronomy 18:21-22 NASB

In the following passage in Isaiah, God challenged the Israelites who were worshiping idols to make those idols show the predictive nature of prophecy. Of course, they couldn't do so because this element of prediction can only be accomplished by God, and through Him, by His prophets:

> **21** "Present your case," the LORD says.
> "Bring forward your strong *arguments*,"
> The King of Jacob says.
> [22]Let them bring forth and declare to us what is going to take place;
> As for the former *events*, declare what they *were*,
> That we may consider them and know their outcome.

Or announce to us what is coming;
²³Declare the things that are going to come afterward,
That we may know that you are gods;
Indeed, do good or evil, that we may anxiously look about us and fear together.
²⁴Behold, you are of no account,
And your work amounts to nothing;
He who chooses you is an abomination.
25 "I have aroused one from the north, and he has come;
From the rising of the sun he will call on My name;
And he will come upon rulers as *upon* mortar,
Even as the potter treads clay."
²⁶Who has declared *this* from the beginning, that we might know?
Or from former times, that we may say, "*He is* right!"?
Surely there was no one who declared,
Surely there was no one who proclaimed,
Surely there was no one who heard your words. Isaiah 41:21-26 NASB

God showed the predictive nature of prophecy again in Isaiah after reasoning with the Jews about their idols:

8 "Remember this, and be assured;
Recall it to mind, you transgressors.
⁹"Remember the former things long past,
For I am God, and there is no other;
I am God, and there is no one like Me,
¹⁰Declaring the end from the beginning,
And from ancient times things which have not been done,
Saying, 'My purpose will be established,
And I will accomplish all My good pleasure';
¹¹Calling a bird of prey from the east,
The man of My purpose from a far country.
Truly I have spoken; truly I will bring it to pass.
I have planned *it, surely* I will do it." Isaiah 46:8-11 NASB

Therefore, there is no biblical validity in the liberal critical scholars' claims that prophecy is not predictive.

Prophets' Inspiration & Understanding

This author believes that the Scriptures are inspired by God. The following two passages are true and cannot be ignored:

> [16]All Scripture is inspired by God and profitable for teaching, for reproof, for correction, for training in righteousness; [17]so that the man of God may be adequate, equipped for every good work. 2 Timothy 3:16-17 NASB

> [20]But know this first of all, that no prophecy of Scripture is *a matter* of one's own interpretation, [21]for no prophecy was ever made by an act of human will, but men moved by the Holy Spirit spoke from God. 2 Peter 1:20-21 NASB

In addition, the Old Testament prophets did not always understand the content of the prophecies that were given to them by God. For instance, Daniel did not fully understand all the prophecies given to him, and he sought clarification repeatedly (Daniel 7:16; 8:15-16). Daniel at times was unable to understand the vision at all (Daniel 8:27). Zechariah also sought clarification (Zechariah 1:19).

According to Peter, the Old Testament prophets tried to understand the prophecies about the Messiah:

> **10** As to this salvation, the prophets who prophesied of the grace that *would come* to you made careful searches and inquiries, [11]seeking to know what person or time the Spirit of Christ within them was indicating as He predicted the sufferings of Christ and the glories to follow. [12]It was revealed to them that they were not serving themselves, but you, in these things which now have been announced to you through those who preached the gospel to you by the Holy Spirit sent from heaven—things into which angels long to look. 1 Peter 1:10-12 NASB

From this passage, even the angels did not understand fully the prophecies regarding the coming of Christ.

Therefore, let us approach the issue of Messianic prophecies from the predications laid in the Old Testament passages as well as the fulfillments that are found in the New Testament. Since we know that the Old Testament prophets and even the angels did not fully understand the coming of Christ, we must rely heavily on the interpretations of those passages by Christ and His apostles. The liberal, critical theologians would never allow Christ and His apostles to interpret the Old Testament. Yet, if we desire to be true to the biblical faith, we must not only allow it, but we must prefer the interpretations of Christ and His apostles.

The Old Testament

The setting of the Old Testament is very ancient. The first five books written in the Old Testament were written by Moses in about 1440 BC. God informed Moses of even more ancient times than his own, and these were described in Genesis, the first book in the Pentateuch. Unfortunately, we don't have the original Pentateuch documents that Moses wrote. If we did have those original documents, they would be nearly 3500 years old. In the same manner, we have none of the original documents of the remaining Old Testament writers.

The preservation of those precious Old Testament documents had to be by the providence of God. Many times the Israelites drifted back into idolatry, beginning at Mount Sinai when God first wrote the 10 commandments on tablets of stone. The book of Judges bears witness to a time of some 300 years when God's chosen people did not know or obey God's Law. Indeed, it was by the grace of God that any of these writings survived the evil kings in both Israel and Judah. Even more amazing, we find these ancient writings somehow survived the destruction of Jerusalem by Babylon in 586 BC. At that time the Jews were scattered over the known world. Yet, somehow, God preserved His precious Scriptures. After 70 years in captivity, Cyrus allowed the Jews to return and rebuild Jerusalem. Ezra the scribe was known for his readings of the Old Testament Scriptures to God's people in Jerusalem. Truly it was by God' grace and providence that He preserved the Old Testament Scriptures through all the ancient times.

With the second destruction of Jerusalem by the Romans in AD 70, the Jewish Temple was completely destroyed, and whatever manuscripts may have been there were destroyed. Yet, there was a knowledge and a fervent desire to preserve the Scriptures wherever the Jews were scattered. They were the people of the Book. There was nothing like their Book in all the world. And God, by His gracious providence and grace, preserved the Hebrew Scriptures, even to this day.

Now I will consider three versions of the Old Testament to show how God preserved His message. This includes an examination of the Greek translation of the Old Testament known as the Septuagint, or the LXX, the Hebrew Scriptures found in the Dead Sea Scrolls, and the Masoretic Text.

The Greek Septuagint

If one comes across a New Testament passage that quotes an Old Testament passage, one will often find some differences between the Old Testament and New Testament passages in our modern Bibles. The reason for this is that nearly 2000 years ago, the New Testament writers routinely used the Septuagint, which is the ancient Greek translation of the Hebrew Old Testament. This is important because our Old Testaments today are *not* based on the ancient Greek Septuagint like the apostles used. Rather, our Old Testaments today are based on the English translation of the Hebrew Masoretic Text.

The Greek translation of the Old Testament that was accomplished at Alexandria in Egypt around 250-200 BC has been called the Septuagint for most of two millennia and was also designated as LXX. "Septuagint" was an abbreviation of the Greek title. The background to this translation included the uncountable numbers of Jews who were born, lived, and died in the Diaspora (that is, in countries outside of Palestine). The languages of these lands were not Hebrew and, as a consequence, many of the Jewish people lost their functional ability to read their own Hebrew Scriptures. The lingua franca during this period was definitely the Greek language and remained so for several centuries, especially in the eastern portions of the Roman Empire. Therefore, a great need existed among the Jewish people for a Greek translation of the Hebrew Scriptures, and this need was fulfilled by the translation of the Septuagint in Alexandria.

Although there are interesting legends about how all this came about, the following is thought to be factual:

1. The Septuagint was produced in Alexandra, Egypt, starting around 250 BC.

2. The Pentateuch was translated first, and the other books followed.
3. The Hebrew rolls that were the source documents for the Greek translation came from Jerusalem.

The quotations from the Septuagint that are found in the New Testament are from a very ancient manuscript, more ancient than any Septuagint manuscript that is known today. Aside from the quotations found in the New Testament, the oldest manuscript of the Septuagint that is known today is from an old Latin translation dated in the second century AD. The importance of the Septuagint is well described in the following quote:

> Its chief value lies in the fact that it is a VS of a Heb text earlier by about a millennium than the earliest dated Heb MS extant (916 AD), a VS, in particular, prior to the formal rabbinical revision of the Heb which took place early in the 2d cent. AD. It supplies the materials for the reconstruction of an older form of the Heb than the MT reproduced in our modern Bibles.[1]

Because the writers of the New Testament used the Septuagint, it was adopted by the Christians in the first century as their Old Testament. When the Christians started citing the Septuagint to prove that Messianic prophecies were fulfilled in Jesus Christ, the Jews became concerned that the Septuagint had errors and they abandoned the Septuagint as their Scriptures.

The Septuagint continued to be the Old Testament for the Christians until the time of Jerome (c 347-420). At that time, the Latin language was predominant over the western Roman Empire, and they needed a Latin translation of the Old Testament. Jerome accomplished that Latin translation. He first translated from the Septuagint for his Old Testament text. However, he later changed his mind and translated from the existing Hebrew Scriptures for what is now called the Latin Vulgate. Jerome met resistance in doing so and was accused of devaluing the Septuagint. Even Augustine was concerned because

---

[1] H. St. J. Thackeray, "Septuagint," in James Orr, John L. Nuelsen, Edgar Y. Mullins, Morris O. Evans, and Melvin Grove Kyle (editors), *The International Standard Bible Encyclopaedia, Volume IV* (Grand Rapids, Mich.: Wm. B. Eerdmans Publishing Co., 1939, 1956), 2722.

the apostles used the Septuagint, and Augustine thought that it was the only Old Testament version, apart from the original, that had God's approval.[2] However, Jerome would not back down on his decision to use the existing Hebrew Scriptures as the basis for the Latin Old Testament.

The Greek Septuagint continued to be used by the Greek speaking people in the eastern portion of the Roman Empire because Latin was not their native tongue. Even today, the Eastern Orthodox Church continues to employ the Septuagint in their studies of the Old Testament.

If you wish to read an English translation of the Septuagint, it is available in print and in e-books.[3] You will most likely be reading from the translation of document B (Vaticanus, at Rome, 4th century AD) since it has been adopted as the standard Septuagint text in all recent editions.[4]

The Dead Sea Scrolls

From 1947 to 1956, a number of ancient manuscripts were found in the region of Khirbet Qumran. These ancient manuscripts were found in the caves and were written in Hebrew, Aramaic, and Greek. Further manuscripts were found in other locations near the Dead Sea from 1951-1965. Among all these manuscripts, some were biblical in nature. Many scholars think that the people living in Qumran were the Essenes. It is thought that these people occupied that location from 150 BC to AD 68.

The biblical scrolls have been translated, and scholars have now been able to recreate the Old Testament as was used by the Essenes at Qumran. These scrolls are much older than the Masoretic Text that is the basis for our modern Old Testaments. Some current English Bible versions of the Old Testament quote from the Dead Sea Scrolls.

---

2   S. Angus, "Vulgate," in James Orr, John L. Nuelsen, Edgar Y. Mullins, Morris O. Evans, and Melvin Grove Kyle (editors), *The International Standard Bible Encyclopaedia, Volume IV* (Grand Rapids, Mich.: Wm. B. Eerdmans Publishing Co., 1939, 1956), 3061.

3   For example, the Septuagint hardback translated by Sir Lancelot Charles Lee Brenton (1807-1862) entitled *The* Septuagint *with Apocrypha: Greek and English* from Hendrickson Publishers, and also an English e-book entitled *Brenton's* Septuagint *Version of the Old Testament*.

4   Thackeray, "Septuagint," in Orr, *et al.*, *The International Standard Bible Encyclopaedia, Volume IV,* 2728.

Overall, the biblical Dead Sea Scrolls largely confirm the later Masoretic Text, which is the basis for our modern English Old Testament. However, some of the Dead Sea Scrolls read more like the Septuagint than the Masoretic Text.[5] For example, Exodus 1:5 reads "seventy" in the Masoretic Text, but both the Septuagint and the Dead Sea Scrolls say "seventy-five," as did Stephen in Acts 7:14. This confirms the need to examine all possible sources of the Old Testament in order to have the best translation.

An English translation that recreates the Old Testament as used by the Essenes at Qumran is now available in print and e-books, and is entitled *The Dead Sea Scrolls Bible: The Oldest Known Bible Translated for the First Time into English.*"[6]

The Masoretic Text (MT)

Before the invention of the improved movable type mechanical printing press by the German printer Johannes Gutenberg in 1450, all documents were copied by hand. Unfortunately, copying manuscripts by hand has always carried with it the high probability of introducing copying errors. This phenomenon can be seen in ancient documents, including biblical documents. The ancient Jewish scholars recognized this, and many tried to guard and preserve the Hebrew Scriptures.

As one can see from the Dead Sea Scrolls, there was not a strict uniformity between copies of a manuscript at that time. This problem persisted until the destruction of Jerusalem in AD 70. However, with the destruction of their precious manuscripts in AD 70, the Jews were all the more dedicated to guarding and preserving their Scriptures.

The ones most notable in their desire to guard and preserve the Scriptures were the Masoretes. This group of Jews did their most notable work from AD 500 to about 900. They are best known for their system of vowels and accents that they applied to the Hebrew Text. Hebrew was written with consonants only. As long as Hebrew was the mother-tongue of the Jews, they had no difficulty reading such a document since the vowels were naturally inferred. However,

---

5　Neil R. Lightfoot, *How We Got the Bible*, second edition (Grand Rapids: Baker Book House, 1963, 1988), 103.

6　*The Dead Sea Scrolls Bible: The Oldest Known Bible Translated for the First Time into English,* Translated by and with Commentary by Martin Abegg, Jr., Peter Flint, and Eugene Ulrich, (HarperCollins, 1999 for the paperback and 2012 for the e-book).

as Hebrew became less and less a mother-tongue for the Jews in the Diaspora, the vowels and the accents of the Masoretes made it possible for Hebrews Scriptures to be pronounced correctly.

The Masoretes were also known for their safeguards that could catch omissions or additions. They carefully numbered the verses, words, and letters of each book. They then calculated the middle verse, the middle word, and the middle letter. When the new copy was completed, all these calculations had to match the new copy, or the new manuscript could not be used.[7]

Time will only tell whether the differences between the Masoretic Text and that of the Dead Sea Scrolls will result in any substantial changes in Old Testament text in our English Bibles. However, the differences are not substantial, and no point of doctrine appears to be at stake. What is amazing is how little difference there is between the Masoretic Text and the Dead Sea Scrolls.

In fact, one can learn the message of the Old Testament from reading English translations of the Septuagint, the Dead Sea Scrolls, or the Masoretic Text. The reading of Isaiah 53 from any of these versions will still bring tears, sorrows, and joy to the eyes of a believer in Christ.

Essential Historical Considerations

During the first 900 years AD, the Jewish understanding of the Messianic passages was similar to the Christian understanding, except that the Jews did not identify Jesus of Nazareth as the Messiah in the Old Testament passages. Yet, both groups agreed that these passages were Messianic.

This shared understanding started to change with the Jewish scholar Saadia Gaon (880-942). He emphasized the concept of the simple, plain, or literal meaning of the Old Testament text.

It was the Jewish biblical commentator named Rabbi Shlomo Yitzkhaki (1040-1105) who truly changed the traditional Jewish interpretations of the Messianic passages. He was better known by the name of Rashi. In his commentaries on the Scriptures and the Talmud, he changed the interpretation of the Messianic passages that

---

7   Lightfoot, *How We Got the Bible*, 2nd edition, 90-93.

Christians used against the Jews by abandoning the traditional Jewish interpretations and insisting on historical sense interpretations. Rashi equated the historical sense with the simple, plain, and literal meaning. Thus, instead of the passage being messianic, Rashi reinterpreted the meaning to an Old Testament person or event. However, Rashi maintained the traditional Messianic interpretations of Jewish Scriptures where the Christians did not recognize these as messianic.

Rashi's approach revolutionized Jewish understanding of what they had previously considered Messianic prophecies. It also galvanized the Jews against the Christians' efforts to convert them using the Hebrew Scriptures.

Even more, Rashi's approach has had a profound effect on critical Christian scholars ever since that time. Initially, critical Roman Catholic scholars and later critical Protestant scholars were deeply influenced by Rashi's treatment of the Messianic prophecies.[8] Now the liberal, critical, Christian scholars have assumed all of Rashi's interpretations of the messianic passages in the Old Testament. The liberal, critical scholars treasure Rashi's understanding of these Messianic prophecies over the teachings of Jesus Christ, the Son of God, and over His inspired apostles and prophets who wrote the New Testament.

The Controversy

Therefore, for about the last 1000 years, that is, from the time of Rashi, the enemies of the biblical Jesus have tried in every way possible to abolish the idea that there were prophecies in the Old Testament which identify the New Testament Jesus as the long-awaited Messiah. At first this opposition was primarily from outside of Christianity and most prominent among unbelieving Jews and people of Islam.

However, during the Age of Enlightenment (c1650-c1800), another attack against biblical Christianity came from within, that is, from its own honored scholars. This movement was greatly augmented by the birth of Friedrich Schleiermacher (1768-1834), and he is called the father of liberal theology. He was given this title because he asserted

---

8   Michael Rydelnik, *The Messianic Hope: Is the Hebrew Bible Really Messianic?* (B&H Publishing Group, 2010), 112-128.

that the experience of God was subjective and introspective and thereby he made the Bible useless. Germany became the hotbed of scholars who were exceedingly critical of the Bible. This movement spread like a cancer over Europe and North America, and to this day its poison has gone out to the four corners of the earth, destroying faith in biblical Christianity.

For example, Dr. Paul Schwartzkopff, a professor of theology in Göttingen, Germany, who wrote more than a century ago, maintained that Christ had mental limitations, was not omniscient, but had a human rather than a divine intellect. Thus, Dr. Schwartzkopff claimed that Christ was imperfect in intellect. He offered three proofs of this as follows:

> Such assumptions of Jesus, as that David was the author of the 110th Psalm, or that he prophetically foresaw the Messiah, or that demons had a personal existence, might be increased by a multitude of similar examples. The first indicates a limitation of His thought with regard to exegesis; the second reveals above all an imperfect notion of the development of prophecy; the third has directly to do with the form in which He grasped the content of His revelation of God. The objective incorrectness of all three notions, however, evidently arose from Jesus' dependence on contemporary ideas both as regards religious and secular matters.[9]

What is the reason for this vast departure from biblical Christianity? It is a lack of faith in the New Testament documents. The critical scholars view the gospels as being without credibility because there are too many detailed observations about Christ. They view Christ's miracles as being impossible because there are no such miracles today. They view the Messianic prophecies in the Old Testament as impossible because foretelling is impossible. Therefore, their assumptions about the deficiencies of the Scriptures are the result of their rejection of the truth of the New Testament.

In 1891, Dr. Dewart wrote a treatise that was "a review and refutation of the negative theory of messianic prophecy." Dr. Workman, a liberal theologian of that time, had adopted this negative

---

9   Paul Schwartzkopff, *The Prophecies of Jesus Christ Relating to His Death, Resurrection, and Second Coming, and Their Fulfilment*, (translated by Neil Buchanan) (Edinburgh: T. & T. Clark, 1897), 5.

theory of Messianic prophecy and was leading many away with his false man-made logic. Dr. Dewart refuted Dr. Workman's logic. It is interesting that the basic issues of this debate have really not changed much since Dewart published his book in 1891.[10]

Liberal critical theologians continue to this day to attack the deity of Christ and the inspiration of the Bible. They, like most of the Jews who don't believe that Jesus was and is the Messiah, often say politely that Jesus was mistaken in His understanding, and that He was neither divine nor was He the fulfillment of the Old Testament Messianic prophecies. Furthermore, on this issue of Messianic prophecies, the critical theologians absolutely refuse to allow the New Testament to interpret anything in the Old Testament. They would much rather make up their own rules and interpret the Old Testament passages as meaning anything EXCEPT what Christ and His apostles said those Scriptures meant.

Therefore, at this point in history, Messianic prophecies, that is, Old Testament Messianic prophecies fulfilled literally by Jesus Christ, are controversial for many people. The present day critical theologians with their low view of Scripture deny that there are any Messianic prophecies in the Old Testament which were fulfilled by Jesus Christ. This position is very well articulated by Dr. John T. Willis of Abilene Christian University as follows:

> There is no unequivocal specific prediction of the coming of Jesus Christ and/or the church in the Old Testament. New Testament speakers reinterpreted and reapplied Old Testament texts to Christ and/or the church.[11]

The critical theologians do not believe that Jesus is the Christ (i.e., the Messiah), the Son of the Living God. They take this stance despite what Christ revealed about Old Testament Messianic prophecies. Indeed, Christ clearly said that the prophets wrote about Him:

---

10 Edward Hartley Dewart, *Jesus the Messiah in Prophecy and Fulfilment: A Review and Refutation of the Negative Theory of Messianic Prophecy* (Toronto: William Briggs, 1891).

11 John T. Willis, "Old Testament Prophecy," in *The Transforming Word* (Editors: Hamilton, Mark W., Cukrowski, Kenneth L., Shankle, Nancy W., Thompson, James, and Willis, John T.) (Abilene: Abilene Christian University Press, 2009), 66.

> ²⁵And He said to them, "O foolish men and slow of heart to believe in all that the prophets have spoken! ²⁶Was it not necessary for the Christ to suffer these things and to enter into His glory?" ²⁷Then beginning with Moses and with all the prophets, <u>He explained to them the things concerning Himself in all the Scriptures</u>. Luke 24:25-27 NASB

> **44** Now He said to them, "These are My words which I spoke to you while I was still with you, that <u>all things which are written about Me in the Law of Moses and the Prophets and the Psalms must be fulfilled</u>." ⁴⁵Then He opened their minds to understand the Scriptures, ⁴⁶and He said to them, "<u>Thus it is written, that the Christ would suffer and rise again from the dead the third day,</u> ⁴⁷<u>and that repentance for forgiveness of sins would be proclaimed in His name to all the nations, beginning from Jerusalem</u>. ⁴⁸You are witnesses of these things. ⁴⁹And behold, I am sending forth the promise of My Father upon you; but you are to stay in the city until you are clothed with power from on high." Luke 24:44-49 NASB

Not only these Scriptures, but our Lord Jesus Christ, when giving His defense of being the Son of God, invoked the writings of the Old Testament saying that <u>those Scriptures "testify about Me"</u> (John 5:39). He also specifically invoked the <u>writings of Moses saying "he wrote about Me"</u> (John 5:46). Hence, there can be no doubt that our Lord Jesus Christ understood that there were Messianic prophecies regarding Himself in the Old Testament.

In addition to Christ's explicit words, His followers clearly understood from the beginning of Christ's public ministry that He was fulfilling Messianic prophecies. A good example comes from Philip just after Jesus called Philip to follow Him. Philip immediately spoke to Nathanael the following words:

> ⁴⁵Philip *found Nathanael and *said to him, "<u>We have found Him of whom Moses in the Law and *also* the Prophets wrote</u>— Jesus of Nazareth, the son of Joseph." John 1:45 NASB

The attacks on the biblical record by the critical theologians have gone on for a long time. Indeed, this kind of theology has been present for about two centuries. However, the Bible-believing Christians must not admit this kind of destructive doctrine. We must remember that the Bible was inspired by God.

Therefore, it seems wise to study this issue carefully. Is the New Testament really wrong? Was Christ so misinformed that He erred in this matter, saying the Messianic prophecies spoke of Him when they really did not speak of Him at all? Are there really no authentic Messianic prophecies in the Old Testament at all? Did Christ and His apostles just make up everything out of thin air? Did Christ and His apostles mislead us? Or did they willingly lie to us? Indeed, this issue demands a very careful examination since the allegations of the critical theologians attack the veracity of the very founder of Christianity.

Messianic Prophecies Are Ancient

It is clear that the Jewish people recognized Messianic prophecies in their own Scriptures long before Christ was born. This is revealed in the following passage:

> **1** Now after Jesus was born in Bethlehem of Judea in the days of Herod the king, magi from the east arrived in Jerusalem, saying, ²"Where is He who has been born King of the Jews? For we saw His star in the east and have come to worship Him." ³When Herod the king heard *this*, he was troubled, and all Jerusalem with him. ⁴Gathering together all the chief priests and scribes of the people, he inquired of them where the Messiah was to be born. ⁵They said to him, "In Bethlehem of Judea; for this is what has been written by the prophet:
>
> ⁶'AND YOU, BETHLEHEM, LAND OF JUDAH,
> ARE BY NO MEANS LEAST AMONG THE LEADERS OF JUDAH;
> FOR OUT OF YOU SHALL COME FORTH A RULER
> WHO WILL SHEPHERD MY PEOPLE ISRAEL.'"
> Matthew 2:1-6 NASB

When Herod asked a question about where the Christ would be born, those Jewish chief priests and scribes immediately responded with a quote from Micah 5:2. Notice that none of these people who knew this Messianic prophecy were disciples or apostles of Jesus Christ, for Jesus had just been born. Therefore, this Scripture proves beyond any doubt that Messianic prophecies were recognized and well known by the Jews from their own Holy Scriptures prior to the birth of Jesus.

Alfred Edersheim (1825-1889) was born a Jew and became an outstanding scholar. Because of his studies, he became a believer that Jesus was the Messiah. In his book, *The Life and Times of Jesus the Messiah*, Edersheim wrote a number of appendices to his book, and in Appendix 9 he detailed a "List of Old Testament Passages Messianically Applied In Ancient Rabbinic Writings." His sources for these 456 passages came from "the *Targumim*, the two *Talmuds*, and the most ancient *Midrashim*" as well as the *Yalkut*, although that resource was a later work.[12] In his listing of the 456 passages, he gave abundant citations showing how these Old Testament passages were interpreted Messianically by the ancient Rabbis.[13]

These are not inspired writings, but rather they were ancient Jewish "commentaries" or explanations regarding the Old Testament. The *Targumim* were first an oral tradition, but later written down, starting in about the second century AD. The same applies to the *Midrashim* and the *Talmuds*. The *Talmuds* were considered to be the Oral Law, second only to the biblical documents.

The oral teachings of the rabbis most likely developed in their fullness during and after the Jewish captivity in Babylon. Prior to the Babylonian captivity, the Jewish people were exceedingly disobedient to God's Law, and this was the reason God sent them into Babylonian captivity for 70 years. The first deportation from Jerusalem was in 606 BC. The destruction of Jerusalem was in 586 BC. Never again would they experience an earthly king after the lineage of David nor an earthly kingdom like Solomon established. When they returned from Babylonian captivity in 536 BC, they considered themselves as slaves to the foreign power and not free people. It was out of this great desolation and loss that the oral traditions of the Jews grew and became so well known to all Jews everywhere. It is no wonder that Edersheim found so many Old Testament passages that the ancient

---

12 Alfred Edersheim, *The Life and Times of Jesus the Messiah* (New Updated Edition, Complete and Unabridged in One Volume) (Hendrickson Publishers, Inc., 1993), 981.
13 Edersheim, *The Life and Times of Jesus the Messiah,* 981-1010.

Rabbis thought were Messianic. Surely they were looking heavenward for their help.

Yet, the recognition that there were Messianic prophecies in the Old Testament must have gone back farther than the Babylonian captivity. As we will soon demonstrate in some detail, these Messianic prophecies reached all the way back to Creation. Peter, inspired by the Holy Spirit, wrote 1 Peter 1:10-12, and it was quoted at the beginning of this Introduction. According to the apostle Peter, the "prophets" understood there would be a Messiah. If so, which prophets? Jesus answered that the oldest writing prophet in the Old Testament wrote about Him and named that prophet specifically—Moses (John 5:46). However, this phenomena goes back further than Moses himself, for Moses wrote in Genesis of times and events which preceded himself by eons of time. The ancient Jewish Rabbis believed that the Messiah was present at Creation.

Therefore, since Messianic prophecies reach deep into antiquity, and surely are far more ancient than the birth of our Savior, it seems wise that we see the fuller extent of these Messianic prophecies so that we might all the more rejoice in what we find in the New Testament. Indeed, God spread the clues about His Messiah throughout the Old Testament so that men are without excuse. Even the ancient Rabbis are witnesses of this, for they found these treasures in the Old Testament. Therefore, let us survey the Old Testament Messianic prophecies and see the majesty of God's revelation about His Son.

This study will continue to use Edersheim's research which identified Old Testament passages that the ancient Jews considered Messianic as well as New Testament claims to Messianic prophecies. Where there are ancient rabbinic evidences, as per Edersheim and others, these will be cited. With each of these will be presented a discussion. In considering this presentation, no claim is made that this is an exhaustive list. Yet, it should be sufficient to convince Christians that there are indeed Messianic prophecies in the Old Testament despite what the critical theologians claim to the contrary.

Christ's Hermeneutics on Prophecies

How then are we to receive the Messianic prophecies from the Old Testament? First, it is very important that we study the Messianic prophecies in their contexts. Second, we must study the use of these Messianic prophecies by the New Testament writers. Third, we need to see that our Savior gives us specific instructions regarding how we should understand these Messianic prophecies.

Now there are three major categories into which these Messianic prophecies fall, which are described below.

Moses Wrote About Me

These prophecies are fulfilled only by Jesus.

Jesus Christ, the Son of the Living God, certainly makes claims on some Messianic prophecies. Besides saying that Moses "...wrote about Me" (John 5:46), He also claimed prophecies in the Law of Moses, the Prophets, and the Psalms (Luke 24:27; 24:44). Indeed, there are Old Testament Messianic prophecies that are fulfilled by Jesus of Nazareth and only Him. They are very important prophecies that teach us much about who Jesus really is, what He was called to do, and how He reigns on the eternal throne of David to this day. They are grand, faith-building prophecies about Christ and Christ alone.

Chief among the magnificent Messianic prophecies is Isaiah 52:13-53:12. This passage captured the heart and mind of the Ethiopian eunuch (Acts 8:26-38), and it has captured the hearts and minds of both Jews and Gentiles ever since.

As With The Father, So With The Son

These are prophecies related to the Godhead.

The eternal pre-existence of Christ is a major doctrine in the New Testament and is succinctly expressed in John's great prologue to his gospel (John 1:1-5).

> 1 In the beginning was the Word, and the Word was with God, and the Word was God. ²He was in the beginning with God. ³All things came into being through Him, and apart from Him nothing came into being that has come into being. ⁴In Him was life, and the life was the Light of men. ⁵The Light

shines in the darkness, and the darkness did not comprehend it. John 1:1-5 NASB

Jesus taught that "I and the Father are one" (John 10:30). He said, "He who has seen Me has seen the Father" (John 14:9). Jesus is called "...the image of the invisible God..." (2 Corinthians 4:4; Colossians 1:15). The unity of God is the very bedrock of the New Testament.

Knowing this, we should not be surprised that Jesus taught His disciples about His own preexistence in the Old Testament, of which the apostles learned through Christ's teachings while He was physically with them. The apostles continued to learn after Christ's ascension because the fulfillment of this promise:

> **12** "I have many more things to say to you, but you cannot bear *them* now. ¹³But when He, the Spirit of truth, comes, He will guide you into all the truth; for He will not speak on His own initiative, but whatever He hears, He will speak; and He will disclose to you what is to come. ¹⁴He will glorify Me, for He will take of Mine and will disclose *it* to you. ¹⁵All things that the Father has are Mine; therefore I said that He takes of Mine and will disclose *it* to you. John 16:12-15 NASB

This was accomplished through the ministry of the Holy Spirit and resulted in the apostles having "all truth" (John 16:13), that is, the perfect understanding of the Holy Scriptures.

Christ said that the Father is greater than the Son (John 14:28). Christ worked just as His Father worked, for whatever He saw His Father do, so He did (John 5:19). The Father Himself wanted all people to honor His Son, so the Father gave His Son the power to raise the dead and to give life. The Father gave all judgment to the Son. The Father did this so all people would honor the Son just as they honor the Father (John 5:21-23).

A number of Old Testament Messianic prophecies exist that are based on this principle of "as with the Father, so with the Son." For instance, when we look back and read a psalm addressed to the LORD (in Hebrew, YHWH), our natural tendency is to assume it was addressed to the Father. However, some of these psalms clearly have definite Messianic properties, and because of this, we must conclude that the preexistent Christ was also, at times, known as the LORD (YHWH).

This is completely consistent with Jesus of Nazareth being divine and eternally present with the Father before the beginning of time.

Something Lesser to Something Greater

These prophecies use typology or type fulfillment.

Although not as striking, this third kind of Messianic prophecy is important because it shows the glory of Christ. It is called "typology" since it compares something lesser to something greater. Jesus gives the formula using the sign of Jonah:

OT

> **17** And the LORD appointed a great fish to swallow Jonah, and Jonah was in the stomach of the fish three days and three nights. Jonah 1:17 NASB

NT

> **38** Then some of the scribes and Pharisees said to Him, "Teacher, we want to see a sign from You." ³⁹But He answered and said to them, "An evil and adulterous generation craves for a sign; and *yet* no sign will be given to it but the sign of Jonah the prophet; ⁴⁰for just as JONAH WAS THREE DAYS AND THREE NIGHTS IN THE BELLY OF THE SEA MONSTER, so will the Son of Man be three days and three nights in the heart of the earth. ⁴¹The men of Nineveh will stand up with this generation at the judgment, and will condemn it because they repented at the preaching of Jonah; and behold, something greater than Jonah is here. ⁴²*The* Queen of *the* South will rise up with this generation at the judgment and will condemn it, because she came from the ends of the earth to hear the wisdom of Solomon; and behold, something greater than Solomon is here. Matthew 12:38-42 NASB

In this passage, Jesus draws a comparison between Himself and Jonah and between Himself and Solomon. In both cases Jesus was "greater than" either of these well-known Old Testament characters.

Therefore, there are many "prophecies" that are structured as a comparison between some Old Testament person with Jesus. Whether the initial reference was David, Solomon, Jonah, or anyone or anything else, the comparison is to show that Christ was and still remains superior.

No person in the history before Christ, and no person after Christ's ascension has been able to compare with Christ in any sense of equality. He was ONE of a kind, and that oneness was superior and remains superior. How can anyone capture this Person with words? How can a man or woman fully understand the magnificence of such a Person? So humble, yet so powerful. So poor, yet so rich. So ordinary, yet so extraordinary. So simple with words, yet so profound with meaning. Again, how can one capture the very essence of this Person and describe Him with words? Yet, that is what the eye-witnesses of Christ had to do. One of their essential tools was to compare the lesser to the greater.

This is called "typology" or "type fulfillment." There was an Old Testament "type," and there is a New Testament "antitype." For example, the Christ of the New Testament was prefigured in the Old Testament. This "prefiguring" reveals a potent descriptor of Christ, and this process is called "fulfillment." The meaning of the first augments the meaning of the second. For example, the marriage relationship typified by Adam and Eve prefigures Christ and His church (Ephesians 5:22-33). There are so many more.

Therefore, with this framework of Messianic prophecies which are fulfilled in Christ alone, and also with multitudes of symbolic fulfillments in Jesus, we can be certain that Jesus is the Christ (Messiah), the Son of the Living God.

Implied Fulfillment

A number of passages inhere in which the biblical writers explicitly state that there was some fulfillment of Messianic prophecy in the New Testament context. In addition, there are other passages where the fulfillment was implied, but not explicitly stated.

For instance, in Peter's sermon in Acts 2, he quotes four passages (Joel 2:28-32; Psalm 16:8-11; Psalm 132:11; Psalm 110:1) from the Old Testament which were all Messianic in nature. He makes no explicit claim that these were Messianic in nature except for Acts

2:31 where Peter says that David "...looked ahead and spoke of the resurrection of the Christ...."

Thus it is certainly possible that a New Testament writer assumed the Messianic nature of a passage without using explicit words such as "fulfilled" to designate it.

The Critical Application & Fulfillment

Since we live in a world now where the liberal, critical Christian scholars do not believe what Christ and the apostles taught concerning Messianic prophecies, we must be alert when we look at Old Testament prophecies. Such scholars will constantly tell us that these so-called Messianic prophecies were *fulfilled* in some event or person in that Old Testament time and were *applied* centuries later to Jesus and the Church.

Indeed, we must be true to biblical context. At times we will see in a Messianic prophecy someone like David who is a type of the Messiah. Such a situation will often cause people to suspect a "double fulfillment," i.e., one with David and one with Christ. However, if that is our stance, then we have devalued what Christ and His apostles have taught us. Rather, let us reintroduce the ancient concept of Scriptural *"application"* and *"fulfillment."* At every occasion like this, we must have the bravery to call so many of these prophecies "Messianic" in the true sense of the word in order to be faithful to our Lord. Let us honestly say that these were real Messianic prophecies that were also *applied* at times to some person or event in the Old Testament. However, in spite of that Old Testament *application*, the prophecy was really meant for the Messiah and was *fulfilled* by Him.[14]

Inevitably, we must choose which of these will become our understanding of such Messianic prophecies. Which will you adopt?

1. The prophecy was *applied* to a person or event in the Old Testament times, but was really meant for the Messiah and *fulfilled* by Him. OR
2. The prophecy was *fulfilled* in a person or event in the Old Testament times, but was later *applied* by Jesus to Himself.

---

14 Dewart, *Jesus the Messiah in Prophecy and Fulfilment*, 191.

The first is *applied* and later *fulfilled* in Christ. This honors Christ and His teachings.

The second is *fulfilled* and then later *applied* to Christ. This honors the unbelieving critical scholars.

You must choose.

Context Is Very Important

Unlike modern manuscripts, ancient books such as those in the Old and New Testaments were limited in manuscript length for practical reasons. For instance, 5 Books made up the Hebrew Psalms: Book I was Psalms 1-41; Book II was Psalms 42-72; Book III was Psalms 73-89; Book IV was Psalms 90-106; and Book V was Psalms 107-150. To have written all the Psalms on one roll would not have been possible or feasible.

This consideration applies to the New Testament documents as well. For example, the Gospels are relatively brief and are not exhaustive biographies of Jesus. Rather, the Gospels concentrate on the last week of Jesus life, including His trials, crucifixion, death, burial, resurrection, and ascension. We know nearly nothing about Jesus in the thirty years before He was baptized by John the Baptist. That doesn't necessarily mean that such information was unknown to the Gospel writers. However, what was inspired by God and was written down by the apostles and prophets in the New Testament took all those factors into account. These documents are certainly sufficient for us today.

Many of the references to the Messianic Prophecies in the New Testament are brief. That doesn't mean that the Messianic Prophecies were not important. Rather, the references to the Messianic Prophecies were just enough to let the reader know that such things about Christ were written long before Christ's ministry on this earth.

In many instances, going back to the Old Testament reference will reveal that the contexts of some prophecies are relatively large. Incredible treasures of ever-expanding vistas that prophesied the Christ event in a much fuller manner are often found in these contexts. Although it is common now to find brief lists of Messianic prophecies and the corresponding fulfillments found in Christ, there is so much more that we should know about this subject. Therefore, I invite the reader to go deeper than that. That deeper look is what this book is about.

Come be amazed at the incredible nature of the evidence.

Prophecies & Fulfillments

Creation (Genesis 1:1)

OT

> **1** In the beginning God created the heavens and the earth. ²The earth was formless and void, and darkness was over the surface of the deep, and the <u>Spirit of God</u> was moving over the surface of the waters. Genesis 1:1-2 NASB

NT

> **1** In the beginning was the Word, and the Word was with God, and the Word was God. ²He was in the beginning with God. ³All things came into being through Him, and apart from Him nothing came into being that has come into being. ⁴In Him as life, and the life was the Light of men. ⁵The Light shines in the darkness, and the darkness did not comprehend it.
>
> **14** And the Word became flesh, and dwelt among us, and we saw His glory, glory as of the only begotten from the Father, full of grace and truth. John 1:1-5, 14 NASB

Discussion: This Old Testament passage does not immediately strike us today as being Messianic. However, when we discover that the ancient Jewish Rabbis before the time of Christ understood the "Spirit of God" to be the "Spirit of King Messiah,"[15] then we realize how John's great prologue to his gospel would have resonated with many Jews in the days of Christ. In addition, Paul's treatment of Christ and the Spirit is completely in tune with this same thought:

---

15 Edersheim, *The Life and Times of Jesus the Messiah*, 980.

¹⁷Now the Lord is the Spirit, and where the Spirit of the Lord is, *there* is liberty. ¹⁸But we all, with unveiled face, beholding as in a mirror the glory of the Lord, are being transformed into the same image from glory to glory, just as from the Lord, the Spirit. 2 Corinthians 3:17-18 NASB

This is a prophecy regarding the Godhead. It follows the principle that as with the Old Testament "Spirit of God" in Genesis 1:1, so it is with the Lord Jesus Who is the Spirit. Even the ancient Jewish rabbis connected these two thoughts long before the birth of Christ.

One Flesh (Genesis 2:24)

OT

²⁴For this reason a man shall leave his father and his mother, and be joined to his wife; and they shall become one flesh. Genesis 2:24 NASB

NT

³¹FOR THIS REASON A MAN SHALL LEAVE HIS FATHER AND MOTHER AND SHALL BE JOINED TO HIS WIFE, AND THE TWO SHALL BECOME ONE FLESH. ³²This mystery is great; but I am speaking with reference to Christ and the church. Ephesians 5:31-32 NASB

Discussion: The Genesis passage is indeed a mystery. In what way did God mean that the man and his wife would be joined together and become one flesh? How can this be? Certainly, marriage among the postmodern peoples carries no sense of this; for if a marriage or even more common, a sexual relationship without marriage, fails as it so often does in this setting, then how does the man and wife become one flesh? Even if they stay together, one man with one woman for life, and they have children as a result; how does the man and his wife become one flesh? Is it the offspring that are the manifestation of this "one flesh" as the child is the fleshly union of the gametes of the man and woman?

The Apostle Paul viewed this Genesis passage as a mystery. However, with the advent of Christ and His church, it became clear to Paul that the mystery of Genesis 2:24 was perfectly fulfilled.

Indeed, nothing aside from Christ and His church could cause full enlightenment. The oneness of Christ and His church is the answer to the mystery of Genesis 2:24. The ESV translates verse 32 as follows: "This mystery is profound, and I am saying that it refers to Christ and the church."

Although we would not ordinarily think of Genesis 2:24 as a prophecy that cannot be completely fulfilled except in Christ, it is easy to see why Paul considered it as such. Certainly, the fact that Paul was inspired by Christ and the Holy Spirit made this connection possible. It is another example of something that was prefigured in the Old Testament as a mystery but brought to full meaning in the New Testament. Typology is surely at work here showing the movement of the lesser to the greater; from marriage of a man and woman to the coming of Christ and His Bride, the Church. Christ Himself solved the mystery.

The Woman's Seed (Genesis 3:15)

OT

> [15] And I will put enmity
> Between you and the woman,
> And between your seed and her seed;
> He shall bruise you on the head,
> And you shall bruise him on the heel." Genesis 3:15 NASB

NT

> [22] Now all this took place to fulfill what was spoken by the Lord through the prophet: [23] "BEHOLD, THE VIRGIN SHALL BE WITH CHILD AND SHALL BEAR A SON, AND THEY SHALL CALL HIS NAME IMMANUEL," which translated means, "GOD WITH US." Matthew 1:22-23 NASB

Discussion: The word "seed" in Genesis 3:15 is from the Hebrew word which can be translated into several different ideas, but the two most common are "offspring" and "seed." The ASV, DNT, DRB, HCSB, KJV, NASB, NKJV, RSV, and YLT all translate this word as "seed." In addition, the same word can be translated in other contexts as semen (e.g., Leviticus 15:16), and this of course must imply that the ovum from the woman's ovary must also be considered "seed." It is important to see that God was speaking about Eve's seed and never mentioned anything about Adam's seed in this Genesis passage. Ordinarily, Old Testament genealogies refer to males in generations and usually do not mention females. However, this is a notable exception.

The passage goes on to say that there would be enmity between the woman's seed and Satan's seed. There would be some battle in which Satan would be defeated, but not before harming the Messiah.

Edersheim showed that the Genesis passage was considered Messianic in the days of the ancient Rabbis, and these Rabbis specifically thought that the "heel" in this passage belonged to the "Messiah."[16]

Since Matthew 1:22-23 refers back to Messianic prophecies in Isaiah 7:14, it may seem inappropriate to link this with Genesis 3:15. However, in Genesis 3:15, God is speaking only of the woman's seed, and this is completely consistent with the virgin birth in Matthew 1:22-23.

The largest New Testament context that is inferred from Genesis 3:15 has to do with the struggle between Christ and Satan. This began with Satan's attempted murder of the Christ child by using his wicked servant, King Herod. The next recorded attempt was Satan's three fold temptation of Christ after His baptism and during His forty day fast in the wilderness (Matthew 4:1-11). This was Satan's attempt to gain control over Christ. It continued with the Jewish elite and their growing opposition and murderous intent against Jesus. It culminated in the gravely unjust beatings, trials, condemnations, and crucifixion of Christ. Satan had struck and killed the Messiah, and he proved that the grave and the fear of death are Satan's most potent weapons against mankind. Or so Satan's power seemed to be so potent.

However, Christ arose from the grave, appeared to more than five hundred people over 40 days (Acts 1:3; 1 Corinthians 15:6), and then ascended to the right hand of God and thereby proved that He was and still is the Son of God, the Lord, and the Messiah (Christ). Because of this, the principalities and powers were disarmed and humiliated, and certainly that would have included Satan. Not only this, but Christ has delivered us from that fear of death through our faith in Him:

---

16 Edersheim, *The Life and Times of Jesus the Messiah*, 981.

14 Therefore, since the children share in flesh and blood, He Himself likewise also partook of the same, that through death He might render powerless him who had the power of death, that is, the devil, ¹⁵and might free those who through fear of death were subject to slavery all their lives. Hebrews 2:14-15 NASB

Therefore, Christ wins and wins big. However, Satan loses big and is enraged because he knows his time is short (Revelation 12:12).

This is an example of typology. The "woman's seed" of Genesis 3:15 prefigures the virgin birth of Christ in the New Testament.

All Nations Blessed (Genesis 22:18)

OT

"¹⁸In your seed all the nations of the earth shall be blessed, because you have obeyed My voice." Genesis 22:18 NASB (see also Genesis 12:3)

NT

"²⁵It is you who are the sons of the prophets and of the covenant which God made with your fathers, saying to Abraham, 'AND IN YOUR SEED ALL THE FAMILIES OF THE EARTH SHALL BE BLESSED'." Acts 3:25 NASB

Discussion: When Peter referred to this Old Testament passage, he was preaching his second sermon and was addressing Jews. In Acts 3:26, Peter made it clear that this passage was fulfilled by God sending Jesus first to bless the Jews through the avenue of repentance. Certainly, the gospel of Christ became a source of blessing among all their remaining tribes. Many Jews throughout the Roman Empire heard the gospel and became Christians in the first century. It is clear from Acts that Jews, because of their knowledge of Scriptures, often became prominent leaders in the church even when the church was more Gentile than Jewish. However, this was only the beginning.

As the gospel spread, millions of diverse peoples believed and even now believe in the historical Lord Jesus Christ. The influence of our Lord Jesus Christ in this world is profound, and there are now few nations who do not have believers within their borders. A nation does not exist that has not, in its history, been blessed because of the Messiah, for He is that unique offspring of Abraham.

Has there ever been in the history of the nations anyone from the lineage of Abraham who has had a more positive and a more beneficial influence on all the families of the earth? If so, who is that person? There has been no other person besides Christ who has had such a civilizing effect on the nations and on individuals. No person can even approach Jesus of Nazareth in this comparison because He is the Messiah through whom all the nations have been blessed.

This is a direct fulfillment of prophecy because only Christ brought blessings to all the nations. There is no descendent of Abraham other than our Lord Jesus Christ who has accomplished this.

Edersheim showed that this passage was considered Messianic in the days of the ancient Rabbis.[17]

Lion of Judah (Genesis 49:9-10)

OT

[9]"Judah is a lion's whelp;
From the prey, my son, you have gone up.
He couches, he lies down as a lion,
And as a lion, who dares rouse him up?
[10]"The scepter shall not depart from Judah,
Nor the ruler's staff from between his feet,
Until Shiloh comes,
And to him *shall be* the obedience of the peoples." Genesis 49:9-10 NASB (see also Isaiah 11:10)

NT

[4]Then I *began* to weep greatly because no one was found worthy to open the book or to look into it; [5]and one of the elders *said to me, "Stop weeping; behold, the Lion that is from the tribe of Judah, the Root of David, has overcome so as to open the book and its seven seals." Revelation 5:4-5 NASB (see also Hebrews 7:14; Romans 15:12; Revelation 22:16)

---

17 Edersheim, *The Life and Times of Jesus the Messiah,* 982.

Discussion: The Messiah would be the Lion, the King. "And to Him shall be the obedience of the peoples." Surely to some extent this describes Judah and his lineage, especially including the kings of Israel. Of course, Jesus was from the royal lineage of Judah as well (Matthew 1:1-17; Luke 1:27). The question is; what Jew from the lineage of Judah had commanded the greatest "obedience of the peoples?" The Israelites destroyed many Gentiles in Palestine when they came into the land. David and Solomon commanded many Gentiles.

However, their records are nothing compared to what our Lord Jesus Christ has done. Although others fulfilled in some respect this prophecy, our Lord Jesus Christ has greatly surpassed them all. Has someone been overlooked? Is there another Jew from the lineage of Judah to whom the Gentiles have given their obedience in a greater measure than to Christ? Therefore, only Christ can be the ultimate and direct fulfillment of this prophecy.

Edersheim showed that Genesis 49:9-10 were Messianic in the days of the ancient rabbis.[18]

Star of the Messiah (Numbers 24:17)

OT

¹⁷"I see him, but not now;
I behold him, but not near;
<u>A star shall come forth from Jacob,</u>
A scepter shall rise from Israel,
And shall crush through the forehead of Moab,
And tear down all the sons of Sheth. Numbers 24:17 NASB

NT

1 Now after Jesus was born in Bethlehem of Judea in the days of Herod the king, magi from the east arrived in Jerusalem, saying, ²"Where is He who has been born King of the Jews? For <u>we saw His star</u> in the east and have come to worship Him." Matthew 2:1-2 NASB

---

18 Edersheim, *The Life and Times of Jesus the Messiah*, 982-983.

16 "I, Jesus, have sent My angel to testify to you these things for the churches. I am the root and the descendant of David, the bright morning star." Revelation 22:16 NASB (see also 2 Peter 1:19)

Discussion: Certainly both Christ and the apostles were aware of this teaching because John quoted Jesus as saying He was the "bright morning star" (Revelation 22:16). Peter seems to refer to it as well in 2 Peter 1:19. The star was the sign of the coming of the Messiah, and the scepter was the symbol of kingly rule that He would exercise. Indeed, John calls Christ the King of Kings and Lord of Lords (Revelation 17:14; 19:16). Christ now sits upon the eternal throne of David (Luke 1:32-33) and has been reigning for nearly 2000 years.

So what was this star that the magi saw which caused them to come so far to see the "King of the Jews?" It is certainly possible that they were familiar with Balaam's prophecy in Numbers 24:17, especially since this verse was known among the ancient Rabbis as pointing to the Messiah. The magi must have known that there was something special in the sky, and that could only mean that the person born under this sign was none other than the Messiah. There are many speculations about the star. If God wanted to use natural phenomena, there were certainly star alignments, as well as comets, that were stunning around the time of Jesus' birth. But these magi, who evidently were astrologers, didn't leave us any notes to tell us. Therefore, it remains a mystery.

Now in regards to Jesus fulfilling Balaam's prophecy, which Jewish king reigned over Israel the longest and had the greatest impact? There is not one except Christ, and His reign on David's throne has now spanned nearly 2000 years. Certainly Jesus Christ should take the first place—surely He was and is the star from Jacob.

The last part of Numbers 24:17 and all of verse 18 speak of the retribution that the Messiah will take against the enemies of Israel. The critics say that Jesus of Nazareth did not bring this kind of deliverance, so He cannot be the Messiah. However, consider history well and answer these questions: Where are the people of Moab now? Where do the sons of Sheth live? Where are the inhabitants of ancient Edom? Where can you find the people who inhabited Seir? What happened to them? Were they not all killed or taken away? Oh, critical theologians who love to attack the Christ, have you taken no note of what King Messiah has been doing over the last 2000 years?

Edersheim shows that there were multiple references from the ancient Rabbis who attribute Numbers 24:17 to the coming of the Messiah.[19]

A Prophet Like Moses (Deuteronomy 18:15, 18)

OT

>**15** "The LORD your God will raise up for you <u>a prophet like me</u> from among you, from your countrymen, you shall listen to him." Deuteronomy 18:15 NASB

>[18]"'I will raise up <u>a prophet from among their countrymen like you</u>, and I will put My words in his mouth, and he shall speak to them all that I command him'." Deuteronomy 18:18 NASB

NT

>[22]Moses said, 'THE LORD GOD WILL RAISE UP FOR YOU A PROPHET LIKE ME FROM YOUR BRETHREN; TO HIM YOU SHALL GIVE HEED to everything He says to you. [23]And it will be that every soul that does not heed that prophet shall be utterly destroyed from among the people.' Acts 3:22-23 NASB (see also Acts 7:37)

Discussion: It appears that the last portion of Acts 3:22 is alluding to Deuteronomy 18:19.

This well-known passage was quoted by both Peter (Acts 3:22) and Stephen (Acts 7:37) as representing a Messianic prophecy. However, the critical theologians say this Old Testament Scripture did not uniquely point to Jesus of Nazareth, but was instead a prophecy that covered all the prophets. Indeed, the singular "a prophet" in this passage is similar in construction to "a king" in Deuteronomy 17:14-20, and thus, grammatically, "a prophet" can represent any of the prophets after Moses. Nevertheless, the text poses a severe limiting factor in the text that greatly restricts who this prophet could

---

19   Edersheim, *The Life and Times of Jesus the Messiah*, 984.

be. Moses said in Deuteronomy 18:15, "a prophet like me." God said to Moses in Deuteronomy 18:18, "a prophet like you." The prophet would have to be "like Moses." Yet, the uniqueness of Moses was extreme, and certainly not all prophets could possibly be a prophet like Moses. The incredible task of being "like Moses" is clearly portrayed in the closing verses of Deuteronomy:

> **9** Now Joshua the son of Nun was filled with the spirit of wisdom, for Moses had laid his hands on him; and the sons of Israel listened to him and did as the LORD had commanded Moses. ¹⁰Since that time no prophet has risen in Israel like Moses, whom the LORD knew face to face, ¹¹for all the signs and wonders which the LORD sent him to perform in the land of Egypt against Pharaoh, all his servants, and all his land, ¹²and for all the mighty power and for all the great terror which Moses performed in the sight of all Israel. Deuteronomy 34:9-12 NASB

We don't know when to date this section of Deuteronomy since it appears that someone besides Moses had to write of Moses' death. However, that is academic and really doesn't matter. The point is that none of the prophets who followed Moses were "like Moses."

Burton Coffman did an excellent job of delineating the uniqueness of Moses in his Commentary:

> (1) in the mighty signs and wonders; (2) in his being the mediator of a Covenant; (3) who knew directly from God what was indeed the divine will; and (4) who actually led the people out of bondage.[20]

Therefore, this situation demands a reasonable answer concerning which prophet or prophets were indeed "a prophet like Moses." First, we should observe that God destroyed those in the desert who thought they were equal to Moses. This was described as Korah's rebellion and it is found in Numbers 16. After this we find no one in the Old Testament who claimed equality with Moses. Now let us ask, which

---

20 Burton Coffman, *Coffman Commentaries on the Old and New Testaments*. This reference is from Coffman's comments on Deuteronomy 34. Coffman Commentaries are available to freely view on the Internet: http://www.studylight.org/com/bcc/view.cgi?book=de&chapter=034.

prophet in the Bible was either equal or superior to Moses in the four paradigms that Coffman delineated above?

Mighty Signs and Wonders

The incredible miracles of Moses in Egypt and in the desert wanderings for 40 years are impressive indeed. The first miraculous signs of Moses were given by God at the burning bush. They include the reversible signs of the staff that became a serpent and the leprous hand. He also was given the power to turn the water of the Nile into blood. (Exodus 4:1-9). The miraculous plagues that Moses as God's prophet wrought were as follows:

1. Water Turned to Blood (Exodus 7:14ff)
2. Frogs (Exodus 8:1ff)
3. Gnats (Exodus 8:16ff)
4. Flies (or "insects") (Exodus 8:20ff)
5. Egyptian Livestock Die (Exodus 9:1ff)
6. Boils (Exodus 9:8ff)
7. Hail (Exodus 9:18ff)
8. Locusts (Exodus 10:1ff)
9. Darkness (Exodus 10:21ff)
10. Death of the Firstborn (Exodus 13:15-16)

In addition to the incredible miracles that essentially destroyed Egypt, God's amazing miracle, through Moses, of the dry crossing of the Red Sea by Israel was divine deliverance (Exodus 14:13ff). However, the same was utter destruction by water for Pharaoh and his army (Exodus 14:26-29; Psalm 135:9; 136:15) when they tried to cross the Red Sea. Bitter waters were made sweet (Exodus 15:22ff), manna was the bread from heaven (Exodus 16:1ff), water gushed from the rock (Exodus 17:1ff), and God's glory filled the tent of meeting (Exodus 40:34ff). It was through Moses that the people received such signs as the cloud by day and the fire by night, clothes that did not wear out during the 40 years of wandering, and the brazen serpent that was lifted up so they might be saved from the bites of the deadly vipers. Are there any Old Testament prophets who could perform the mighty signs and wonders that Moses did? Was he not unique in the Old Testament?

How then did Jesus measure up to Moses in regards to mighty signs and wonders? I count 59 mighty signs and wonders associated with Him.[21] God brought forth miracles before the conception of Jesus. The miraculous conception of Jesus was indeed a unique miracle. God brought forth miracles during His gestation. God brought forth miracles during His infancy. Most of all, Jesus performed countless miracles during His ministry. Jesus performed miracles even while He was on the cross. Jesus healed any and every malady, whether physical or spiritual. Jesus had power to change physical substance from one thing into another (John 2:1-11). Jesus took a small amount of food and fed thousands of people with it and even have an abundance left over. Jesus walked on water. Jesus calmed a raging storm with two words. Jesus raised the dead. Jesus cast out demons. Christ's foremost miracles were shown in His own resurrection from the dead and His own miraculous ascension. Indeed, Christ said that His Father had given Him the authority to lay His life down, and also the authority to take it up again. Was Moses able to do these things? Did not Christ do so much more regarding miracles than Moses?

Therefore, there was no one in the Old Testament who could be "a prophet like Moses" in regard to working mighty signs and wonders "like Moses." Only Jesus could answer the description of "a prophet like Moses" in regard to mighty works and wonders. Furthermore, there can be no doubt that Jesus far exceeded Moses in this regard.

The Mediator of a Covenant with God

Moses was the mediator of God's Covenant with the Israelites. Moses' role in this was so central that this covenant is often called the "Mosaic Covenant," although it was not referred to as such in the Bible. In New Testament terms, it was the "old" covenant, whereas the "new" covenant is that which was revealed by Christ and His apostles.

The Mosaic Covenant occupied the vast majority of the Old Testament. It started in the book of Exodus, and it continued through and even after the book of Malachi. As we look closely at all the prophets in the Old Testament, it is clear than none of them brought a covenant that nullified the covenant given by God to Moses. Rather, God continued to expect the terms of His Covenant with the Israelites

---

21 Victor Vadney, *God's Covenants and Restorations* (Abilene: Desert Willow Publishing, 2011), 90-92.

to be in force regardless of changes in culture. Although God's Covenant with David occurred after God's Covenant with Israel, His covenant with David in no way changed the terms of the Mosaic Covenant.

However, Jeremiah (Jeremiah 31:31-34) prophesied that there would be a "new covenant" that would not be like the Mosaic Covenant. In this "new covenant" God would place His law within their hearts, and they would all know God. The people in this covenant would not have to be taught to "know the LORD," because they all would know Him. This means no one could get into this covenant without faith. No one could be physically born into this covenant because all in this covenant would know God. In this "new covenant," God would forgive their iniquity and sins.

The only covenant given for all people is found in the New Testament, and it is the Covenant that is through our Lord Jesus Christ. Unlike the Old Covenant, the New Covenant is for all people, in all places, and at all times. The New Covenant is very different from the Old Covenant. First, it is based on what Christ taught (Matthew 28:20; John 14:6) as well as what His apostles taught (John 15:20; 16:13-14). John portrays dramatically the difference between the persons and the covenants in the following:

> [17]For the Law was given through Moses; grace and truth were realized through Jesus Christ. John 1:17 NASB

Because of the extraordinary meanings of Christ's atoning death on the cross and His victorious resurrection from the dead, the continuance of the Mosaic Covenant became impossible. The following will show this.

First, Jesus bore our sins in His body on the tree (1 Peter 2:24), and by the shedding of His blood, He procured for us eternal redemption which is the forgiveness of our sins (Romans 3:24; Ephesians 1:7; Colossians 1:14; Hebrews 9:12). So Christ died as the offering for all people—all people of that time, all people who had ever lived, and all people who would ever live. Yet, no human sacrifice was allowed in the Mosaic Covenant. If Christ is the eternal atoning sacrifice for all who have faith in Him, then there must be a change in the Mosaic Law.

Jesus Christ became the High Priest of all those in the New Covenant. He became a High Priest after the order of Melchizedek (Psalm 110:4; Hebrews 5:6, 10; 6:20; 7:11, 17). However, there were no priests after the order of Melchizedek in the Mosaic Covenant that God gave to the Israelites at Mount Sinai. Rather, all the priesthood had to come from the tribe of Levi, and more specifically, from the lineage of Aaron. Yet Christ was not from the lineage of Levi/Aaron, but was from the lineage of Judah. Therefore, in order for the Lord Jesus Christ to become our eternal High Priest, there must have been a change in God's Law (Hebrews 7:12).

Not only the High Priest, but also the entire priesthood was completely changed by the coming of Jesus. As mentioned above, the priesthood was strictly limited in the Mosaic Covenant. Not just any Israelite could become a priest according to that Law. Rather, only those who were in the lineage of Levi/Aaron could be priests. However, in the New Covenant, all those who come to Jesus are priests (1 Peter 2:9; Revelation 1:6; 5:10; 20:6).

Jesus Himself in His Sermon on the Mount (Matthew 5:1-7:28) said He came to "fulfill" the Law (Matthew 5:17). For example, He deepened our understanding of the sixth commandment, namely, "You shall not murder," by showing that we will be judged for anger or insults we display (Matthew 5:21-26).

Jesus deepened our understanding of the seventh commandment, namely, "You shall not commit adultery," by showing that we must not even tolerate lust in our lives (Matthew 5:27-30). When we read these now, we realize that Jesus truly did change the sixth and seventh commands by making them more inclusive.

Further, Jesus imposes a serious limitation on the Mosaic Law of divorce by saying that the only approved reason for divorce is adultery (Matthew 5:31-32). Jesus also struck down the Mosaic Law of Oaths (Leviticus 19:12; Numbers 30:2; Deuteronomy 23:21; Ecclesiastes 5:4) by prohibiting oaths (Matthew 5:33-37).

In addition, in Matthew 5:43-48 Jesus also struck down the Mosaic Law of retaliation (Exodus 21:24; Leviticus 24:20; Deuteronomy 19:21) by forbidding retaliation.

Jesus also struck down the Jewish practice of hating one's enemies (Matthew 5:43-48). Although there does not appear to be a straightforward command in the Mosaic Law that one should hate his

A Prophet Like Moses (Deuteronomy 18:15, 18)

or her enemies, it appears to be an implied deduction by at least some of the Jews based on the Scriptures (Deuteronomy 23:3-6; 25:17-19; Psalms 109:1-31; 137:7-9; 139:19-24).[22] One should remember that at the time of Jesus, the Jews were living under an oppressive and unfair Roman government. Loving the Roman invaders was no small task.

Therefore, Jesus indeed changed God's Law with the New Covenant. The entire sacrificial system that is presented in such detail in Leviticus was completely retired. The priesthood of the Mosaic Law was completely retired. Much, if not most of the 613 laws in the Mosaic Covenant were either modified or retired. In fact, it was determined by apostolic authority in Acts 15:1-35 that the Gentiles who came to Christ did not have to obey the Mosaic Law. Truly, Jesus had fulfilled "the Law" and "the Prophets," and by doing so He delivered a New Covenant, one that was clearly different from the Mosaic Law.

Now the whole reason for this discussion is to show that Jesus Christ was the "mediator of a new covenant." Besides Moses, who was the mediator of the Mosaic Covenant, there was no other covenant mediated by any other prophet in the Old Testament. Jesus Christ was the only prophet who, like Moses, was the mediator of a new covenant. Therefore, in regard to making a New Covenant, Jesus was the only prophet who was a "prophet like Moses."

Direct Communication with God

Moses was unlike the other Old Testament prophets in that he communicated with God "face to face, just as a man speaks to his friend" (Exodus 33:11). We see this description regarding Moses also in Deuteronomy 34:10. We find this strongly portrayed in Numbers 12:1-8—

> 1 Then Miriam and Aaron spoke against Moses because of the Cushite woman whom he had married (for he had married a Cushite woman); ²and they said, "Has the LORD indeed spoken only through Moses? Has He not spoken through us as well?" And the LORD heard it. ³(Now the man Moses was very humble, more than any man who was on the face of the earth.) ⁴Suddenly the LORD said to Moses and Aaron and to Miriam,

---

22 Jack P. Lewis, *The Living Word Commentary: The Gospel According to Matthew, Part I* (Abilene: ACU Press, 1976, 1984), 96.

"You three come out to the tent of meeting." So the three of them came out. ⁵Then the LORD came down in a pillar of cloud and stood at the doorway of the tent, and He called Aaron and Miriam. When they had both come forward, ⁶He said,

> "Hear now My words:
> If there is a prophet among you,
> I, the LORD, shall make Myself known to him in a vision.
> I shall speak with him in a dream.
> ⁷"Not so, with My servant Moses,
> He is faithful in all My household;
> ⁸With him I speak mouth to mouth,
> Even openly, and not in dark sayings,
> And he beholds the form of the LORD.
> Why then were you not afraid
> To speak against My servant, against Moses?"
> Numbers 12:1-8 (NASB)

Note that God spoke with Moses "face to face." However, with other prophets God spoke to them in visions or dreams. This is entirely consistent with the Old Testament and New Testament because God spoke in visions to Jacob (Genesis 46:2), Ezekiel (Ezekiel 1:1), Daniel (Daniel 8:2; 10:8, 16), Zechariah (Luke 1:11, 22), Peter (Acts 10:11), and Paul (Acts 22:17). Likewise, God spoke in dreams to Abimelech (Genesis 20:6), Jacob (Genesis 31:10-11), Solomon (1 Kings 3:5), and Joseph (Matthew 1:20). Job commented also that God communicates to man in dreams and visions (Job 33:15), and God answered Job "out of the whirlwind" (Job 38:1).

But how did God speak with Jesus? The New Testament never says that the Father spoke to His only begotten Son in visions and dreams. Nor does it say that the Father spoke to His Son "face to face." Rather, Jesus claimed the ultimate oneness with the Father (John 10:30; 17:11, 22). Everything Jesus spoke and all the wonders He displayed were by the word and will of His Father (John 4:34; 5:30; 6:38; 8:28; 14:10) in Whom Christ dwelt and Who also dwelt in Christ. Now this was and still remains an infinitely greater measure of intimacy than speaking to a person "face to face, just as a man speaks with his friend."

Therefore, we find that the direct communication Jesus had with His Father was infinitely greater than the communication Moses or any other Old or New Testament prophet had with God. This once again shows that only Jesus Christ can be the "prophet like Moses."

He Led the People Out of Bondage

God led His people out of Egyptian captivity, and Moses was God's servant in this matter. Throughout the wilderness wanderings, it was God who led His people Israel through His pillar of cloud by day or His pillar of fire by night (Exodus 13:21-22). Yet it was Moses who continually stood between God and the Israelites. Indeed, had Moses not accepted that place of service and honor, the Israelites would have been destroyed by God's wrath since they were so hardheaded and stiff necked. Moses definitely led the people through those 40 years of wilderness wanderings and did not vacate his position until the Israelites were at the river Jordan, fully ready to march into the promised land.

Even with Moses' death in the land of Moab, his leadership did not cease. The books of Moses, namely Genesis, Exodus, Leviticus, Numbers, and Deuteronomy, remained as a witness to the Israelites. Moses continued to lead the Israelites for hundreds of years through his writings. These same writings are treasured by faithful Jews as well as faithful Gentile Christians to this day.

When we consider the rest of the prophets in the Old Testament, we definitely see their leadership. However, none of them could truly claim to have the same level of leadership as Moses, for they all made it clear that they were restoring a covenant, not starting a new one. Again, these cannot be described as "a prophet like Moses."

However, when we consider the leadership of Jesus Christ, He far exceeds anyone else in the Bible. Consider that Jesus led multitudes on earth, and the Jews sought Him from every quarter. Jesus also has been leading His people for the past 2,000 years. Furthermore, countless millions of people from every tribe on this earth have given themselves to the Christ and trust Him to guide them through His Word, the New Testament, as well as through His Spirit and His Providence. His leadership is not finished! He continues to lead us.

Moses led Israel out of a physical bondage. However, Christ led people from every tribe and nation out of spiritual bondage and into spiritual peace, even in the face of imminent physical death. With His blood He has cleansed us of our sins. By His resurrection from the dead He has freed us from the fear of death (Hebrews 2:15). Assuredly, we now have full confidence that we too will rise again at His call, just as Lazarus did (John 11:25-26; 39-44). Truly, Christ has led us out of bondage and will continue to lead us until the end of this world.

In conclusion, there is no prophet other than Christ who can truly be "a prophet like Moses." He is the second Moses, He is the very One and the only One who can fulfill this prophecy in Deuteronomy 18:15, 18. This is a Messianic prophecy, and it was fulfilled and is still being fulfilled by King Messiah, known to us as Jesus of Nazareth.

Hanged on The Tree (Deuteronomy 21:22-23)

OT

22 "If a man has committed a sin worthy of death and he is put to death, and you hang him on a tree, ²³his corpse shall not hang all night on the tree, but you shall surely bury him on the same day (for <u>he who is hanged is accursed of God</u>), so that you do not defile your land which the LORD your God gives you as an inheritance. Deuteronomy 21:22-23 NASB

NT

10 For as many as are of the works of the Law are under a curse; for it is written, "CURSED IS EVERYONE WHO DOES NOT ABIDE BY ALL THINGS WRITTEN IN THE BOOK OF THE LAW, TO PERFORM THEM." ¹¹Now that no one is justified by the Law before God is evident; for, "THE RIGHTEOUS MAN SHALL LIVE BY FAITH." ¹²However, the Law is not of faith; on the contrary, "HE WHO PRACTICES THEM SHALL LIVE BY THEM." ¹³Christ redeemed us from the curse of the Law, having become a curse for us—for it is written, "CURSED IS EVERYONE WHO HANGS ON A TREE"— ¹⁴in order that in Christ Jesus the blessing of Abraham might come to the Gentiles, so that we would receive the promise of the Spirit through faith. Galatians 3:10-14 NASB

Discussion: Paul frequently used excerpts from the Old Testament in his epistles. The passage he quoted from, Deuteronomy 21:23, is no exception. We do not see any prophecy intended in Deuteronomy 21:23. However, Paul used this passage in a Messianic context. In addition, Paul showed that what was prefigured in the Old Testament was fulfilled in Christ. However, this typology is even more than what meets the eye. Christ was not just cursed by hanging on the tree, but was cursed because He bore the sins of every person in His body on the tree. Yes, this passage in Deuteronomy would apply to anyone hanged on a tree. But no one except Christ was so accursed because only He bore all of our uncountable sins. Therefore, Paul was reasoning from those who were accursed in a <u>lesser</u> sense to Christ who received the <u>ultimate</u> curse so that we could be blessed instead of cursed.

The ancient Rabbis did understand that the Christ must suffer. However, they did not realize that Christ would have to die accursed and disgraced by hanging on a tree. Paul gives meaning to this by showing that Christ redeemed us from the curse of the Law by becoming a curse for us. The curse of the Law was that the Jews could not abide by and perform ALL things written in the book of the Law. Thus, both the Jews and the Gentiles stood accursed before God.

Therefore, Paul used typology to point from the lesser to the greater. In doing so, Christ was and still is exalted.

He Shall Be A Son To Me (2 Samuel 7:12-16)

OT

> [12]"When your days are complete and you lie down with your fathers, I will raise up your descendant after you, who will come forth from you, and I will establish his kingdom. [13]He shall build a house for My name, and I will establish the throne of his kingdom forever. [14]<u>I will be a father to him and he will be a son to Me</u>; when he commits iniquity, I will correct him with the rod of men and the strokes of the sons of men, [15]but My lovingkindness shall not depart from him, as I took *it* away from Saul, whom I removed from before you. [16]Your house and your kingdom shall endure before Me forever; your throne shall be established forever." 2 Samuel 7:12-16 NASB

NT

> 5 For to which of the angels did He ever say,
> "You are My Son,
> Today I have begotten You"?
>
> And again,
>
> "I will be a Father to Him
> And He shall be a Son to Me"? Hebrews 1:5 NASB

Discussion: The passage in 2 Samuel 7 is addressed to King David and includes God's continuing Covenant relations with the lineage of kings from David. Although this passage was not identified by Edersheim as having Messianic significance to the ancient Rabbis, they clearly thought that the Messiah would come through the lineage of David.

In Hebrews 1, the writer gives us several Messianic prophecies including this one in Hebrews 1:5b. The other Messianic references in that chapter and throughout the New Testament will be discussed in accordance with their appearance in the Old Testament.

The words of this Old Testament passage promised a Father/Son relationship to all the Davidic Kings. There is not a specific reference to Jesus Christ. However, if it applied to these Davidic Kings, then how much more does it find its greatest fulfillment to the most important of all the Davidic kings? Who sits on the eternal throne of David now? Who has been sitting on the eternal throne of David for nearly two millennia? Was it not Jesus Christ who was given the throne of David (Matthew 1:1; Luke 1:32, 69; Acts 2:30; Revelation 3:7)? So if it applied to all those Old Testament Davidic kings, it must certainly be fulfilled in Jesus Christ in an infinitely greater sense.

Against the Lord and His Christ (Psalm 2:1-3)

OT

> 1 Why are the nations in an uproar
> And the peoples devising a vain thing?
> ²The kings of the earth take their stand

And the rulers take counsel together
<u>Against the L<small>ORD</small> and against His Anointed</u>, saying,
³"Let us tear their fetters apart
And cast away their cords from us!" Psalm 2:1-3 NASB

NT

23 When they had been released, they went to their own *companions* and reported all that the chief priests and the elders had said to them. ²⁴And when they heard *this*, they lifted their voices to God with one accord and said, "O Lord, it is You who M<small>ADE THE</small> H<small>EAVEN AND THE</small> E<small>ARTH AND THE</small> S<small>EA</small>, <small>AND ALL THAT IS IN THEM</small>, ²⁵who by the Holy Spirit, *through* the mouth of our father David Your servant, said,

'W<small>HY DID THE</small> G<small>ENTILES RAGE</small>,
<small>AND THE PEOPLES DEVISE FUTILE THINGS</small>?
²⁶'T<small>HE KINGS OF THE EARTH TOOK THEIR STAND</small>,
<small>AND THE RULERS WERE GATHERED TOGETHER</small>
<u><small>AGAINST THE</small> L<small>ORD AND AGAINST</small> H<small>IS</small> C<small>HRIST</small></u>.'
Acts 4:23-26 NASB

Discussion: The oldest known version of the Old Testament is a Greek translation called the Septuagint. It was produced starting in the third century BC. It is of interest that the ancient Jewish scholars who produced this Greek translation from the Hebrew translated their Hebrew word for "anointed" in Psalm 2:2 into the Greek word Χριστός (*Christos*).[23] This word can mean "anointed" as with the Hebrew word, but it can also mean the proper name for Jesus of Nazareth, namely "Christ."[24]

Of the English New Testaments I have, 7 translate Acts 4:26 as "**Messiah**" (CEV, GWT, HCSB, NLT, NRSV, TEV and TMSG). There are also 9 other English translations that translate this word as "**Christ**" (DNT, DRB, ICB, ISVNT, KJV, NASB, NCV, NKJV, and YLT). There are 6 that translate this word as "**Anointed**" (ASV, ESV, MSNT, NAB, NIV, RSV).

---

23 Sir Lancelot C. L. Brenton, *The Septuagint with Apocrypha: Greek and English* (Hendrickson Publishers), 699.
24 J. P. Louw & E. A. Nida, *Vol. 1: Greek-English lexicon of the New Testament: Based on semantic domains* (electronic ed. of the 2nd edition.) (New York: United Bible Societies, 1996), 542.

The Septuagint became the popular Bible for the Jews before Christ since most of the Jews in the Dispersion did not know how to read Hebrew. The Septuagint also became the Scriptures for the Gentiles since it was written in Greek, the language they understood. It became the Scriptures for the early Christians. However, when the Christians started showing how the Septuagint supported Jesus of Nazareth as the Messiah, the Jews rejected the Septuagint. Many of the quotes and allusions of the Old Testament as found in the New Testament are actually quotations and allusions from the Septuagint version of the Old Testament.[25]

Edersheim documented that the ancient Rabbis viewed these Old Testament verses in Psalm 2 to be Messianic. In fact, they viewed all of Psalm 2 to be Messianic.[26] Were the ancient Rabbis right? Or are the critical theologians right when they say it applies only to David or one of his immediate descendents? Did Psalm 2 really apply to Jesus of Nazareth or not? The key is found in Psalm 2:8 which reads,

> [8]'Ask of Me, and I will surely give the nations as Your inheritance,
> And the *very* ends of the earth as Your possession.
> Psalm 2:8 NASB

Hence we should ask, who among David and his lineage of kings ruled over all the nations of the earth? There was not even one in the Old Testament. However, who is the descendent of David who reigns to this day on the eternal throne of David, and who has followers in all the nations, yes, to the ends of the earth? There is only one, and He is our Lord Jesus Christ!

Therefore, since Jesus Christ is the only One who could fulfill Psalm 2:8, we can be confident that Psalm 2 is indeed Messianic, just as the ancient Rabbis believed. Furthermore, we can be confident that only Jesus could fulfill all the aspects of this Psalm.

---

25 Brenton, *The Septuagint with Apocrypha: Greek and English* (Hendrickson Publishers), Preface.
26 Edersheim, *The Life and Times of Jesus the Messiah*, 986-987.

You Are My Son (Psalm 2:7)

OT

> 7"I will surely tell of the decree of the LORD:
> He said to Me, '<u>You are My Son,</u>
> <u>Today I have begotten You</u>. Psalm 2:7 NASB

NT

> **5** So also Christ did not glorify Himself so as to become a high priest, but He who said to Him,
> "YOU ARE MY SON,
> TODAY I HAVE BEGOTTEN YOU"; Hebrews 5:5 NASB

We are in the same Psalm as the last discussion, and all those comments about it being a Messianic Psalm that foretold Jesus Christ are still valid. The statement in Psalm 2:7 could potentially refer to David and all the kings in his lineage. However, this Psalm can only be fulfilled by Jesus Christ because of Psalm 2:8. Once again, just as cited previously, Edersheim showed that the ancient rabbis held all of Psalm 2 to be Messianic.

Psalm 2:7 is also found quoted in Acts 13:33 and Hebrews 1:5, and are defended as Messianic prophecies on the same basis.

Out of the Mouths of Infants (Psalm 8:1-2)

OT

> **1** O LORD, our Lord,
> How majestic is Your name in all the earth,
> Who have displayed Your splendor above the heavens!
> ²<u>From the mouth of infants and nursing babes</u> You have established strength
> Because of Your adversaries,
> To make the enemy and the revengeful cease.
> Psalm 8:1-2 NASB

NT

> ¹⁵But when the chief priests and the scribes saw the wonderful things that He had done, and the <u>children who were shouting</u> in the temple, "Hosanna to the Son of David," they became indignant ¹⁶and said to Him, "Do You hear what these *children* are saying?" And Jesus *said to them, "Yes; have you never read, 'OUT OF THE MOUTH OF INFANTS AND NURSING BABIES YOU HAVE PREPARED PRAISE FOR YOURSELF'?" Matthew 21:15-16 NASB

Discussion: If we read this passage in its context, many if not most of us would not immediately infer a Messianic prophecy. In fact, we would attribute the first words as referring to YHWH, for that indeed is what the Hebrew text has. But when we come to Matthew 21:15-16, we find that Jesus quotes Psalm 8:2 as applying to the praise He was receiving from the children. Indeed, the children were shouting that Jesus was King Messiah. Was Jesus wrong to quote this passage? Was He stealing praise from God Almighty? Was Jesus reinterpreting and reapplying Old Testament texts to Himself as the liberal, critical theologians so eagerly allege? Is Psalm 8:2 not really an Old Testament Messianic prophecy?

One of the most basic beliefs of Christianity is that the Son coexisted with the Father before the beginning of time (John 1:1-4). This belief was well articulated in the Nicene Creed of AD 325:

> We believe in one God, the Father Almighty, Maker of all things visible and invisible.
>
> And in one Lord Jesus Christ, the Son of God, begotten of the Father the only-begotten, i.e., of the essence of the Father, God of God, and Light of Light, very God of very God, begotten, not made, being of one substance with the Father....²⁷

Therefore, praise for the Father from before the beginning of time was also received by the Son, for "I and the Father are one." (John 10:30; 17:11, 22; see also John 5:19; 14:10). Not only this, but the early Christians understood that Christ was clearly visible in the Old Testament. As examples of this see Isaiah 6:1 with John 12:41; Exodus

---

27 Philip Schaff, *History of the Christian Church, Volume 3* (Peabody: Hendrickson Publishers, Inc.), 668-669.

17:6 with 1 Corinthians 10:1-4; Numbers 21:4-9 with 1 Corinthians 10:9; see also Hebrews 11:26 and John 3:13-14.

Therefore, we should not be surprised or taken aback by Christ appearing to assume the role of YHWH in some aspects. After all, He clearly taught that "I and the Father are one." To doubt this belief is to doubt one of the most basic tenets of Christianity.

The word "praise" in Matthew 21:16 shows that this quotation was from the Septuagint since the Hebrew text has the word "strength."[28]

Not to Undergo Decay (Psalm 16:8-10)

OT

> [8]I have set the LORD continually before me;
> Because He is at my right hand, I will not be shaken.
> [9]Therefore my heart is glad and my glory rejoices;
> My flesh also will dwell securely.
> [10]For You will not abandon my soul to Sheol;
> <u>Nor will You allow Your Holy One to undergo decay</u>.
> Psalm 16:8-10 NASB

NT

> **22**"Men of Israel, listen to these words: Jesus the Nazarene, a man attested to you by God with miracles and wonders and signs which God performed through Him in your midst, just as you yourselves know— [23]this *Man*, delivered over by the predetermined plan and foreknowledge of God, you nailed to a cross by the hands of godless men and put *Him* to death. [24]But God raised Him up again, putting an end to the agony of death, since it was impossible for Him to be held in its power. [25]For David says of Him,
>
>> 'I SAW THE LORD ALWAYS IN MY PRESENCE;
>> FOR HE IS AT MY RIGHT HAND, SO THAT I WILL NOT BE SHAKEN.
>> [26]'THEREFORE MY HEART WAS GLAD AND MY TONGUE EXULTED;
>> MOREOVER MY FLESH ALSO WILL LIVE IN HOPE;
>> [27]BECAUSE YOU WILL NOT ABANDON MY SOUL TO HADES,

---

28 Jack P. Lewis, *The Living Word Commentary: The Gospel According to Matthew, Part II* (Abilene: ACU Press, 1976, 1984), 88.

> NOR ALLOW YOUR HOLY ONE TO UNDERGO DECAY.
> [28]'YOU HAVE MADE KNOWN TO ME THE WAYS OF LIFE;
> YOU WILL MAKE ME FULL OF GLADNESS WITH YOUR PRESENCE.'
> Acts 2:22-28 NASB

Discussion: This Old Testament prophecy is quoted in Acts 2:25-28, 31; 13:35. Each time, the purpose is to show that the resurrection of Christ was an Old Testament necessity. In both Acts 2 and 13, Peter and Paul stress that David did die and undergo decay. Therefore, the prophecy could not apply to David or anyone in his kingly lineage in the Old Testament. The only one it could apply to was Jesus of Nazareth who did not undergo decay but was resurrected from the dead.

Of course, the liberal, critical theologians deny the New Testament rendering of this prophecy and say that David was simply saying that death will not separate him from God. They deny that David was teaching about resurrection in these verses.[29] They thereby imply that the apostolic handling of this Psalm was wrong, even if the apostles were inspired by the Holy Spirit.

Edersheim confirmed Psalm 16:9 was Messianic in the writings of the ancient rabbis.[30]

The Crucifixion of Christ (Psalm 22)

The critical theologians disagree that there are Messianic prophecies fulfilled by Christ, and this is especially so in Psalm 22. As an example of their utter disregard for the teachings of Christ and His inspired apostles and prophets on this matter, here is what Dr. Anthony Ash of Abilene Christian University said about Psalm 22:

> Rather than viewing it as a prediction, it is better to say that an OT sufferer spoke in language that would later appropriately describe the Messiah.[31]

---

29   Anthony L. Ash and Clyde M. Miller, *Living Word Commentary on the Old Testament*: *Psalms*, Editor John T. Willis (Abilene: ACU Press, 1980, 1984), 75.
30   Edersheim, *The Life and Times of Jesus the Messiah*, 987.
31   Ash and Miller, *Living Word Commentary on the Old Testament*: *Psalms*, 91.

We should not be fooled by these well-crafted words. These words are diametrically opposed to what Christ and His inspired apostles and prophets taught about this Psalm.

To the contrary, Psalm 22 is truly a Messianic Psalm. The New Testament writers pointed explicitly to Psalm 22:1, 8, 18, and 22. Edersheim documented that the ancient Rabbis treated verses 7 and 15 as Messianic.[32] It is clear in reading the Psalm that it is filled with language that simply could not have been fulfilled completely by David or any other person in the Old Testament. In fact, this language is fulfilled in Christ, and only in Him.

Why Have You Forsaken Me?

OT

> **1** My God, my God, why have You forsaken me?
> Far from my deliverance are the words of my groaning.
> Psalm 22:1 NASB

NT

> [46]About the ninth hour Jesus cried out with a loud voice, saying, "ELI, ELI, LAMA SABACHTHANI?" that is, "MY GOD, MY GOD, WHY HAVE YOU FORSAKEN ME?" Matthew 27:46 NASB

Discussion: This cry of Christ on the cross is also found in Mark 15:34.

The cry of Christ on the cross is the most haunting cry in all the literature of men. It pierces my soul each time I read it or hear it read. It brings tears to my eyes because I know what was happening. God had laid upon Christ my sins, our sins, all the sins of every person who has ever lived and would ever live. He was bearing in His body on the cross every murder, every rape, every lie, every refusal of the grace of God, every sin (1 Peter 2:24). He was being blamed and punished for every sin that ever was or ever would be committed. He was accursed and horribly afflicted. He was pierced for our transgressions. He was crushed for our iniquities. The LORD caused our iniquity to fall on Him. Is it any wonder that He cried out in such utter agony?

Another thing Christ's cry on the cross does is bring our attention to Psalm 22. In so doing, our Savior told us far more about His crucifixion than we could ever had anticipated.

---

32 Edersheim, *The Life and Times of Jesus the Messiah,* 988.

Isolated from the rest of the Psalm, we might be tempted to say that Psalm 22:1 is simply a "type fulfillment." However, we must avoid coming to any premature conclusion.

They Mocked and Insulted Him

OT

6 "But I am a worm and not a man,
A reproach of men and despised by the people.
⁷All who see me sneer at me;
They separate with the lip, they wag the head, *saying*,
⁸"Commit *yourself* to the LORD; let Him deliver him;
Let Him rescue him, because He delights in him."
Psalm 22:6-8 NASB

11 Be not far from me, for trouble is near;
For there is none to help.
¹²Many bulls have surrounded me;
Strong *bulls* of Bashan have encircled me.
¹³They open wide their mouth at me,
As a ravening and a roaring lion.
Psalm 22:11-13 NASB

NT

³⁹And those passing by were hurling abuse at Him, wagging their heads ⁴⁰and saying, "You who *are going to* destroy the temple and rebuild it in three days, save Yourself! If You are the Son of God, come down from the cross." ⁴¹In the same way the chief priests also, along with the scribes and elders, were mocking *Him* and saying, ⁴²"He saved others; He cannot save Himself. He is the King of Israel; let Him now come down from the cross, and we will believe in Him. ⁴³HE TRUSTS IN GOD; LET GOD RESCUE *Him* now, IF HE DELIGHTS IN HIM; for He said, 'I am the Son of God.'" ⁴⁴The robbers who had been crucified with Him were also insulting Him with the same words. Matthew 27:39-44

Discussion: After being mocked, insulted, and beaten at the house of Caiaphas (Matthew 26:67), Jesus was mocked by Herod (Luke 23:11). Then He was mocked, insulted, and abused by the Roman soldiers in the Praetorium. Finally, He was mocked and insulted by the Jewish leaders, the soldiers, and those crucified with Him as He hung on the cross (Matthew 27:39-44; Mark 15:29-32; Luke 23:35-37).

Again, if we look at this in isolation from the rest of the Psalm, we would be tempted to say this is simply a "type" fulfillment. However, that would be premature.

Christ's Death By Crucifixion

OT

> [14]I am poured out like water,
> And all my bones are out of joint;
> My heart is like wax;
> It is melted within me.
> [15]My strength is dried up like a potsherd,
> And my tongue cleaves to my jaws;
> And You lay me in the dust of death.
> [16]For dogs have surrounded me;
> A band of evildoers has encompassed me;
> They pierced my hands and my feet.
> [17]I can count all my bones.
> They look, they stare at me;
> [18]<u>They divide my garments among them,</u>
> <u>And for my clothing they cast lots.</u>
> Psalm 22:14-18 NASB

NT

> **23** Then the soldiers, when they had crucified Jesus, took His outer garments and made four parts, a part to every soldier and *also* the tunic; now the tunic was seamless, woven in one piece. [24]So they said to one another, "Let us not tear it, but cast lots for it, *to decide* whose it shall be"; *this was* to fulfill the Scripture: "THEY DIVIDED MY OUTER GARMENTS AMONG THEM, AND FOR MY CLOTHING THEY CAST LOTS." John 19:23-24

Discussion: The oldest Christian interpretation of Psalm 22 is that this Psalm is Messianic and points clearly to Jesus Christ. This is certainly the position taken in the New Testament. However, the critical theologians view the affliction of the psalmist as being something unknown, and "...that no particular illness or distressful situation can be identified."[33] They really don't know what was wrong with the psalmist. They refuse to see the crucifixion of Christ being predicted in Psalm 22.

Abundant and conflicting literature exists regarding Christ's cause of death on the cross. Unfortunately, these theories are all suspect because death by crucifixion has never been studied *in vivo*. This is because this form of torture and execution is ancient. In addition, the moment of His death was of His choosing and not according to the will of his executioner:

> [17]For this reason the Father loves Me, because I lay down My life so that I may take it again. [18]No one has taken it away from Me, but I lay it down on My own initiative. I have authority to lay it down, and I have authority to take it up again. This commandment I received from My Father." John 10:17-18 NASB

However, we can correctly infer that Jesus experienced significant suffering while on the cross because He was human. Psalm 22:14-18 portrays this intense suffering.

"Poured out like water" (Psalm 22:14) is to be without strength. It speaks of extreme physical weakness, so weak that one would lay prostrate on the ground and not be able to rise. This is the kind of weakness that Christ experienced. Scourging was brutal and was frequently used in Roman executions. The victim was stretched out on a frame so that all portions of his or her body could receive the blows. The scourge was an instrument used to beat the one who was convicted as part of their execution. Both sticks and whips could be used. Commonly, this scourging resulted in severe injuries, even down to exposed bone and with substantial blood loss. There was no limit to the number of stripes that could be administered under Roman law. Such scourging frequently killed the prisoner by profuse blood loss and shock. The Scriptures do not inform us as to the severity of Christ's scourging. But the degree of weakness portrayed in Psalm 22 would imply His scourging was severe. The Romans caused Jesus to bear His own cross (John 19:17), but then caused Simon of Cyrene to bear it (Matthew 27:32; Mark 15:21; Luke 23:26). We infer from this

---

33   Ash and Miller, *Living Word Commentary on the Old Testament: Psalms*, 91.

that Christ was unable to carry it because of His profuse injuries and severe blood loss.

His bones were "out of joint" (Psalm 22:14) and "I can count all my bones" (Psalm 22:17). Not a part of His body was spared from the scourging. Every part of His body was racked in pain. With iron spikes driven through His upper and lower extremities, we can understand why He could count all His bones. His upper extremities could be "out of joint." God did not design our upper extremities to hold up our weight for extended periods of time. Shoulder, elbow, and wrist dislocations would not be unreasonable to assume. Dislocation of the wrists was almost a certainty when the iron spikes were driven in. However, we know that Christ as our Passover Lamb (1 Corinthians 5:7) could not sustain a bony fracture because the bones of Passover lamb could not be broken (Exodus 12:46; Numbers 9:12). The explicit reference is as follows:

OT

[20]He keeps all his bones,
Not one of them is broken. Psalm 34:20 NASB

NT

[36]For these things came to pass to fulfill the Scripture, "NOT A BONE OF HIM SHALL BE BROKEN." John 19:36 NASB

His heart was like "melted" wax. Again, extreme weakness in the very depths of his body is portrayed. Nothing is firm, nothing is strong, nothing is right in His body. Some take this to mean that Jesus died of heart failure. However, Jesus had complete control over when to die and when to resurrect as John 10:17-18 shows.

Again, His strength is "dried up like a potsherd." A potsherd is a broken piece of pottery, and what could be more dry than that? This suggests severe dehydration, and is consistent with severe blood loss. When Jesus said, "I am thirsty," He again was fulfilling Scripture (John 19:28; Psalm 69:21).

"You lay me in the dust of death" (Psalm 22:15) is the most common translation here. Simply put, the One being described in the Psalm is dying. His injuries are severe and lethal. Hope of continuing life has vanished. The grave was ready to receive Him.

The "dogs" are the "evildoers" who surround Him and stare at Him. It is the evildoers who "pierced my hands and my feet." This phrase describes crucifixion, a practice unknown to David. It would not appear for hundreds of years past his time. Yet, David saw it through his spiritual eyes, through the eyes of a prophet of God. If there is any doubt about Psalm 22 being a Messianic psalm, this phrase, "pierced my hands and my feet" should erase it. The oldest version of the Old Testament is the Septuagint, and those Jewish scholars clearly translated the Hebrew word into "pierced."[34] This translation was finished long before the birth of Christ and was well-known to the Jews. Unfortunately, critical theologians cannot abide any idea of predictive prophecy, especially where it might involve Christ and His church. So they want to say that a lion or a pack of wild dogs attacked the psalmist's hands and feet.[35]

All the major English translations of the Old Testament use "pierced" in Psalm 22:16. These include, but are not limited to, the ASV, ESV, KJV, NASB, NIV, NKJV, RSV, and YLT.[36] Those NOT using "pierced" in Psalm 22:16 include the CEV, DRB, ICB, NCV, NRSV, TEV, and TMSG.

We now come to the passage that speaks of the evildoers dividing and casting lots for His clothing (Psalm 22:18). As previously mentioned, this is found in John 19:23-24 and John clearly says that this is a fulfillment of prophecy. Of course, this took place during Christ's crucifixion. We should note that most of the fulfillments of this and other aspects of Christ's crucifixion were unwittingly brought about by the unbelieving Jews as well as the unbelieving Romans who crucified Him.

"It is finished!"

The ancient Christians' understanding of the last section of Psalm 22 was that it speaks of Christ's resurrection and Christ's church. That is, the ancient Christians viewed all of Psalm 22 as thoroughly Messianic.

The psalmist pleads with the LORD for help and deliverance in Psalm 22:19-21. The dangers are from people who are symbolically

---

34 Brenton, *The Septuagint with Apocrypha: Greek and English*, 710.
35 Ash and Miller, *Living Word Commentary on the Old Testament: Psalms*, 93.
36 Other less well known translations that use "pierced" in Psalm 22:16 include the DNT, GWT, HCSB, NLT, and TLB.

called the dog, the lion's mouth, and the horns of the wild oxen. God's answer comes at this point:

> ^{21}Save me from the lion's mouth;
> From the horns of the wild oxen You answer me.
> Psalm 22:21 NASB

It is at the last moment of life when God answered Christ, for Christ had accomplished the redemption for all who would believe in Him through His bloody sacrifice, and He had secured eternal forgiveness of sins for all those who come to Him. Instead of being forsaken as the sacrificial lamb who bears and takes away the sin of the world, He says,

> "It is finished!" John 19:30 NASB

> "Father, INTO YOUR HANDS I COMMIT MY SPIRIT."
> Luke 23:46 NASB

Notice how Jesus, with His last words on the cross, continued to use words from the Old Testament to emphasize the prophetic nature of the Old Testament concerning the Messiah: "INTO YOUR HANDS I COMMIT MY SPIRIT." Christ's words came from Psalm 31:5.

Christ and His Church

The psalmist praises God for His great deliverance in Psalm 22:22-25. Notice that the writer of Hebrews clearly saw Psalm 22:22 as being fulfilled by Jesus:

OT

> **22** I will tell of Your name to my brethren;
> In the midst of the assembly I will praise You.
> Psalm 22:22 NASB

NT

> ^{12}"I WILL PROCLAIM YOUR NAME TO MY BRETHREN,
> IN THE MIDST OF THE CONGREGATION I WILL SING YOUR PRAISE."
> Hebrews 2:12 NASB

Surely this implies Christ's adoration of His heavenly Father for His own deliverance! His Spirit was immediately with His Father! The angels shouting praise for the greatest and most moving event in the whole history of man! The Son has won! He has crushed the head of the serpent! He has redeemed man with His own blood! Amen! Amen! Amen! Forever will the Son praise the Father for this great deliverance for Him, the typical Man, standing before the Father on behalf of all His people!

It should be noted that the Hebrew word translated "assembly" in Psalm 22:22 was translated by the 70 Jewish scholars into the Greek word ἐκκλησία (ekklēsia) in the Septuagint, and this Greek word is translated into the English word "church" in the New Testament. It is this very same Greek word that is translated into "congregation" in Hebrew 2:12. Therefore, a prominent English translation of the Septuagint reads as follows:

> [22]I will declare thy name to my brethren: in the midst of the church I will sing praise to thee. Psalm 21:22 Septuagint[37]

Now it is very difficult to pass over the significance of this. If we cannot see the church prophesied symbolically in typological terms in the Old Testament, then we must have blinders on our eyes. This Greek translation by the 70 Jewish scholars of the Hebrew Scriptures was written long before the birth of Christ.

We should reflect for a moment on the worship we find in the Old Testament and realize that the symbolism and even some of the actual elements are reflected in New Testament worship. The first worship we find is with Abel and involved animal sacrifice (Genesis 4:4). Noah also built an altar and offered animal sacrifice (Genesis 8:20-21). Abraham built a number of altars for animal sacrifice in his moving from place to place (Genesis 12:7-8; 13:4; 22:9). The last reference was to the altar Abraham made to sacrifice Isaac, and there Abraham clearly combined sacrifice and worship (Genesis 22:5). Isaac built an altar for animal sacrifice (Genesis 26:25). Jacob built an altar for animal sacrifice (Genesis 33:20; 35:3, 7).

Moses built altars for animal sacrifice (Exodus 17:15; 24:4-6), and in the Law of Moses God gave regulations regarding altars (e.g., Exodus 20:24-26; 27:1-8). In these regulations, the place of sacrifice was confined to the Tent of Meeting where the altar was located (Leviticus 17:1-9; Deuteronomy 12:13-14). In the times of the Judges, the worship and sacrifice to God was at Shiloh (1 Samuel 1:3) for that

---

37   Brenton, *The Septuagint with Apocrypha: Greek and English*, 710.

was where the Tabernacle of the LORD was located (1 Samuel 1:9) as well as the Ark of the Covenant (1 Samuel 4:3). It was David who moved the Ark of the Covenant to Jerusalem (2 Samuel 6:12). There David restored the Mosaic Covenant in regard to all sacrifices and worship (1 Chronicles 16). David built an altar for animal sacrifice (1 Chronicles 21:18). David greatly desired to build a Temple for God, but God did not allow him to do so (1 Chronicles 17:4). However, David prepared for the building of the Temple by a massive stock piling of various items (1 Chronicles 22:1-19). King Solomon, son of David, built the Temple (2 Chronicles 3-4). There are 303 verses with reference to "altar" in the Old Testament.

The worship in the ancient Temple was filled with massive temporal stimuli. The building was glorious with gold within and without. The phenomenal and beautiful clothing of the chief priest and all the priests attending the offerings must have been a delight to the eyes. The singers and all the incredible sounds of the musical instruments and the blasts from the silver trumpets must have been an incredible experience. The blood of many sacrifices gushing out and then being thrown on the sides of the altar and placed on the horns of the altar must have been shocking to the senses. However, even with all this sensory stimulation, it was insufficient to keep alive the faith in the one and only God and the obedience to that one and only God.

Although restored by good kings like Hezekiah and Josiah, the Temple worship fell into disuse because of the attraction of idolatry. Finally, God brought the Babylonians who conquered both Judah and Jerusalem. The Jewish people were deported and the Temple was then destroyed in 586 BC.

It was in Babylonian captivity that the Jewish people turned back to God and sought His will. In the absence of the physical Temple with all its phenomenal sensory input, the Synagogue arose as the place to worship God and have fellowship with fellow believers. There was only one Temple, but the idea of the Synagogue spread rapidly among the Jewish people. Even when the Jewish captives returned to Jerusalem to rebuild the Temple in 536 BC, the idea of the Synagogue went with them. Synagogues were built throughout the Jewish dispersion and even in Jerusalem where the second Temple was built. By the time of Christ, Synagogues were a very important part of Jewish worship throughout the known world.

In contrast to the Temple, the worship in the Synagogue was rational and included the following items:

1. The Reciting of the Shema (the confession of God's unity)
2. Prayers
3. Reading from the Law and the Prophets
4. The Sermon
5. Giving alms
6. Singing without musical instruments[38]
7. The Benediction[39]

This scheme of rational worship became the norm for all faithful Jewish people and continued to be the standard after the destruction of the second Temple by the Romans in AD 70.

When we compare this rational Synagogue worship to the non-miraculous aspects of Christian worship, we find that the rational Synagogue worship and rational Christian worship are very similar. The rational Christian worship involved the following:

1. Worship was planned
2. Worship involved singing without instruments[40]
3. Worship involved praying
4. Worship involved teaching and preaching from the Bible
5. Worship involved the Lord's Supper
6. Worship involved giving
7. Worship involved fellowship[41]

Therefore, we see the hand of God in all matters concerning the Christian assembly, the Christian congregation, and yes, the Christian church. Typology is at work here. The type is the Temple and the Synagogue. The antitype is the rational worship of the Church.

---

38 Everett Ferguson, *A Cappella Music in the Public Worship of the Church*, fourth edition (Abilene: Desert Willow Publishing, 2013), 46.
39 Paul Levertoff, "Synagogue," in *The International Standard Bible Encyclopaedia*, Volume IV (James Orr, John L Nuelsen, Edgar Y. Mullins, Morris O. Evans, Melvin Grove Kyle, editors) (Grand Rapids, Michigan: WM. B. Eerdmans Publishing CO., 1939, 1956), 2879. (Levertoff described all the list except for "singing.")
40 Ferguson, *A Cappella Music in the Public Worship of the Church*, fourth edition, 26.
41 Victor Vadney, *The Arrogant Journey: Hermeneutics and Church History* (Abilene, Texas: Desert Willow Publishing, 2012), 75, 76.

In Psalm 22:26-31, the psalmist writes about the exceeding benefits of God's answer toward God's people. David writes of a time when "The afflicted will eat and be satisfied...." (Psalm 22:26 NASB), and this was fulfilled in Christ's feeding of the 5,000 (Matthew 14:13-21; Mark 6:33-44; Luke 9:12-17; John 6:1-15) as well as Christ's feeding of the 4,000 (Matthew 15:32-38; Mark 8:1-10). In addition, David writes that "All the prosperous of the earth will eat and worship...." (Psalm 22:29 NASB), a clear prophetic reference to the Lord's Supper. "Prosperous" implies salvation in this passage, that is, spiritual rather than physical prosperity.

However, one of the most striking elements in this passage is the following:

> [27]All the ends of the earth will remember and turn to the LORD,
> And all the families of the nations will worship before You.
> [28]For the kingdom is the LORD's
> And He rules over the nations.
> Psalm 22:27-28 NASB

Now we should ask ourselves, under which Jewish king did all the ends of the earth turn to the LORD? Certainly this did not happen during the reign of the Jewish kings. When, then, did the Gentiles turn to Him and worship Him? Was it during the time of the Babylonian captivity? Yes, it is clear that the Gentile pagan kings such as Nebuchadnezzar (Daniel 1:1 to 4:37), Darius (Daniel 6:1-28), Cyrus (2 Chronicles 36:22; Ezra 1:1-8; 3:7; Isaiah 45:1-4; Daniel 6:28) as well as Artaxerxes (Ezra 7:11-26) seemed to have some knowledge of God, but their realms could hardly be considered bastions of monotheism. Was it during the time of the rebuilding of the second Temple? Was it during the time of the Maccabees? No, the fulfillment of this passage simply did not happen in the Old Testament.

However, King Messiah, even our Lord Jesus Christ, fulfilled this passage and is still fulfilling this passage during His reign as our heavenly King. He has been the King of kings and Lord of lords for nearly 2000 years. He sits on the eternal throne of David. It is Jesus who has accomplished this great feat of bringing the Gentiles to faith, repentance, and obedience. It is only in Jesus Christ that Psalm 22:27-28 is fulfilled. Behold the millions of Gentiles who say they believe in Him!

I ask you, who can compare to our King Messiah in this matter?

They Hate Me Without A Cause (Psalm 35:19)

OT

¹⁹Do not let those who are wrongfully my enemies rejoice over me;
Nor let <u>those who hate me without cause</u> wink maliciously.
Psalm 35:19 NASB

⁴<u>Those who hate me without a cause</u> are more than the hairs of my head;
Those who would destroy me are powerful, being wrongfully my enemies;
What I did not steal, I then have to restore.
Psalm 69:4 NASB

NT

²²"If I had not come and spoken to them, they would not have sin, but now they have no excuse for their sin. ²³He who hates Me hates My Father also. ²⁴If I had not done among them the works which no one else did, they would not have sin; but now they have both seen and hated Me and My Father as well. ²⁵*But they have done this* to fulfill the word that is written in their Law, '<small>THEY HATED ME WITHOUT A CAUSE</small>.'" John 15:22-25 NASB

Discussion: Christ Himself quoted this saying which is found in Psalms 35 and 69, and said it was a fulfillment. Indeed, it was a fulfillment. David was hard pressed, but Christ was pressed harder. David died in old age despite what his enemies tried to do to him. However, Christ's enemies succeeded in their plans to utterly humiliate Him and make Him accursed. It was not the Romans, but the Jews who cried out repeatedly, "Crucify Him!" (See Matthew 27:22-23; Mark 15:13-14; Luke 23:21; John 19:6, 15.)

It was hatred without a cause. Christ murdered no one. Christ robbed no one. Christ stole from no one. Christ committed no adultery or fornication. Christ was not a liar. Christ was not a cheat. It was hatred without a cause. In all His incredible miracles, not one person was abused, not one person had to pay for his or her healing, not one person had to hand over his treasures to Christ because Christ raised him from the dead. The unfruitful fig tree died at His word, the brute forces of nature were forced to obey Him instantly, and the evil spirits cried out in terror at His approach and pleaded for His mercy. He was without mercy to them. But to man, Christ was a prophet, a healer, a Savior, a precious friend. It was hatred without a cause.

Therefore, this is a type—antitype fulfillment. David is the type, Christ is the antitype. It is to illustrate the movement from lesser to greater. One was mistreated. The other was humiliated, beaten, scourged, mocked, crucified, accursed, and judicially murdered.

Can we point to anyone else who was so humiliated and accursed? Which descendent of David, which "King of the Jews," was hung on a tree? Truly, the leaders of the Jews hated Jesus of Nazareth and hated Him with a perfect hatred. They cried out, "Crucify Him," and this was perfect hatred perfectly fulfilled.

It is as Jesus said: It was a fulfillment. It was hatred without a cause.

Offerings Not Required (Psalm 40:6-8)

OT

6 <u>Sacrifice and meal offering You have not desired</u>;
My ears You have opened;
<u>Burnt offering and sin offering You have not required</u>.
⁷Then I said, "Behold, I come;
<u>In the scroll of the book it is written of me</u>.
⁸I delight to do Your will, O my God;
Your Law is within my heart."
Psalm 40:6-8 NASB

NT

1 For the Law, since it has *only* a shadow of the good things to come *and* not the very form of things, can never, by the same sacrifices which they offer continually year by year,

make perfect those who draw near. ²Otherwise, would they not have ceased to be offered, because the worshipers, having once been cleansed, would no longer have had consciousness of sins? ³But in those *sacrifices* there is a reminder of sins year by year. ⁴For it is impossible for the blood of bulls and goats to take away sins. ⁵Therefore, when He comes into the world, He says,

> "SACRIFICE AND OFFERING YOU HAVE NOT DESIRED,
> BUT A BODY YOU HAVE PREPARED FOR ME;
> ⁶IN WHOLE BURNT OFFERINGS AND *sacrifices* FOR SIN YOU HAVE TAKEN NO PLEASURE.
> ⁷"THEN I SAID, 'BEHOLD, I HAVE COME
> (IN THE SCROLL OF THE BOOK IT IS WRITTEN OF ME)
> TO DO YOUR WILL, O GOD.'"

⁸After saying above, "SACRIFICES AND OFFERINGS AND WHOLE BURNT OFFERINGS AND *sacrifices* FOR SIN YOU HAVE NOT DESIRED, NOR HAVE YOU TAKEN PLEASURE *in them*" (which are offered according to the Law), ⁹then He said, "BEHOLD, I HAVE COME TO DO YOUR WILL." He takes away the first in order to establish the second. ¹⁰By this will we have been sanctified through the offering of the body of Jesus Christ once for all. Hebrews 10:1-10 NASB

Discussion: In these quotations, we find that the writer of Hebrews is showing that the one-time sacrifice of Jesus Christ makes burnt offerings and sin offerings unnecessary. This fundamental change in the Law necessitates the New Covenant. He is quoting from the Septuagint as the second line shows.

However, this change in sacrifice did not take place during the reign of David or any other king in his lineage as found in the Old Testament. This change did not occur until Christ died on the cross as an atoning sacrifice for all people.

In addition, the phrase, "In the scroll of the book it is written of me" is entirely Messianic and cannot refer to David. There is nothing in the Pentateuch that speaks of David. However, as we have already covered, there are multiple references to Christ in the Pentateuch. Therefore, this sentence cannot refer to anyone except Christ.

Psalm 40 as a whole is considered by some to be Messianic. Certainly the ancient Rabbis considered Psalm 40:7 to be Messianic.[42] In fact, there is much to commend the proposition that the whole of Psalm 40 is Messianic.

However, the words of verse 12 appear at first to disallow all of Psalm 40 to be Messianic throughout:

> [12]For evils beyond number have surrounded me;
> <u>My iniquities have overtaken me</u>, so that I am not able to see;
> They are more numerous than the hairs of my head,
> And my heart has failed me.
> Psalm 40:12 NASB

Since Jesus was without sin (John 8:46; 14:30; Hebrews 4:15; 7:26; 1 Peter 2:22; 1 John 3:5), "My iniquities" cannot apply to Him in any ordinary and simple manner. Although the Hebrew word translated "iniquities" in Psalm 40:12 can mean "sin," "guilt," or "punishment,"[43] the Septuagint uses the Greek words ἀνομία μου which means "my lawlessness"[44] and this does not carry the meaning of "punishment." In addition, all the major English translations that are available to me translate Psalm 40:12 as "my sins" or "my iniquities." Only the DNT has a footnote indicating that "mine iniquities" could be translated as "my punishments."

However, Christ "bore our sins in His body on the cross" (1 Peter 2:24; Isaiah 53:5, 11; Hebrews 9:28). He was the atoning sacrifice bearing our sins, being blamed for our sins, and dying because of our sins. God even made Him to be sin:

> [21]He made Him who knew no sin *to be* sin on our behalf, so that we might become the righteousness of God in Him.
> 2 Corinthians 5:21 NASB

Therefore, in this sense, David's "my iniquities" become a type, and the antitype is Christ bearing all the iniquities of every person who ever lived and will ever live in His own body. Once again, this would show <u>the lesser to the greater</u>, even to the infinite.

---

42 Edersheim, *The Life and Times of Jesus the Messiah*, 988.
43 James A. Swanson, *Dictionary of Biblical Languages with Semantic Domains: Hebrew (Old Testament)* (electronic ed.) (Oak Harbor: Logos Research Systems, Inc., 1997), 6411.
44 Swanson, *Dictionary of Biblical Languages with Semantic Domains : Hebrew (Old Testament)*, 490.

Others will object to the Messianic nature of Psalm 40 because of verses 14 and 15. Here David asks God to shame, humiliate, turn back, dishonor, and appall those who seek his harm. There are multiple psalms which have similar language, and they are called the "imprecatory psalms." More than 20 psalms have prayers against the wicked, and the most prominent are Psalms 35, 69, and 109.[45] However, the psalmists wrote with God fully centered in their minds. It was the reign of God that was at stake.

We should remember that God has never been ashamed to judge those who violate His covenant, whether they be in the Old Testament or the New Testament. God never allowed Israel to go its own way. He has always been patient, but judgment always awaited those who rebelled against His word and would not repent. Recall that He sent the Northern Kingdom into Assyrian captivity. Recall that He sent the Southern Kingdom into Babylonian captivity. Apparently, they had difficulty learning from history, for He again destroyed Jerusalem and Palestine in AD 70 and sent His Jewish people into the Dispersion.

Jewish history is not unique, and Christian History is just as disappointing. Consider the massive unauthorized changes in Christ's Church over the first seven centuries. Islam arose and waged war on Christendom and captured every Christian center except Rome. What was considered "Christianity" at that time was subjugated and decimated by the Islamic hordes. Was this not a judgment of God against those who had broken His New Covenant? Was not the Protestant Reformation a similar judgment? Were not the 100 years of religious wars in Europe a manifestation of God's judgment on both the Roman Catholics as well as Protestants?

Therefore, we should not be ashamed of the Psalmists when they prayed against the wicked. It was and still remains that God's honor is at stake.

---

45 John Richard Sampey, "Book of Psalms," in *The International Standard Bible Encyclopaedia* (Editors: James Orr, John L. Nuelsen, Edgar Y. Mullins, Morris O. Evans, Melvin Grove Kyle), Volume IV (Grand Rapids: WM. B. Eerdmands Publishing Company, 1939, 1956), 2494.

He Who Eats My Bread (Psalm 41:9)

OT

> ⁹Even my close friend in whom I trusted,
> Who <u>ate my bread</u>,
> Has <u>lifted up his heel against me</u>. Psalm 41:9 (NASB)

NT

> ¹⁸I do not speak of all of you. I know the ones I have chosen; but *it is* that the Scripture may be fulfilled, 'HE WHO EATS MY BREAD HAS LIFTED UP HIS HEEL AGAINST ME.' ¹⁹From now on I am telling you before *it* comes to pass, so that when it does occur, you may believe that I am *He*. John 13:18-19 NASB (see also Matthew 26:23; Luke 22:21)

Discussion: Psalm 41 is a Psalm of David. Evidently during an illness or some other serious trouble, a trusted friend betrayed David and this hurt David greatly. David asked for strength from God, and God gave strength to David.

Although David did not specify who this traitor was, we might suspect that it could have been his son Absalom who conspired to kill David and take his throne, or David's trusted counselor Ahithophel the Gilonite who joined Absalom in this rebellion (2 Samuel 15).

This betrayal and suffering of David and David's restoration to his throne became a type, and the betrayal by Judas and the sufferings of Christ and His Kingdom became the antitype. David had to flee from his son Absalom, and he suffered great sorrow when Absalom was killed in the battle. However, he was able to recover his kingdom. As the antitype, Christ was betrayed by one of His apostles and suffered infinitely more than David, even to the point of death by torture with severe cruelty. Yet, Christ arose from the dead on the third day and received His own Kingdom and was seated at the right hand of God, seated forever on the eternal throne promised to David.

Therefore, Jesus rightly said that the "Scripture may be fulfilled" because the typology applied to King David as God's suffering servant was completely fulfilled in King Messiah whom we call Christ.

Your Throne, O God (Psalm 45:6-7)

OT

> **6** <u>Your throne, O God, is forever and ever;</u>
> A scepter of uprightness is the scepter of Your kingdom.
> ⁷You have loved righteousness and hated wickedness;
> Therefore God, Your God, has anointed You
> With the oil of joy above Your fellows. Psalm 45:6-7 NASB

NT

⁸But of the Son *He says*,

> "Your throne, O God, is forever and ever,
> And the righteous scepter is the scepter of His kingdom.
> ⁹"You have loved righteousness and hated lawlessness;
> Therefore God, Your God, has anointed you
> With the oil of gladness above Your companions."
> Hebrews 1:8-9 NASB

Discussion: According to the ancient rabbis, the entirety of Psalm 45 was deemed Messianic.[46] The first century Christians certainly viewed it this way as Hebrews 1:8-9 reveals. The early Christian commentators like Augustine viewed this psalm as Messianic also.[47] This interpretation has continued to this day, and Burton Coffman gave an excellent presentation of this view in his commentary.[48] However, the liberal, critical theologians deny that this psalm refers to Christ.[49]

This psalm is addressed "to the King." However, no king is named. The psalmist speaks very highly of the King, and says the King is blessed by God. Indeed, the psalmist writes that the King is above "the sons of men." We can understand that poetic exaggeration might be at work concerning this unique King in David's lineage being the recipient of the psalm in the first five verses. However, when we reach verse 6, something extraordinary is written. The psalmist

---

46   Edersheim, *The Life and Times of Jesus the Messiah*, 988, 989.
47   Augustine of Hippo, "Expositions on the Book of Psalms" (A. C. Coxe, Trans.), in *A Select Library of the Nicene and Post-Nicene Fathers of the Christian Church, First Series, Volume VIII: Saint Augustine: Expositions on the Book of Psalms* (P. Schaff, Ed.) (New York: Christian Literature Company, 1888), 155.
48   Burton Coffman, *Coffman Commentaries on the Old and New Testaments*, http://www.studylight.org/com/bcc/view.cgi?book=ps&chapter=045#8 .
49   Ash and Miller, *Living Word Commentary on the Old Testament, Psalms*, 163.

says to the King, "Your throne, O God, is forever and ever...." So this King is called "O God," something that was never done in all the rest of the Old Testament in regards to kings in the lineage of David. The Hebrews simply did not view their kings as "God." The only reasonable solution to this is to view the psalm as Messianic, and identify the King of this psalm with the Messiah. Otherwise, verse 6 cannot be explained and resolved.

If we accept this obvious solution to verse 6, then this psalm becomes a symbolic representation of Christ and His church. Symbolism is used throughout the Old Testament, particularly with the writings of the Psalms and the Prophets. For example, Psalm 23 is rich in symbolism because David calls the LORD his shepherd, and speaks as if he was one of His sheep as God directs, protects, and cares for him. Symbolic language is profuse in the Old Testament, and particularly in the Psalms.

Therefore, just as we have discovered the pattern of the Messianic types/antitypes found repeatedly in the Old/New Testaments, they are also found in the poetry of Psalm 45 and have the corresponding antitypes in the New Testament.

Psalm 45:1—"My heart overflows with a good theme" suggests divine inspiration for this Psalm. It reminds us that "All Scripture is inspired by God" as found in 2 Timothy 3:16.

Psalm 45:2a—"Grace is poured upon Your lips" reminds us of extraordinary and undeserved favor we have in Christ. The word "upon" in this passage can also be translated "through." The reading from the Septuagint is "grace has been shed forth on thy lips."[50] Jesus came not to be served, "...but to serve and to give His life a ransom for many" (Mark 10:45). Jesus was "full of grace" (John 1:14). From Him we have received "grace upon grace" (John 1:16). We are "saved through the grace of the Lord Jesus" (Acts 15:11). We are "justified as a gift by His grace through the redemption which is in Christ Jesus" (Romans 3:24 and see also Titus 3:7). It was the "gift by the grace of the one Man, Jesus Christ" (Romans 5:15). It was "the grace of God which was given you in Christ Jesus" (1 Corinthians 1:4). It was "the grace of our Lord Jesus Christ" (2 Corinthians 8:9). God called us "by the grace of Christ" (Galatians 1:6). It was "to the praise of the glory of His grace, which He freely bestowed on us in the Beloved"

---

50 Brenton, *The Septuagint with Apocrypha: Greek and English*, 724.

(Ephesians 1:6). It is "by grace you have been saved through faith" (Ephesians 2:8). This grace was prophesied by the prophets (1 Peter 1:10), and we find it here in Psalm 45:2.

Psalm 45:2b—"Therefore God has blessed You forever" (see also Psalm 21:6). This could certainly apply to David. However, how much more would it apply to King Messiah, even our Lord Jesus Christ? He is seated at the right hand of God (Luke 22:69; Colossians 3:1; Hebrews 8:1; 12:2) on the eternal throne of David (Luke 1:32) with His heavenly Father (Revelation 22:1, 3).

Psalm 45:3—"Your sword." Here the Messianic King has a sword, and He also has arrows in verse five. The liberal, critical theologians don't believe in a God who will punish or who will bring about vengeance or who will send a person to hell. They deny there is even a hell.[51] However, such things the God of both the Old and New Testaments will most certainly do. Jesus prophesied of the destruction of Jerusalem, and everything He prophesied came to pass:

> **20**"But when you see Jerusalem surrounded by armies, then recognize that her desolation is near. [21]Then those who are in Judea must flee to the mountains, and those who are in the midst of the city must leave, and those who are in the country must not enter the city; [22]because these are days of vengeance, so that all things which are written will be fulfilled. [23]Woe to those who are pregnant and to those who are nursing babies in those days; for there will be great distress upon the land and wrath to this people; [24]and they will fall by the edge of the sword, and will be led captive into all the nations; and Jerusalem will be trampled under foot by the Gentiles until the times of the Gentiles are fulfilled." Luke 21:20-24 NASB

There can be no doubt that this sword represented the judgment of God upon the Jews. No doubt exists that God used the Roman army to destroy Jerusalem just as God used the Assyrians and the Babylonians to accomplish similar things for Him in the past. Long before that, God sent Moses to humiliate Pharaoh and enrage him so

---

51 R.. Albert Mohler, "Air Conditioning Hell: How Liberalism Happens," *IX Marks Ministries eJournal* (January/February 2010) (can be read online at http://www.albertmohler.com/2010/01/26/air-conditioning-hell-how-liberalism-happens/)

He could triumph over Pharaoh in the Red Sea (Exodus 14:13-14; Psalm 136:15).

However, King Messiah has an even more powerful sword, for it is the "sword of the Spirit, which is the word of God" (Ephesians 6:17). This sword is sharper than any two-edged sword for it enters the deepest depths of the human soul and judges the thoughts and intentions of the heart (Hebrews 4:12). In Revelation the Christ is pictured as having a sharp two-edged sword that comes out of His mouth (Revelation 1:16; 19:15). Christ warns the sinners at the church of Pergamum in this manner:

> [16]Therefore repent; or else I am coming to you quickly, and I will make war against them with the sword of My mouth. Revelation 2:16 NASB

Psalm 45:4—"...ride...for the cause of truth and meekness and righteousness." In an amazing irony, this warrior, this great King, stands for **truth** and **meekness** and **righteousness**. Indeed, it would describe King David and his lineage in the Old Testament in some partial way. But, it describes King Messiah, Jesus of Nazareth, in a profound way.

Truth

Now regarding "truth," Jesus was described as being "full of grace and truth" (John 1:14). John adds that "grace and truth were realized through Jesus Christ" (John 1:17). Jesus told His disciples that if they continued in His word, they would "know the truth, and the truth will make you free" (John 8:31-32). Not all accepted the truth, for Jesus says, "But because I speak the truth, you do not believe Me" (John 8:45). Again, John recounts Christ's own words:

> [6]Jesus *said to him, "I am the way, and the truth, and the life; no one comes to the Father but through Me. John 14:6 NASB

Meekness

The meaning of the English words "meek" and "meekness" have changed in recent times. In the English language, "meek" and "meekness" often implies weakness rather than strength. In prior times the English word "meekness" did not imply weakness, but rather strength. This becomes clear when we consider the prior descriptions of Moses (Numbers 12:3) and Christ (Matthew 11:29) as being "meek" in the Authorized Version (KJV). Although the English meanings have changed, the Greek words formerly translated "meek" do not imply weakness.

Therefore, the most common Greek words formerly translated "meek" and "meekness" do not find exact English counterparts at this time. The words speak primarily of a condition of heart and mind that brings forth certain actions. Such a person does not strive against God or man.[52] In prior times the English words "meek" and "meekness" would have been a good fit, but now we have a number of English words that approximate the Greek meaning, including gentle, humble, considerate, unassuming, and meek in the former favorable sense.[53]

Of course, our primary interest is in showing that the "meekness" found in Psalm 45:4 describes Christ. The Septuagint translates the Hebrew word in Psalm 45:4 into the same Greek word that is used to describe the "meekness" of Christ in 2 Corinthians 10:1.[54] Christ described Himself with the word for "meekness" in Matthew 11:29. This same word He commended to His disciples in Matthew 5:5 that we might also be "meek." In addition to these occurrences, the "meekness" of Jesus is manifest in His condescension so beautifully expressed in Philippians 2:5-8—

> [5]Have this attitude in yourselves which was also in Christ Jesus, [6]who, although He existed in the form of God, did not regard equality with God a thing to be grasped, [7]but emptied Himself, taking the form of a bond-servant, *and* being made in the likeness of men. [8]Being found in appearance as a man, He humbled Himself by becoming obedient to the point of death, even death on a cross. Philippians 2:5-8 NASB

---

52 W. E. Vine, *An Expository Dictionary of New Testament Word with their Precise Meanings for English Readers*, Volume III (Old Tappan: Fleming H. Revell Company), 56. This can be accessed without cost at http://www2.mf.no/bibel/vines.html .

53 Walter Bauer, Frederick W. Danker, William F. Arndt, F. Wilbur Gingrich (BDAG), *A Greek-English Lexicon of the New Testament and Other Early Christian Literature*, second edition (Chicago: The University of Chicago Press, 1957, 1979), 699.

54 Brenton, *The Septuagint with Apocrypha: Greek and English*, 724.

More specifically, we should remember His condescension in being "in subjection" to Joseph and Mary (Luke 2:51), and His condescension to live in poverty "though He was rich" (2 Corinthians 8:9).

Therefore, the "meekness" spoken of in Psalm 45:4 is a type of the "meekness" that Christ displayed as an antitype. However, His gentleness, humility, as well as His unassuming and considerate mind and actions are far more impressive than anything we find displayed in the lineage of the Davidic kings in the Old Testament. So vast is the difference that we should consider this more than just an antitype. Indeed, it must be none other than the literal fulfillment of this Old Testament Psalm in Jesus Christ.

Righteousness

The Greek word δικαιοσύνη is translated "justice" or "righteousness" and occurs 92 times in the New Testament. It is the word found in the Septuagint translation of Psalm 45:4. This Greek word has four major meanings in the New Testament as follows:

1. The uprightness and justice that characterizes a judge (Acts 17:31; Hebrews 11:33; Revelation 19:11).
2. In the moral and religious sense which God requires of men, including obeying His statutes (Matthew 3:15; 5:20; 6:1f; Philippians 3:6), and as a principle for conducting our lives (Matthew 5:6; 21:32; Luke 1:75; Acts 10:35; 24:25; Romans 6:13, 16, 18; 14:17; 2 Corinthians 6:7, 14; Ephesians 4:24; 5:9; 1 Timothy 6:11; 2 Timothy 2:22; 3:16; 4:8; Hebrews 1:9; 12:11; James 1:20; 2 Peter 2:5, 21; 3:13; 1 John 2:29; 3:7, 10; Revelation 22:11).
3. Christ as our righteousness through faith, which is found primarily in the Pauline Epistles (Romans 1:17; 3:21, 22, 25, 26; 4:3, 5, 9, 11, 13, 22; 5:17; 8:10; 9:30; 10:4; 1 Corinthians 1:30; Galatians 3:6; 5:5; Hebrews 11:7; James 2:22-23; 2 Peter 1:1).
4. "Righteousness" viewed as virtue and a near equivalent to "Christianity" (Matthew 5:10; 1 Peter 2:24; 3:14).[55]

---

55 BDAG, *A Greek-English Lexicon of the New Testament and Other Early Christian Literature*, second edition, 196-197.

Christ lived a righteous life in every respect, and unlike David and the kings in his lineage in the Old Testament, no one could convict Him of sin. Not only this, but Christ and His apostles taught that we must be righteous in the moral and religious sense. However, true and faultless righteousness must be imputed to us by God on the basis of our faith in Christ, and not our faith in our own exercise of righteousness.

Was there anyone in the history of man who was more righteous than Christ? Was there anyone who taught the necessity of personal righteousness more than Christ? Was there anyone besides Christ who had the power to impute ultimate and vicarious righteousness to His disciples based on their faith in Him?

Therefore, **Truth**, **Meekness**, and **Righteousness** in their fullness uniquely belong to Jesus Christ.

Psalm 45:6—This was addressed on pages 76-77.

Psalm 45:7a—"You have loved righteousness" (see above on "Righteousness").

Psalm 45:7a— "and hated wickedness...." Christ loved righteousness and hated wickedness according to Hebrews 1:9. Likewise, we as followers and imitators of Him, must also place our relationship with Him as primary, more important than any other relationship and even more important than our own lives (Luke 14:27).

Psalm 45:7b—"Your God has anointed You with the oil of joy above your fellows." Just as the Davidic kings were anointed by the prophets with oil as a sign of their earthly kingships and reigns, so Christ was also anointed with the Holy Spirit. This referred to the coming of the Holy Spirit upon Christ after His baptism, and the divine pronouncement by the Father that Jesus was His Son (Matthew 3:16-17; Luke 3:21-22; John 1:29-34). Therefore, we have the picture of the Davidic kings' anointing with oil by a prophet as the type, and the far superior anointing of Christ by God the Father with the Holy Spirit and with the Father's own verbal ratification. Furthermore, just as the Davidic kings were anointed "above your fellows," so Christ was anointed to become the "King of kings" and "Lord of lords" (Revelation 17:14; 19:16), "...far above all rule and authority and power and dominion, and every name that is named..." (Ephesians 1:21). We see again the typology that moves from the lesser to the

Your Throne, O God (Psalm 45:6-7)

greater, from that which was grand to that which is breathtaking, from the temporal to the eternal, from the Davidic kings to Christ.

Psalm 45:8a—"Your garments are *fragrant with* myrrh and aloes *and* cassia...." Surely, the Davidic kings were dressed in the best looking and best smelling clothes. How ironic it is to find that Christ's grave clothing consisted of linen wrappings with 100 pounds of myrrh and aloes (John 19:39-40). Previously, the typology was from the lesser to the greater. Here the typology is from the greater to the lesser, from the unique and expensive to that which was common and customary for even a poor, dead Jew. However, the irony would change because Jesus resurrected from the dead, and none of the Davidic kings in the Old Testament did that. What the world saw as defeat, God saw as only a step to glory!

Psalm 45:8b—"Out of ivory palaces stringed instruments have made you glad." It was Solomon who built an ivory throne for himself (2 Chronicles 9:17). Perhaps jealous of this, Ahab in the Northern Kingdom, later built a house of ivory for himself (1 Kings 22:39). Ivory must have become a symbol of wealth to flaunt since others later did the same and were rebuked by the prophet Amos (Amos 3:15). "Stringed instruments" used in Temple worship were popularized by David (1 Chronicles 15:16, 28; 16:42). Evidently, a fuller expression of this is found in Psalm 150. David himself played the lyre, and it drove the harmful spirit from Saul temporarily (1 Samuel 16:23). When there were restorations of the Mosaic Covenant, often after generations of neglect, such musical instruments also were restored (2 Chronicles 29:25; 34:12).[56] These instruments were the physical and literal signs of the Old Testament.

However, with the conviction that Psalm 45:6 makes this psalm Messianic, and with the support of the ancient Rabbis who agree with the same, and with the validation of the inspired writer of the New Testament book of Hebrews showing that Psalm 45:6-7 points to Jesus Christ, we should press on to discover the meaning of Psalm 45:8b. There are no ivory houses mentioned in the New Testament. However, our Savior is in heaven, which is a pure paradise and beyond the understanding of mortals. It was from heaven that He came to earth to

---

56 James Miller, "Music," in *The International Standard Bible Encyclopaedia* (Editors; James Orr, John L. Nuelsen, Edgar Y. Mullins, Morris O. Evans, Melvin Grove Kyle), Volume III (Grand Rapids: WM. B. Eerdmands Publishing Company, 1939, 1956), 2094-2101.

become the incarnated Son of God and suffer and die for us all. It was to heaven that He returned after His death, burial, and resurrection. Undoubtedly, this is what Henry Barraclough had in mind when he wrote the hymn, *My Lord Has Garments* (Ivory Palaces). The chorus is, "Out of the ivory palaces, Into a world of woe, Only His great eternal love...Made my Savior go."[57] Now Barraclough was not inspired as the biblical writers were, but he must have understood that the symbolism of Psalm 45:8b pointed to Christ and heaven.

Regarding the "stringed instruments" in Psalm 45:8b, the figurative language found in Revelation employs this symbolism, calling them "harps" (Revelation 5:8; 14:2-3; 15:2). Just as the golden bowls full of incense were symbolic of the prayers of the saints (Revelation 5:8), so the harps were symbolic of their songs and praises to God (Revelation 14:2-3). We should not try to force a literal meaning on the bowls or the harps because they are spiritual symbols. If we demand literal harps in Revelation, then we must also be convinced that God has a cat-gut factory in heaven to replace the worn-out strings of the literal harps.

Unlike the explicit commands of the Old Testament (e.g., Psalm 150), instrumental music was never authorized in Christian worship in the New Testament. It was well-understood by the church in the following centuries that instrumental music was not a part of Christian worship. Instrumental music in worship originated in the Western arm of the Catholic Church. The Eastern Orthodox Church, which separated from the Roman Catholic Church in AD 1054, believed and still holds that instrumental music was never authorized in the New Testament, and they remained non-instrumental in their worship for centuries after the Great Schism.

> Since the Eastern Orthodox tradition bans instrumental music, or accompaniment, the singing is always a cappella, with only a few exceptions admitted by Westernized parishes in America. The idea behind the ban is based upon the practice of worship in the New Testament; i.e., only the natural aptitudes

---

57 Henry Barraclough, "My Lord Has Garments," in *Great Songs of the Church*, Number Two (Chicago: Great Songs Press, 1972), hymns 154, 155.

of the living congregation are viewed as capable of expressing praise that is worthy of God.[58]

A very scholarly treatment of *a cappella* music in the church was written by Dr. Everett Ferguson and should be read thoroughly in order to understand the ancient documents that bear witness on this subject. In concluding his comments on the vast evidence from the ancient manuscripts, Dr. Ferguson says that instrumental music was introduced in about AD 1000 in the form of an organ. He adds that the organ was then a separate item in the worship service. The chant as a hymn left no room for the organ, and it was not until new styles of music developed that the organ could accompany actual singing. He also points out that the great majority of the Eastern churches still do not use instrumental music, and that all these things testify to the "purely vocal style of early Christian worship."[59]

Therefore, the Jewish type was "ivory palaces," and the Christian antitype is heaven. The stringed instruments of the Jewish Temple were the type, and the Christian antitype is the non-instrumental vocal praise of God. Clearly then we have entered into Christ's church as the antitype of the Mosaic system.

Psalm 45:9-15 is a description of the King's daughters, the queen, and the virgins. They are symbolic of Christ's church. John the Baptist was the first to express this so clearly.

> **25** Therefore there arose a discussion on the part of John's disciples with a Jew about purification. [26]And they came to John and said to him, "Rabbi, He who was with you beyond the Jordan, to whom you have testified, behold, He is baptizing and all are coming to Him." [27]John answered and said, "A man can receive nothing unless it has been given him from heaven. [28]You yourselves are my witnesses that I said, 'I am not the Christ,' but, 'I have been sent ahead of Him.' [29]<u>He who has the bride is the bridegroom</u>; but the friend of the bridegroom, who stands and hears him, rejoices greatly because of the bridegroom's voice. So this joy of mine has been made full. [30]He must increase, but I must decrease. John 3:25-30 NASB

---

58 Monks at Decani Monastery in Kosovo, *The Doctrine of the Orthodox Church: Worship & Sacraments*, http://orthodoxinfo.com/general/doctrine3.aspx

59 Ferguson, *A Cappella Music in the Public Worship of the Church*, fourth edition, 96-98.

Using this same metaphor, Paul compares the intimate relationship of Christ and His church to the relationship between a husband and wife.

> **25** Husbands, love your wives, just as Christ also loved the church and gave Himself up for her, [26]so that He might sanctify her, having cleansed her by the washing of water with the word, [27]that He might present to Himself the church in all her glory, having no spot or wrinkle or any such thing; but that she would be holy and blameless. [28]So husbands ought also to love their own wives as their own bodies. He who loves his own wife loves himself; [29]for no one ever hated his own flesh, but nourishes and cherishes it, just as Christ also *does* the church, [30]because we are members of His body. [31]FOR THIS REASON A MAN SHALL LEAVE HIS FATHER AND MOTHER AND SHALL BE JOINED TO HIS WIFE, AND THE TWO SHALL BECOME ONE FLESH. [32]This mystery is great; but I am speaking with reference to Christ and the church. Ephesians 5:25-32 NASB

The apostle John continued this metaphor of Christ and His Bride as well as the marriage supper of the Lamb in Revelation 19:7-9. In Revelation 21:2 the new Jerusalem coming down out of heaven is likened to a bride adorned for her husband. In Revelation 21:9-10, the new Jerusalem is called the "bride, the wife of the Lamb." In Revelation 22:17, it is the "Spirit and the bride" who give the invitation, "Come."

It is obvious that the inspired writers of the New Testament knew that the church was the bride of Christ. Therefore, in this psalm the "type" is represented by the king's queen, daughters, and virgins. The New Testament antitype is Christ and His church. Once again we see the metaphor move from the lesser to the greater, from the carnal to the spiritual, from the Jewish king to the Ruler of the universe.

Psalm 45:10-11 deserves further comment:

> **10** Listen, O daughter, give attention and incline your ear:
> Forget your people and your father's house;
> [11]Then the King will desire your beauty.
> Because He is your Lord, bow down to Him. Psalm 45:10-11 NASB

Regarding the "forgetting" of precious relationships, this was fulfilled in Christ's teachings (Matthew 10:37; Luke 14:26; 16:13; John 12:25-26). Christ must be the first, and if others disagree, He is to be the only relationship that must be preserved and cherished.

Concerning "the King will desire your beauty," the very sending of Christ and His atoning death on the cross for all people shows the incredible nature of God's love for us. If we love Christ, God loves us and desires for us to have fellowship with Him forever.

"Because He is your Lord, bow down to Him." This is worship. Surely, we must bow down before the Son of God, and surely, we must worship Him. He proved His love and His Lordship on the cross. This incredible act for our eternal salvation should make us bow before Him.

Psalm 45:16 is another one of the verses that only Christ can fulfill:

16 In place of your fathers will be your sons;
<u>You shall make them princes in all the earth</u>. Psalm 45:16 NASB

We must ask which king in the line of David made his sons "princes in all the earth?" Definitely the kings made their sons princes in Palestine. David's and Solomon's rule extended even farther. However, none of Old Testament kings caused their sons to become princes "in all the earth." Yet in Christ's Kingdom, His Church, He has made His spiritual sons "princes in all the earth." Yes, we are sons of the King! We are heirs of God and joint heirs with Christ (Romans 8:17)!

Psalm 45:17 is yet another in a long list of verses that <u>only</u> Christ can fulfill:

[17]<u>I will cause Your name to be remembered in all generations</u>;
Therefore <u>the peoples will give You thanks forever</u> and ever.
Psalm 45:17 NASB

From the opening phrase, "I will cause," it would appear that either the psalmist or God is now speaking to the King. Certainly, the English first person singular is expressed in Psalm 45:1, and there it seemed natural to assume that it was the poet speaking. However, when the psalmist is under God's control, it is God who ultimately is speaking.

The Septuagint clearly has "They shall make" instead of "I will cause," referring to the sons of the King. Contextually, this third person plural Greek verb makes sense as the sons continue to give testimony in "all generations," and surely would have a greater voice than the psalmist.

Regardless of the "I" or "They," what is promised is that the King will be remembered in all generations and by the "peoples." This is obviously not confined to the Jews. Rather, the work of the Messiah would include the Gentiles as depicted in Isaiah 2:2; 56:7; and Zechariah 8:22.

This being the case, which king in the lineage of David tried to include the Gentiles in his ministry? Which king accomplished the goal of Gentile inclusion into the kingdom? Which king accomplished the goal of praise from the Gentiles for the one and only God of heaven? I submit that there were none who succeeded in this except King Messiah, even Jesus of Nazareth, who commanded that the Great Commission include all the nations of the earth (Matthew 28:19). It is only King Messiah who has accomplished the vast dispersion of the Gospel and who has brought so many Gentiles into His Kingdom. "All generations" and "all peoples:" Is there anyone other than Jesus of Nazareth who has accomplished this?

A Word About Psalm 69

Psalm 69 has four verses that are quoted in the New Testament as fulfillments. Psalm 69:4 has already been quoted with Psalm 35:19 (They Hate Me Without A Cause). Psalm 69:9 (Zeal For Your House), Psalm 69:21 (They Gave Me Vinegar To Drink), and Psalm 69:25 (Let No One Dwell In It) will be discussed next. However, Psalm 69 is not like Psalm 45. Psalm 45 is regarded by many as a Messianic psalm from beginning to end. Yet, in spite of the four references from Psalm 69, it does not appear to be Messianic throughout. Psalm 69 portrays the great sufferings David went through and his confidence that God would deliver him.

Yet, this was a fertile field for the Holy Spirit to highlight the sufferings of Christ to His followers. The usage of these verses by the inspired apostles and prophets of the New Testament was not of their own choosing. Rather, it was by the overruling of the Holy Spirit that these verses were chosen and used.

The basic reasoning used by the Holy Spirit was "as it was for David, so it was for Christ." It is fitting to see that both the head of the Davidic lineage and the Head of the New Covenant should have endured suffering that was parallel in nature. This, once again, is typology where there is a type in the Old Testament (David) and an antitype in the New Testament (Christ).

Nearly 2000 years ago, a man named Jesus of Nazareth appeared on the scene of history. He was wonderful in every way. God Almighty spoke from heaven twice saying that this Jesus was His Son. His powers over diseases, demons, death, life, matter, and even the brute forces of Nature were shocking and phenomenal. His teachings were very different, extremely challenging, and at the same time comforting. He spoke with authority in every way. He taught His followers that He was fulfilling the Old Testament. This Person who was wonderful beyond explanation was taken captive by His enemies, given an unlawful trial and verdict, then brutalized and murdered on the basis of false evidence. Yet, according to His own prophecy, He rose from the dead on the third day. He appeared alive to His followers multiple times over 40 days and then ascended into heaven with numerous people as witnesses.

Nothing like this had ever happened. No one else like this had ever lived on the earth. Therefore, it was not surprising that the inspired apostles and prophets who wrote the New Testament were led by the Holy Spirit to bring all things into submission to Him. This included the Old Testament which this phenomenal Person testified with all gravity, "spoke about" Him.

Zeal And Reproach (Psalm 69:9)

OT

> [9]For <u>zeal for Your house has consumed me,</u>
> And <u>the reproaches of those who reproach You have fallen on me</u>. Psalm 69:9 NASB

Jesus Christ *Fulfills* Messianic Prophecies

NT

13 The Passover of the Jews was near, and Jesus went up to Jerusalem. ¹⁴And He found in the temple those who were selling oxen and sheep and doves, and the money changers seated *at their tables*. ¹⁵And He made a scourge of cords, and drove *them* all out of the temple, with the sheep and the oxen; and He poured out the coins of the money changers and overturned their tables; ¹⁶and to those who were selling the doves He said, "Take these things away; stop making My Father's house a place of business." ¹⁷His disciples remembered that it was written, "ZEAL FOR YOUR HOUSE WILL CONSUME ME." John 2:13-17 NASB

1 Now we who are strong ought to bear the weaknesses of those without strength and not *just* please ourselves. ²Each of us is to please his neighbor for his good, to his edification. ³For even Christ did not please Himself; but as it is written, "THE REPROACHES OF THOSE WHO REPROACHED YOU FELL ON ME." Romans 15:1-3 NASB

Discussion: This short passage in Psalm 69:9 has two different citations in the New Testament. Both John and Paul said, "it is written." So, there cannot be any reasonable objection that such were considered prophecies in the mind of the Holy Spirit or the minds of John and Paul.

David's statement is in the past tense in Psalm 69:9 in both the Hebrew and the Septuagint. The Temple had not yet been constructed. David had fled from King Saul and had gone to the Tabernacle in Nob. There Ahimelech the priest inquired of the LORD for David, gave David some of the holy bread, and also gave David the sword of Goliath (1 Samuel 21:1-9). When Saul heard about this (1 Samuel 22:6-23), he commanded that all the priests and the entire city of Nob to be killed. Doeg the Edomite carried this out, and also murdered all the other people in Nob. Surely, this must have been a heavy burden for David to bear, knowing that his actions led to the slaughter of the priests as well as the city of Nob. Such knowledge "consumed" him.

The parallel statement in John 2:17 is in the future tense, "will consume." This is because the Passion of Christ on the cross was still in the future when He cleansed the Temple.

We have typology at work here. As it was with David, so it was with Christ. David is the type and Christ is the antitype. It is a contrast in degree from the lesser to the greater. David was consumed with grief over the consequences of his trip to the tabernacle in Nob. However, the consuming of Christ because of His zeal for God's Kingdom/House was infinitely greater: He was crucified, He bore the sins and was blamed and punished for the sins of every human being, and He died to save us from our sins on that horrible cross.

The second reference is to David's statement, "the reproaches of those who reproach You have fallen on me." Saul's reproach of God by murdering His priests fell upon David. David must have remembered that incident until he died.

Paul used David's statement in the context of his argument that the strong must bear the weaknesses of those who have no strength because that is what Christ did for us. We all have reproached God with our sins. God took all that reproach and put it on His Son. Thus, "the reproaches of those who reproach You have fallen on me" describes Christ supremely. Just as He bore our weaknesses in His body on the cross, we also are commanded to bear each others' weaknesses. Here the implications of the typology are very personal.

They Gave Me Gall & Vinegar (Psalm 69:21)

OT

²¹They also gave me <u>gall for my food</u>
And for my thirst they gave me <u>vinegar to drink</u>. Psalm 69:21 NASB

NT

28 After this, Jesus, knowing that all things had already been accomplished, <u>to fulfill the Scripture,</u> *said, "I am thirsty." ²⁹A jar full of sour wine was standing there; so they put a sponge full of the sour wine upon *a branch of* hyssop and brought it up to His mouth. ³⁰Therefore when Jesus had received the sour wine, He said, "It is finished!" And He bowed His head and gave up His spirit. John 19:28-30 NASB (see also Matthew 27:34, 48; Mark 15:23, 36; Luke 23:36)

Discussion: David's statement may have been literal or figurative in Psalm 69:21. The Hebrew word translated "gall" can also be translated as "poison." It can also be translated as "bitterness" in terms of life experience.[60] It is not implausible to think that David's enemies tried to poison his food and drink. Again, there may have been some bitterness in David because of his life experiences. Regardless, the Holy Spirit took David's statement and applied it to Christ.

In Matthew 27:34 and Mark 15:23, Jesus was given wine mixed with gall before His crucifixion. After tasting it, He refused to drink it. In Matthew 27:48, Mark 15:36, and Luke 23:36, Jesus was given "sour wine" just before His death on the cross.

Once again we are dealing with typology with David as the type and Christ as the antitype. As it was for David, so it was for Christ. Again we find that it illustrates a movement from the lesser to the greater. David was inconvenienced or perhaps even harmed in some way. However, David did not die as a result. On the other hand, Christ was brutalized and judicially murdered. In the first instance David was inconvenienced but lived to a ripe old age. However, Christ's sufferings were far greater and even lethal. Thus this passage regarding suffering was truly fulfilled in Christ.

Let His Homestead Be Desolate (Psalm 69:25)

OT

²⁵May their camp be desolate;
May none dwell in their tents. Psalm 69:25 NASB

NT

15 At this time Peter stood up in the midst of the brethren (a gathering of about one hundred and twenty persons was

---

60 James Swanson, *Dictionary of Biblical Languages with Semantic Domains: Hebrew* (Old Testament) (electronic ed.) (Oak Harbor: Logos Research Systems, Inc., 1997), definition 8032.

there together), and said, ¹⁶"Brethren, <u>the Scripture had to be fulfilled, which the Holy Spirit foretold by the mouth of David concerning Judas</u>, who became a guide to those who arrested Jesus. ¹⁷For he was counted among us and received his share in this ministry." ¹⁸(Now this man acquired a field with the price of his wickedness, and falling headlong, he burst open in the middle and all his intestines gushed out. ¹⁹And it became known to all who were living in Jerusalem; so that in their own language that field was called Hakeldama, that is, Field of Blood.) ²⁰"<u>For it is written in the book of Psalms,</u>

'LET HIS HOMESTEAD BE MADE DESOLATE,
AND LET NO ONE DWELL IN IT';
and,
'LET ANOTHER MAN TAKE HIS OFFICE.' Acts 1:15-20 NASB

Discussion: The last line of Acts 1:20 is from Psalm 109:8, and that prophecy will be discussed when we reach that Psalm.

Psalm 69:25 is part of David's prayer against the wicked in verses 22-28. His suffering was covered in verses 1-21, and he briefly restated that in verse 29. David then ends Psalm 69 with praise to God in verses 30-36.

Peter says that the "Holy Spirit foretold by the mouth of David concerning Judas...." From these inspired apostolic words, we must understand that we are dealing with a prophecy in Psalm 69:25 regarding Judas. Typology is again present. Just as David was betrayed, so Christ was betrayed. Just as there were imprecations against those who betrayed David, so there are imprecations against the one who would betray Christ. If you see the one, you see the other. The imprecation in Psalm 69:25 is applied to Judas. The implications of the "book of life" in Psalm 69:28, including who are and who are not named in that book, are alluded to in several New Testament passages.

Of course, this gives new emphasis for our need to understand the imprecatory psalms. Just as imprecations were upon those who stood against David, so the same imprecations are against those who stand against Christ. Now the critical theologians might faint at this because they do not believe in the hell that Jesus taught about in the Gospels. They don't believe in a God who would condemn anyone to eternal punishment. Yet, the Scripture is exceedingly clear:

⁶For after all it is *only* just for God to repay with affliction those who afflict you, ⁷and *to give* relief to you who are afflicted and to us as well when the Lord Jesus will be revealed from heaven with His mighty angels in flaming fire, ⁸dealing out retribution to those who do not know God and to those who do not obey the gospel of our Lord Jesus. ⁹These will pay the penalty of eternal destruction, away from the presence of the Lord and from the glory of His power.... 2 Thessalonians 1:6-9 NASB

Jesus Spoke In Parables (Psalm 78:2)

OT

²<u>I will open my mouth in a parable</u>;
I will utter dark sayings of old.... Psalm 78:2 NASB

NT

34 All these things Jesus spoke to the crowds in parables, and He did not speak to them without a parable. ³⁵*This was* to fulfill what was spoken through the prophet:

"I WILL OPEN MY MOUTH IN PARABLES;
I WILL UTTER THINGS HIDDEN SINCE THE FOUNDATION OF THE WORLD." Matthew 13:34-35 NASB

Discussion: Psalm 78 has a heading indicating that it is "A Maskil of Asaph." This psalm is a history lesson based on Israelite history from Jacob, through Egypt and God's great deliverance for His people Israel, through their wilderness wanderings, through their entry into the promised land, and ending with God's choice of David. Throughout this history, the Jewish people were known for their disobedience.

Asaph calls this a "parable" in verse 2. In the Septuagint, the Greek word used in Psalm 78:2 is the same word that is translated "parable" in the Gospels. In both Hebrew and Greek, "parable" is defined as a "short narrative with a symbolic meaning."[61,62] In Asaph's parable, the narrative was historical, but the symbolic meaning was the pressing need to recognize and obey God's Law and honor the king that God had chosen. As in all times and seasons, those who wanted to hear the ancient parable would understand, but those who did not want to listen would become a stubborn, rebellious, and faithless generation, just as their ancient fathers had been in the wilderness.

The context for Matthew 13:34-35 is the whole of Matthew 13, for here Matthew presents several parables taught by Jesus. The parables are The Sower And The Soils (Matthew 13:3-9, 18-23), The Tares Among the Wheat (Matthew 13:24-30, 36-43), The Mustard Seed (Matthew 13:31-32), The Leaven (Matthew 13:33), The Hidden Treasure (Matthew 13:44), The Costly Pearl (Matthew 13:45-46), and The Dragnet (Matthew 13:47-50). Jesus explained His use of parables in Matthew 13:10-17 and this included a quote from Isaiah 6:9-10. The verses from Isaiah will be considered when we discuss the Messianic prophecies in Isaiah.

In essence, Christ used parables in a similar way of Asaph so that those who were earnest seekers would understand, and those who were not earnest would not understand. Those who understood would become wiser, but the opposite would be for those who would not understand.

Once again we find that typology explains the New Testament fulfillment. Asaph spoke a parable so that the faithful could understand their need to obey God. Christ spoke parables for the same reason. In both cases, those with stubborn hearts and minds would not be able to assimilate the symbolic meaning of the parables. So we find the type in Asaph and the antitype in Christ. Again there is a comparison from the lesser to the greater. How many people know of Asaph? How many know of Christ? Asaph was a good teacher with sound instruction. Jesus was the master teacher whose instructions are like food and water to a starving and thirsty world. At God's command, we must listen to Jesus Christ, His Son (Matthew 17:5; Mark 9:7;

---

61 Swanson, *Dictionary of Biblical Languages with Semantic Domains: Hebrew* (Old Testament), 5442.

62 J. P. Louw & E. A. Nida, *Vol. 1: Greek-English lexicon of the New Testament: Based on semantic domains* (electronic ed. of the 2nd edition.) (New York: United Bible Societies, 1996), 390.

Angels Worship Him (Psalm 97:7)

OT

> 7 Let all those be ashamed who serve graven images,
> Who boast themselves of idols;
> <u>Worship Him, all you gods</u>. Psalm 97:7 NASB

NT

> ⁶And when He again brings the firstborn into the world, He says,
>
> > "AND LET ALL THE ANGELS OF GOD WORSHIP HIM." Hebrews 1:6 NASB

Discussion: The Septuagint translation of Psalm 97:7 has "...worship him, all ye his angels."[63] It would appear that the author of Hebrews was using the Septuagint translation in Hebrews 1:6. Some concerns have arisen that the writer of Hebrews was quoting from the Septuagint translation of Deuteronomy 32:43. However, the words quoted there have no equivalent thought in the Hebrew text, so this is unlikely.

Psalm 97 extols the reign, the majesty, and the awesome power of the LORD. The people are exhorted to abandon their idols because God is far above all. They are exhorted to "hate evil" and worship God.

The writer of Hebrews exalts Christ in Hebrews 1, and there can be no doubt that he portrays God as commanding all the angels to worship His firstborn Son, that is, Christ. Only the critical theologian would dare to challenge the writer of Hebrews regarding his authority in this matter.

The writer of Hebrews was certainly not the only one in ancient Christianity to interpret this psalm Messianically. Concerning the heading of this psalm in the Syriac version, Adam Clarke said,

---

63 Brenton, *The Septuagint with Apocrypha: Greek and English*, 757.

The Syriac has, "A Psalm of David, in which he predicts the advent of Christ, (i.e., in the flesh,) and through it his last appearing, (i.e., to judgment.")[64]

Early Christian writers like Augustine the Bishop of Hippo (354-430), certainly understood that all of Psalm 97 referred to Christ:

> 1. ... This Psalm is entitled, "A Psalm of David's, when his land was restored." <u>Let us refer the whole to Christ</u>, if we wish to keep the road of a right understanding: let us not depart from the corner stone, lest our understanding suffer a fall: in Him let that become fixed, which wavered with unstable motion; let that rest upon Him, which before was waving to and fro in uncertainty.[65]

At least six times the Hebrew text of Psalm 97 refers to "LORD," or "YHWH." If indeed this psalm is Messianic throughout, then we find again that Jesus of Nazareth is pictured as YHWH in the Old Testament. Regarding this phenomenon, please see my discussion on Psalm 8:1-2.

Barnes pointed out that there is nothing in Psalm 97 that could prove this psalm is not referring to the Messiah. He also pointed out that two famous rabbis, Raschi and Kimchi, assert that Psalms 93 through 101 are Messianic.[66]

You Founded The Earth (Psalm 102:25-27)

OT

²⁵"Of old You founded the earth,
And the heavens are the work of Your hands.

---

64 Adam Clarke, *The Adam Clarke Commentary*, Psalm XCVII, http://www.studylight.org/com/acc/view.cgi?book=ps&chapter=097.

65 Augustine of Hippo, *Expositions on the Book of Psalms* (A. C. Coxe, Trans.), In P. Schaff (Ed.), *A Select Library of the Nicene and Post-Nicene Fathers of the Christian Church, First Series, Volume VIII: Saint Augustin: Expositions on the Book of Psalms* (P. Schaff, Ed.) (New York: Christian Literature Company, 1888), 475.

66 Albert Barnes, *Barnes' Notes on the New Testament*, http://www.studylight.org/com/bnn/view.cgi?book=heb&chapter=001.

Jesus Christ *Fulfills* Messianic Prophecies

²⁶"Even they will perish, but You endure;
And all of them will wear out like a garment;
Like clothing You will change them and they will be changed.
²⁷"But You are the same,
And Your years will not come to an end. Psalm 102:25-27 NASB

NT

¹⁰And,

"You, Lord, in the beginning laid the foundation of the earth,
And the heavens are the works of Your hands;
¹¹They will perish, but You remain;
And they all will become old like a garment,
¹²And like a mantle You will roll them up;
Like a garment they will also be changed.
But You are the same,
And Your years will not come to an end." Hebrews 1:10-12 NASB

Discussion: Psalm 102 is addressed to the Lord, or "YHWH," and the psalmist addresses Him as such seven times in this psalm. The psalmist puts forward his personal plight in poetic detail as well as the urgent needs of Israel and pleads for the favor of God. The psalmist takes comfort that God lives forever and that He will show compassion on Israel. This will cause praise in future generations.

The writer of Hebrews in chapter 1 uses multiple Messianic references from the Old Testament to exalt Christ and confirm that He is the Son of God. In Hebrews 1:10-12, it is clear that the writer of Hebrews is equating Jesus with the Lord or "YHWH," The principle is simple: As with the Father, so with His Son. Regarding this phenomenon, please see the Introduction as well as my discussion on Psalm 8:1-2. Once again, only those who do not recognize that the writer of Hebrews had inspired authority will disagree with his use of Psalm 102:25-27.

Let Another Take His Office (Psalm 109:8)

OT

> [8]Let his days be few;
> Let another take his office. Psalm 109:8 NASB

NT

> [20]"For it is written in the book of Psalms,
>> 'LET HIS HOMESTEAD BE MADE DESOLATE,
>> AND LET NO ONE DWELL IN IT';
>
> and,
>> 'LET ANOTHER MAN TAKE HIS OFFICE.' Acts 1:20 NASB

Discussion: Like Psalm 69, Psalm 109 is an imprecatory psalm where David prays against the wicked. Although David had shown love to these particular people, they betrayed him and repaid him with evil. The distinct majority of the 31 verses in this psalm contain multiple imprecations. The liberal scholars often scoff at such. However, it is clear in the New Testament that those who do not obey God will face eternal suffering in hell (Matthew 5:22, 29, 30).

As I noted in the discussion of Psalm 69:25, Peter's use of Acts 1:20 contains two Old Testament passages. The first portion of Acts 1:20 was discussed with Psalm 69:25. We now focus on Peter's usage of Psalm 109:8 which is used in the second portion of Acts 1:20.

Both of these imprecations or curses in Acts 1:20 had in one sense already taken effect on Judas, because he had already committed suicide. The point of Peter quoting these Scriptures was to show not only the divine judgment that was given against Judas, but also to show the divine authority for selecting someone else to fill the office of apostle in place of Judas. This is the only time an apostle was replaced, because it was the only time that "LET ANOTHER MAN TAKE HIS OFFICE" could apply.

Once again, all this takes place within a typology. Just as David was persecuted, Christ was persecuted and Christ also was persecuted and suffered to the point of death. Just as David prayed that God would judge the wicked, so Judas had already passed into his condemnation. Jesus prophesied regarding this:

> ²⁴The Son of Man *is to* go, just as it is written of Him; but woe to that man by whom the Son of Man is betrayed! It would have been good for that man if he had not been born." Matthew 26:24 NASB

The LORD says to my Lord (Psalm 110:1)

OT

> 1 The LORD says to my Lord:
> "Sit at My right hand
> Until I make Your enemies a footstool for Your feet." Psalm 110:1 NASB

NT

> **41** Now while the Pharisees were gathered together, Jesus asked them a question: ⁴²"What do you think about the Christ, whose son is He?" They *said to Him, "*The son* of David." ⁴³He *said to them, "Then how does David in the Spirit call Him 'Lord,' saying,
>
>> ⁴⁴'THE LORD SAID TO MY LORD,
>> "SIT AT MY RIGHT HAND,
>> UNTIL I PUT YOUR ENEMIES BENEATH YOUR FEET"'?
>
> ⁴⁵If David then calls Him 'Lord,' how is He his son?" Matthew 22:41-45 NASB

Discussion: Psalm 110:1 is frequently quoted in the New Testament, and the above quotes are from Christ Himself. Psalm 110:1 is quoted or alluded to in Matthew 22:44; 26:64; Mark 12:36; 14:62; Luke 20:42-43; 22:69; Acts 2:34; Hebrews 1:3; 10:12-13. This shows us the great importance of this quotation. It should be noted that the ancient rabbis found that "Ps. 110 is throughout applied to the Messiah."[67]

---

67 Edersheim, *The Life and Times of Jesus the Messiah*, 991.

Without exception, the New Testament references uniformly proclaim that the One sitting down at the right hand of God is Christ and not David. In addition, the heading for this Psalm is "A Psalm of David." Therefore, David was writing about someone besides himself who was being seated at the right hand of God. The person being seated is Christ, and David's psalm is about Christ.

Early Christianity did not deny the New Testament witness but confessed that Christ indeed was revealed in the Psalms and most especially in Psalm 110. Augustine of Hippo (354-430) wrote,

> 1.... This Psalm is one of those promises, surely and openly prophesying our Lord and Saviour Jesus Christ; so that we are utterly unable to doubt that Christ is announced in this Psalm, since we are now Christians, and believe the Gospel.[68]

However, the critical theologians love to contradict Christ and His apostles, saying that this psalm was not written *by* David, but by someone else *about* David,[69] thus dethroning Christ and substituting the typical Davidic king in the place of Christ. By any means possible they will deny that this is a Messianic prophecy fulfilled only and uniquely by Jesus Christ.

A Priest Forever (Psalm 110:4)

OT

> **4** The LORD has sworn and will not change His mind,
> "You are a priest forever
> According to the order of Melchizedek." Psalm 110:4 NASB

NT

> ⁶just as He says also in another *passage*,
> "YOU ARE A PRIEST FOREVER
> ACCORDING TO THE ORDER OF MELCHIZEDEK." Hebrews 5:6
> NASB (see also Hebrews 7:17, 21)

Discussion: In Psalm 110:4 we find that King Messiah, who is seated at the right hand of God (Psalm 110:1), is also declared by

---

68 Augustine of Hippo, *Expositions on the Book of Psalms*, 541.
69 Ash and Miller, *Living Word Commentary on the Old Testament, Psalms*, 367.

God to be a "priest forever." This priesthood is not after the levitical/Aaronic priesthood but after the priesthood of Melchizedek. There were countless levitical/Aaronic priests attending in the Temple who died and had to be replaced continually. However, Christ, who is our High Priest after the order of Melchizedek, serves forever because He always lives to intercede for us (Hebrews 7:25). Since Christ, who was in the lineage of Judah rather than Levi, represented such a dramatic change in the priesthood according to the Law of Moses, the Law of Moses also had to be changed (Hebrews 7:12).

However, the liberal, critical theologians insist that this priesthood was not unique to Christ, and they deny that the writer of Hebrews was correct. Rather, they say that David and Solomon functioned as priests after the order of Melchizedek, citing 2 Samuel 6:13-15 and 1 Kings 8:62; 9:25.[70] These state that David and Solomon "offered" certain sacrifices, and these critical theologians assume that means David and Solomon, as priests after the order of Melchizedek, performed the duties of the priest in these offerings. They seem to overlook the laws that regulated these offerings. In brief, Leviticus details the following regarding the roles of the worshipper and the roles of the priest in the following sacrifices:

Burnt Offerings: The worshipper was to "offer" the sacrifice, lay his hand on the bull's head, and kill the bull. The priest was to collect the bull's blood and throw the blood against the sides of the altar, arrange the fire, wash the bull's entrails and legs with water, and burn all of it on the altar (Leviticus 1).

Grain Offerings: The worshipper brought the grain offering, poured oil on it, put frankincense on it, and then gave it to the priest. The priest offered the memorial portion, and the rest became food for the priests (Leviticus 2).

Peace Offerings: The worshipper brought the peace offering from the herd or flock, without blemish, and "offered" it before the Lord. The worshipper laid his hands on the head of the sacrifice and then killed the sacrifice. The priest threw the blood of the sacrifice against the walls of the altar. The fatty portions were removed by the priest and offered to the Lord by fire (Leviticus 3).

Sin Offerings: The worshipper "offered" the bull without blemish, laid his hands on the head of the bull, and then killed the

---

70 Ash and Miller, *Living Word Commentary on the Old Testament, Psalms*, 368.

bull. The priest took some of the blood of the bull, sprinkled it before the LORD, placed some of the blood on the horns of the altar, and then poured the rest of the blood at the base of the altar. The priest removed the fatty portions and burnt them on the altar. The rest of the sacrifice was burnt outside the camp (Leviticus 4:1-5:13).

Guilt Offerings: The one who committed the breach offered the ram and had to make restitution (Leviticus 5:14-6:7).

The point is this: It was the worshipper who always offered the sacrifice, laid his hands on the animal's head, and killed the animal. The role of the priest was to cast the blood where the Law said and otherwise process the body of the animal according to the Law.

In 2 Samuel 6:13-15 and 1 Kings 8:62; 9:25, nothing suggests that David and Solomon did anything more than what the ordinary worshipper did when he brought an offering. David and Solomon, just like every Jewish worshipper, *offered* and slaughtered these animals. Nothing suggests that they served as priests by processing the blood and the body of the sacrifice. To do so would break the Law of Moses, for the work of the priests could only be done by the sons of Aaron (Leviticus 1:7; 3:13; 6:18; 7:10; 7:33; 21:1).

There were times when the Jewish kings tried to usurp the role of the priests, but they suffered for it. These included Saul (1 Samuel 10:8; 13:8-13) and Uzziah (2 Chronicles 26:16-21). Therefore, it is ridiculous to say that David and Solomon were allowed to violate the Mosaic Law by being priests without being the "sons of Aaron." The priest after the order of Melchizedek did not appear until Jesus Christ. This radical change in the priesthood mandated a substantial change in the Law of Moses (Hebrews 7:12).

Jesus Christ is the only One who could become a priest after the order of Melchizedek and be that priest forever. All the other priests after the order of Aaron died. The biblical role of the Jewish priesthood completely disappeared with the destruction of the Temple in Jerusalem in AD 70. However, Christ's role of High Priest in the order of Melchizedek has continued for nearly 2,000 years without any lapse. He is our Priest forever. No one else can compare with Christ, and no one else can be "a priest forever."

Jesus Christ is the only One who could fulfill the Messianic prophecy of Psalm 110:4.

The Rejected Stone (Psalm 118:22-23)

OT

> **22** <u>The stone which the builders rejected</u>
> <u>Has become the chief corner *stone*</u>.
> ²³This is the LORD's doing;
> It is marvelous in our eyes. Psalm 118:22-23 NASB

NT

> **42** Jesus *said to them, "Did you never read in the Scriptures,
>
> > 'THE STONE WHICH THE BUILDERS REJECTED,
> > THIS BECAME THE CHIEF CORNER *stone*;
> > THIS CAME ABOUT FROM THE LORD,
> > AND IT IS MARVELOUS IN OUR EYES'"?
>
> ⁴³Therefore I say to you, the kingdom of God will be taken away from you and given to a people, producing the fruit of it. ⁴⁴And he who falls on this stone will be broken to pieces; but on whomever it falls, it will scatter him like dust." Matthew 21:42-44 NASB

Discussion: Psalm 118 was a psalm of thanksgiving for God's mighty works of salvation. Although it is not attributed to David, it certainly fits David. "Nations" opposed him, but he prevailed because of God's intervention. The great troubles between David and King Saul prior to David becoming king could be the context. In addition, David was later rejected by those who wanted David's son Absalom to be king. In both instances, there was the joyous and momentous entry of David into Jerusalem.

Psalm 118:22-23 is quoted by Jesus in Matthew 21:42. The context here is that Jesus had taught the Jewish people, including their chief priests and elders (Matthew 21:23), the parable of the landowner. This involved the vine-growers illegally taking possession of the vineyard and even murdering the son of the landowner so that there would be no heir. Thus, it was symbolic for what the chief priests and elders (i.e., the vine-growers) were about to do to Jesus (i.e., the landowner's son), that is, they would soon be responsible for His crucifixion. The Jewish leaders realized what should be done to the vine-growers in the parable, but did not grasp that they were like the vine-growers in

The Rejected Stone (Psalm 118:22-23)

Christ's parable. This is when Jesus quoted Psalm 118:22-23 showing that He, though rejected by the builders, would become the chief cornerstone. This involved the taking away of the kingdom from the Jewish leaders and giving it to another people who would produce the proper fruit.

There is no mention of "fulfillment" in Matthew. Psalm 118:22-23 is quoted also in Mark 12:10, Luke 20:17, Acts 4:11; 1 Peter 2:7. Not one of these passages invoked the word "fulfillment." However, it seems clear that both Christ and His apostles understood that Christ indeed fulfilled Psalm 118:22-23. Their very usage implied that the Old Testament passage was fulfilled in Christ. Peter's sermon in Acts 2 used four Messianic prophecies (Acts 2:17-21, 25-28, 30, 34-35), and by so doing there were 3000 Jews who were baptized because they believed that Jesus was indeed the Messiah. Other than saying that David "...looked ahead and spoke of the resurrection of Christ...", Peter did not mention the word "fulfillment" in any form when citing the Old Testament texts. However, the context implies that such fulfillment was understood. Therefore, the lack of the word "fulfillment" in any form does not disallow the use of Psalm 118:22-23 as a Messianic prophecy in the New Testament because it was fulfilled in Christ.

This passage is a perfect example of typology also. In Psalm 118, David was rejected and yet became and continued to be king with great rejoicing. In the same manner, Christ was rejected and yet became the King of kings and Lord of lords (Revelation 17:14; 19:16) with the rejoicing of saints and angels on earth and in heaven for nearly 2,000 years. It is from the lesser to the greater, from the sinner forgiven to the Master of the universe who forgives, from the material king to the Spiritual King, from the earthly royalty to the sublime and eternal Magnificence. On this basis we can certainly view Psalm 118:22-23 as enjoying a beautiful fulfillment in Christ.

Blessed Is He Who Comes (Psalm 118:26)

OT

²⁶Blessed is the one who comes in the name of the LORD; We have blessed you from the house of the LORD. Psalm 118:26 NASB

NT

37 "Jerusalem, Jerusalem, who kills the prophets and stones those who are sent to her! How often I wanted to gather your children together, the way a hen gathers her chicks under her wings, and you were unwilling. ³⁸Behold, your house is being left to you desolate! ³⁹For I say to you, from now on you will not see ME until you say, 'BLESSED IS HE WHO COMES IN THE NAME OF THE LORD!' " Matthew 23:37-39

Discussion: For the setting of Psalm 118, see the previous discussion on Psalm 118:22-23.

The setting in Matthew was on Tuesday during the Passion Week.[71] Jesus spoke the above quote just after His eight woes against the Pharisees.

Now, many prophets in the Old Testament came and spoke in the name of the LORD, and they were surely blessed for so doing. This would include David and certainly the author of Psalm 118, if he wasn't David. Yet how much more does this apply to Christ? If it applied to those ancient prophets, then it certainly applies to the Lord as well. So again, we have typology at work with the "type" found in Psalm 118:26 and the "antitype" found in Jesus Christ in Matthew 23:39. It is again a portrayal of the lesser compared to the greater.

The passage in Psalm 118:26 is also quoted by Jesus in Luke 13:35. This was earlier, during the Perean ministry, when certain Pharisees warned Jesus to flee because Herod was planning to kill Him.[72] Therefore, we find Jesus speaking a similar message in different

---

71 William Arnold Stevens and Ernest De Witt Burton, *A Harmony of the Gospels for Historical Study* (New York: Charles Scribner's Sons, 1932), 184. (This book is available as a free EPUB e-book download from Barnes and Noble.)

72 Stevens and Burton, *A Harmony of the Gospels for Historical Study*, 148.

places and times. We should not be surprised at this, for Jesus was not teaching one doctrine at one place and changing it in another place.

This passage is also quoted by the people during Christ's triumphal entry to Jerusalem (Luke 19:38). John also records this same incident in John 12:13 where it was the people shouting what Jesus had undoubtedly spoken many times. Thus, Christ spoke these words on many occasions and in many places, so much so that the crowds could shout it at the time of His triumphal entry.

Surely we should also say of Him today, "BLESSED IS HE WHO COMES IN THE NAME OF THE LORD!" Unlike His predecessors, we can continue to express it in the present tense, for He is alive and listening from the throne of David where He reigns to this day.

The LORD Has Sworn To David (Psalm 132:11)

OT

> ¹¹The LORD has sworn to David
> A truth from which He will not turn back:
> "Of the fruit of your body I will set upon your throne.
> ¹²"If your sons will keep My covenant
> And My testimony which I will teach them,
> Their sons also shall sit upon your throne forever." Psalm 132:11-12 NASB (see also 2 Samuel 7:12-16; Psalm 89:3-4)

NT

> **29** "Brethren, I may confidently say to you regarding the patriarch David that he both died and was buried, and his tomb is with us to this day. ³⁰And so, because he was a prophet and knew that GOD HAD SWORN TO HIM WITH AN OATH TO SEAT *one* OF HIS DESCENDANTS ON HIS THRONE, ³¹he looked ahead and spoke of the resurrection of the Christ, that HE WAS NEITHER ABANDONED TO HADES, NOR DID His flesh SUFFER DECAY. Acts 2:29-31 NASB

Discussion: Psalm 132 is one of the Songs of Ascents. The author remembered how David was so dedicated to God and asked God to bless that lineage on the throne of Israel and bless Israel. The psalmist realized that the kingly rule of Davidic lineage was conditional according to their obedience.

Peter's statements are made in the context of his sermon on the day of Pentecost when he used Old Testament prophecies to convince the Jews that Jesus was both Lord and Christ. Peter focused on God's oath to David in Acts 2:30. Now the word "one" in this verse is not in the Hebrew or the Greek text, but is inferred in the English text in Acts 2:30 because of what Peter says in Acts 2:31, namely, that David "...looked ahead and spoke of the resurrection of the Christ...." Therefore, according to the inspired Peter and surely what had been taught to him by Christ, what was written in Psalm 132:11 was to have it's grandest fulfillment in Jesus Christ. Indeed, Jesus was and still remains the ultimate singularity, for He is the only one who had the authority to lay down His life and the authority to take it up again (John 10:17-18).

Therefore, at the very least, we have the fulfillment of typology where the Davidic kings were the type and Jesus Christ was the antitype. It again is a comparison of that which was important and royal to the One who was of the greatest importance and immanently imperial.

Yet, it is more than just a fulfillment of typology. David did look ahead and spoke of the resurrection of Christ in Psalm 16:10 as Peter relates in Acts 2:31. Although the critical theologians will not allow it, the Bible states clearly that David did believe in resurrection, and since he had not yet experienced it, the only One who can fulfill Psalm 16:10 is Jesus Christ. See further discussion at Psalm 16:8-10.

Isaiah Saw Christ's Glory (Isaiah 6:1-3)

OT

> 1 In the year of King Uzziah's death I saw the Lord sitting on a throne, lofty and exalted, with the train of His robe filling the temple. ²Seraphim stood above Him, each having six wings: with two he covered his face, and with two he covered his feet, and with two he flew. ³And one called out to another and said,

> "Holy, Holy, Holy, is the LORD of hosts,
> The whole earth is full of His glory." Isaiah 6:1-3 NASB

NT

> ⁴¹These things Isaiah said because he saw His glory, and he spoke of Him. John 12:41 NASB

Discussion: Isaiah 6 is a record of Isaiah's vision of God (6:1-7), and it is also God's prophetic commission which He gave to Isaiah (6:8-13). The vision of God was full of wonder and amazement, but also for Isaiah, fear and trembling. Knowing his own imperfections, he cried out that he was ruined,

> For my eyes have seen the King, the LORD of hosts. Isaiah 6:5b NASB

The inspired apostle John, after quoting from Isaiah 6, said that Isaiah saw the glory of Christ and spoke with Christ. This is another example of "As with the Father, So with the Son." There are other Old Testament examples of this same phenomenon where we assume we are reading about the Father, and then discover through the apostles that we are reading about the Son. As mentioned previously, the unity of the Father, Son, and Holy Spirit is taught repeatedly in the New Testament. It is clear from this that the LORD (i.e., YHWH) is at times the Son. Please see the Introduction for further information on this.

Yet there are some who refuse to allow Christ to be in Isaiah 6. Who, besides a critical theologian with a low view of Scriptures, would question the veracity of the apostle John? A good example of this unbelief is Dr. Willis who says,

> As to John 12:40-41, it is not clear that the "glory" which Isaiah saw was that of Christ as distinguished from the Father.[73]

Although for Dr. Willis this is not clear, there was no such confusion in the inspired writings of the Christ-appointed apostle John.

---

73 John T. Willis, *Living Word Commentary: Isaiah* (Austin: Sweet Publishing Company, 1980), 143.

Why Jesus Taught In Parables (Isaiah 6:8-10)

OT

⁸Then I heard the voice of the Lord, saying, "Whom shall I send, and who will go for Us?" Then I said, "Here am I. Send me!" ⁹He said, "Go, and tell this people:

'Keep on listening, but do not perceive;
Keep on looking, but do not understand.'
¹⁰"Render the hearts of this people insensitive,
Their ears dull,
And their eyes dim,
Otherwise they might see with their eyes,
Hear with their ears,
Understand with their hearts,
And return and be healed." Isaiah 6:8-10 NASB

NT

10 And the disciples came and said to Him, "Why do You speak to them in parables?" ¹¹Jesus answered them, "To you it has been granted to know the mysteries of the kingdom of heaven, but to them it has not been granted. ¹²For whoever has, to him *more* shall be given, and he will have an abundance; but whoever does not have, even what he has shall be taken away from him. ¹³Therefore I speak to them in parables; because while seeing they do not see, and while hearing they do not hear, nor do they understand. ¹⁴<u>In their case the prophecy of Isaiah is being fulfilled</u>, which says,

'YOU WILL KEEP ON HEARING, BUT WILL NOT UNDERSTAND;
YOU WILL KEEP ON SEEING, BUT WILL NOT PERCEIVE;
¹⁵FOR THE HEART OF THIS PEOPLE HAS BECOME DULL,
WITH THEIR EARS THEY SCARCELY HEAR,
AND THEY HAVE CLOSED THEIR EYES,
OTHERWISE THEY WOULD SEE WITH THEIR EYES,
HEAR WITH THEIR EARS,

AND UNDERSTAND WITH THEIR HEART AND RETURN,
AND I WOULD HEAL THEM.'

¹⁶But blessed are your eyes, because they see; and your ears, because they hear. ¹⁷For truly I say to you that many prophets and righteous men desired to see what you see, and did not see *it*, and to hear what you hear, and did not hear *it*. Matthew 13:10-17 NASB (see also Mark 4:12; Luke 8:10; John 12:37-41)

Discussion: Jesus and John explicitly state that Jesus fulfilled the prophecy found in Isaiah 6:9-10. Now there can be no doubt that this passage had an immediate meaning for the prophet Isaiah. God wanted the prophet Isaiah to understand the hardness of the hearts that he was facing with his fellow Jews, and from the very beginning, understand that like a farmer who tries to grow a crop on bedrock, there would be little fruit from his labors.

The fulfillment of this passage in the New Testament was based on the fact that the Jews had not changed from the time of Isaiah to the time of Christ and still had hearts of stone. In spite of the incredible evidence that Jesus presented in His mighty works and wonders and signs, and most especially in His resurrection from the dead, the majority of the Jewish people were not convinced that He was the Messiah. To graphically illustrate this, after Christ's ascension, there were only 120 souls who gathered themselves with the apostles prior to the day of Pentecost (Acts 1:15). Even after Peter's initial sermon in Acts 2 and the apostles' subsequent ministry among the Jews, it was only a minority of the Jewish population who believed that Jesus was the Messiah.

This situation concerning the Jews and Jesus continues to this very day. It still remains that only a minority of Jews today believe that Jesus of Nazareth is the Messiah.

Therefore, let us, as Christians, not harden our hearts as the Jews did toward Jesus. Indeed, there has arisen a great hardening of the hearts of Gentiles in the First World countries. In this part of the earth, doubt about the Bible is pervasive and atheism is gaining ground. With the joining of the liberal, critical theologians with their low view of Scriptures and the atheistic biologists' handling of the fictitious and statistically impossible theory of evolution, people have been led away from the God of the Bible by the millions. Beware, for just as the passage in Isaiah 6:9-10 applied to the Jews in the times of Isaiah and the apostles, it now applies to the Gentiles' First World countries.

This "fulfillment" is based in typology. First, Isaiah was the type and Christ is the antitype. This is a movement from the lesser to the greater. Second, the Jews at the time of Isaiah were the type, and the Jews at the time of Jesus were the antitype. The stoney hearts of the Jews in Isaiah's time became as hard as diamonds in Jesus' time.

For this reason, Jesus taught in parables.

The Virgin & Her Son Immanuel (Isaiah 7:14)

OT

10 Then the LORD spoke again to Ahaz, saying, ¹¹"Ask a sign for yourself from the LORD your God; make *it* deep as Sheol or high as heaven." ¹²But Ahaz said, "I will not ask, nor will I test the LORD!" ¹³Then he said, "Listen now, O house of David! Is it too slight a thing for you to try the patience of men, that you will try the patience of my God as well? ¹⁴Therefore the Lord Himself will give you a sign: <u>Behold, a virgin will be with child and bear a son, and she will call His name Immanuel</u>. ¹⁵He will eat curds and honey at the time He knows *enough* to refuse evil and choose good. ¹⁶For before the boy will know *enough* to refuse evil and choose good, the land whose two kings you dread will be forsaken. Isaiah 7:10-16 NASB

NT

18 Now the birth of Jesus Christ was as follows: when His mother Mary had been betrothed to Joseph, before they came together she was found to be with child by the Holy Spirit. ¹⁹And Joseph her husband, being a righteous man and not wanting to disgrace her, planned to send her away secretly. ²⁰But when he had considered this, behold, an angel of the Lord appeared to him in a dream, saying, "Joseph, son of David, do not be afraid to take Mary as your wife; for the

Child who has been conceived in her is of the Holy Spirit. ²¹She will bear a Son; and you shall call His name Jesus, for He will save His people from their sins." ²²Now all this took place to fulfill what was spoken by the Lord through the prophet: ²³"BEHOLD, THE VIRGIN SHALL BE WITH CHILD AND SHALL BEAR A SON, AND THEY SHALL CALL HIS NAME IMMANUEL," which translated means, "GOD WITH US." ²⁴And Joseph awoke from his sleep and did as the angel of the Lord commanded him, and took *Mary* as his wife, ²⁵but kept her a virgin until she gave birth to a Son; and he called His name Jesus. Matthew 1:18-25 NASB

Discussion: The background to this prophecy is that Ahaz, king of Judah, was being threatened by the alliance of Pekah, king of Israel, and Rezin, king of Aram. Pekah and Rezin had invaded Judah and tried to capture Jerusalem and overthrow Ahaz, but they were not successful. They were planning another attack in hopes of deposing Ahaz and putting a man named Tabeel on Ahaz's throne. God's message to Ahaz through His prophet Isaiah was that this plan of Pekah and Rezin would fail. Instead, both Aram and Israel would be invaded by the Assyrians and the Assyrian invasion would even reach Jerusalem. However, God chose to spare Jerusalem from conquest by the Assyrian horde because of the petition of the righteous King Hezekiah (see all of Isaiah 7 as well as Isaiah 36 & 37).

God, through His prophet Isaiah, communicated with King Ahaz not to be afraid of Pekah and Rezin and assured Ahaz that these kings would not succeed and instead would be defeated. He told Ahaz to choose a sign that these things would come true, but Ahaz declined. It is as that point that Isaiah gave the prophecy regarding Immanuel.

The context of Isaiah 7 clearly shows that Immanuel was a real child born at that time and would still be a child when Pekah and Rezin would be defeated. So at first glance, the prophecy regarding Immanuel seems to fit that time and place with no necessity for another fulfillment 700 years later. However, as we dig further into the prophecy of this child, we find that there is something that transcends that time and place. If fact, we find that this prophecy cannot be truly fulfilled without Christ.

His Name

His name was "Immanuel." In the Old Testament, this name is only found in Isaiah 7:14 and 8:8. This name is never directly or indirectly applied to any king or prophet in the Old Testament. The meaning of "Immanuel" is found in Isaiah 8:10—"God with us." This is not some soft and cuddly name. "God with us" in Isaiah carries with it a description of great trial and suffering. It was a time for God's judgment on His people. Even Judah was taken by the Assyrians. The Assyrian emperor wrote that he had shut up Hezekiah in Jerusalem like a bird in a cage.[74]

The use of Immanuel in Isaiah 7:14 is simply the name of an infant boy. However, in Isaiah 8:6-8, the LORD speaks of the future massive Assyrian invasion that will "...fill the breadth of your land, O Immanuel." This may simply be a symbolic reference to Immanuel living in the land, just like I live in the USA, and it is figuratively "my land." However, such a statement is of no practical use, for no one can lawfully build a house on land that he doesn't own, neither now nor in the times of Isaiah. The land in question was Judah (Isaiah 8:8). Therefore, God's statement to Immanuel regarding "your land" seems to imply that Immanuel is the lord of the land, even the owner of the land of Judah. This could not be said of any king over Judah, not even David. The only one who possessed the land of Judah was God. Therefore, Immanuel, who was "God with us," is that very possessor of that land, for He is divine.

The last usage of "Immanuel" is in Isaiah 8:10. In this verse, the phrase "God is with us" has exactly the same Hebrew characters as the name "Immanuel" in Isaiah 7:14 and 8:8. The word is to all the "peoples" on earth, and they are told that no amount of preparation, planning, or rhetoric will prevail because of Immanuel. Here, the sphere of Immanuel's rule had vastly broadened from Judah to all peoples of the earth.

Immanuel, or "God with us, " is a name that is more than mere rhetoric. It identifies the bearer of that name as divine. As such, the meaning of this name cannot truly be fulfilled in the absence of Jesus of Nazareth, the Messiah.

---

74 Anonymous, *Wikipedia*, "Taylor and Sennacherib Prisms," http://en.wikipedia.org/wiki/Sennacherib%27s_Prism, accessed 01/01/2013.

His Mother

Regarding Immanuel's mother, we have very little information. Modern Jewish translations of the Hebrew Scriptures describe her as a "young woman" or "maiden." However, Christian Bibles almost always translate her as being a "virgin." Some historical perspective is helpful in understanding this difference. In fact, the debate regarding "young woman" versus "virgin" goes back at least to the second century AD when Irenaeus made the following observations regarding certain disruptive Jewish translations of Isaiah 7:14:

> 1. God, then, was made man, and the Lord did Himself save us, giving us the token of the Virgin. But not as some allege, among those now presuming to expound the Scripture, [thus:] "Behold, a young woman shall conceive, and bring forth a son," as Theodotion the Ephesian has interpreted, and Aquila of Pontus, both Jewish proselytes. The Ebionites, following these, assert that He was begotten by Joseph; thus destroying, as far as in them lies, such a marvellous dispensation of God, and setting aside the testimony of the prophets which proceeded from God.[75]

When we try to go back to the most reliable Hebrew manuscripts available for us now, we find that the Masoretic text of the Hebrew Scriptures date back only to the 9th century AD.[76] However, the Dead Sea Scroll entitled *The Great Isaiah Scroll* (1QIsaa) is dated at c 100 BC, and there are only minor variations between this ancient Hebrew text and the much later Masoretic text.[77] The English translations of the two Hebrew texts show that the Jewish scholars translate Isaiah 7:14 as "young woman."[78]

This Hebrew word is ʿăl·mā(h) and according to Hebrew lexicons, it means "young woman" who may or may not be sexually active. This same word is also used in Genesis 24:43; Exodus 2:8; Psalm

---

75 Irenaeus of Lyons, "Irenæus against Heresies," in A. Roberts, J. Donaldson & A. C. Coxe (Eds.), *The Ante-Nicene Fathers, Volume I: The Apostolic Fathers with Justin Martyr and Irenaeus* (A. Roberts, J. Donaldson & A. C. Coxe, Ed.) (Buffalo, NY: Christian Literature Company, 1885), 451.
76 Lightfoot, *How We Got the Bible*, , 90.
77 Lightfoot, *How We Got the Bible*, second edition, 100.
78 *The Digital Dead Sea Scrolls, Great Isaiah Scroll*, http://dss.collections.imj.org.il/chapters_pg, ©The Israel Museum, Jerusalem, 1995-2012.

68:25; Proverbs 30:19; Song of Solomon 1:3; 6:8.[79] The point is that this Hebrew word may be translated "virgin" depending on the context.

The oldest version of the Hebrew Scriptures is the Greek translation known as the Septuagint. The Greek word that was used in Isaiah 7:14 was παρθένος (parthenos) which is most commonly translated "virgin."[80]

Of the versions of the New Testament that I own, the following translate this Hebrew word as "virgin" in Isaiah 7:14—ASV, CEV, DNT, DRB, ESV, GWT, HCSB, ICB, KJV, NAB, NASB, NCV, NIV, NKJV, NLT, TLB, TMSG, and YLT. Only the RSV, NRSV, and TEV translate this word as "young woman."

Therefore, we should understand that Matthew's quote of Isaiah 7:14 as "virgin" was based on the Septuagint. This Greek translation of the Hebrew Scriptures by prominent and knowledgeable Jewish scholars was completed long before the birth of Christ. We should also understand that this Hebrew word can be fairly translated into "virgin" by looking at its usage elsewhere in the Old Testament.

It is possible this passage only represents a fulfillment in typology. The mother in Isaiah 7:14 is the type, and the Virgin Mary is the antitype. Again, the Immanuel of Isaiah 7:14 is the type, and the Christ is the antitype. However, it seems to be deeper and wider and higher than just a type fulfillment.

Just as the divine name of Immanuel points us to something supernatural, so does the description of Immanuel's mother. True, a real woman at the time of King Ahaz gave birth to a real child and named him Immanuel. But the connotations of this mother and child reach far beyond that age, and a complete fulfillment of this ancient prophecy is not possible without the Virgin Mary and her son, Jesus Christ. The inspired apostle Matthew knew this, and for this reason he spoke of it as a fulfillment of Messianic prophecy.

Convictions regarding the spiritual and the intellectual integrity of the inspired writers of the New Testament should increase as we see the scores of Messianic prophecies that were written down by

---

[79] Swanson, *Dictionary of Biblical Languages with Semantic Domains : Hebrew (Old Testament), (electronic ed.)* definition 6625.

[80] Swanson, *Dictionary of Biblical Languages with Semantic Domains: Greek (New Testament)* (electronic ed.) definition 4221.

the prophet Isaiah. He, more than any other prophet, announced the coming of the Messiah.

The Rock of Offense (Isaiah 8:14)

OT

¹³"It is the LORD of hosts whom you should regard as holy.
And He shall be your fear,
And He shall be your dread.
¹⁴"Then He shall become a sanctuary;
But to both the houses of Israel, <u>a stone to strike and a rock to stumble over</u>,
And a snare and a trap for the inhabitants of Jerusalem.
¹⁵"Many will stumble over them,
Then they will fall and be broken;
They will even be snared and caught." Isaiah 8:13-15 NASB

NT

4 And coming to Him as to a living stone which has been rejected by men, but is choice and precious in the sight of God, ⁵you also, as living stones, are being built up as a spiritual house for a holy priesthood, to offer up spiritual sacrifices acceptable to God through Jesus Christ. ⁶For *this* is contained in Scripture:

"BEHOLD, I LAY IN ZION A CHOICE STONE, A PRECIOUS CORNER *stone*,
AND HE WHO BELIEVES IN HIM WILL NOT BE DISAPPOINTED."

⁷This precious value, then, is for you who believe; but for those who disbelieve,

"THE STONE WHICH THE BUILDERS REJECTED,
THIS BECAME THE VERY CORNER *stone*,"

⁸and,

"A STONE OF STUMBLING AND A ROCK OF OFFENSE";

for they stumble because they are disobedient to the word, and to this *doom* they were also appointed. 1 Peter 2:4-8 NASB

Discussion: The inspired apostle Peter presents three different Old Testament references regarding this Rock of Offense. All of the references combined portray a picture of the Messiah which is fulfilled in Christ. In Isaiah 8:13-15, the Lord (YHWH) was the One who, if feared, became a sanctuary. However, the Lord also became, for those who did not fear Him, "a stone to strike and a rock to stumble over."

In a parallel manner, in 1 Peter 2:4-8, it was Christ who became the precious cornerstone for those who believe, but "a stone of stumbling and a rock of offense" (verse 8) for those who do not believe.

This is another example of a prophecy which demonstrates the principle of "as with the Father, so with the Son." Please see the Introduction for more detail on this class of prophecies.

Peter's quotation, "BEHOLD, I LAY IN ZION..." will be discussed at Isaiah 28:16. "THE STONE WHICH THE BUILDERS..." is found in Psalm 118:22 and was discussed previously.

I and the Children (Isaiah 8:16-18)

OT

16 Bind up the testimony, seal the law among my disciples. ¹⁷And I will wait for the Lord who is hiding His face from the house of Jacob; I will even look eagerly for Him. ¹⁸Behold, I and the children whom the Lord has given me are for signs and wonders in Israel from the Lord of hosts, who dwells on Mount Zion. Isaiah 8:16-18 NASB

NT

10 For it was fitting for Him, for whom are all things, and through whom are all things, in bringing many sons to glory, to perfect the author of their salvation through sufferings. ¹¹For both He who sanctifies and those who are sanctified are all from one Father; for which reason He is not ashamed to call them brethren, ¹²saying,

> "I WILL PROCLAIM YOUR NAME TO MY BRETHREN,
> IN THE MIDST OF THE CONGREGATION I WILL SING YOUR PRAISE."

¹³And again,

> "I WILL PUT MY TRUST IN HIM."

And again,

> "BEHOLD, I AND THE CHILDREN WHOM GOD HAS GIVEN ME."
> Hebrews 2:10-13 NASB

Discussion: Psalm 22:22 is referenced in Hebrews 2:12 and was discussed in the section dedicated to Psalm 22. See that discussion regarding the New Testament church conceptualized in the Old Testament. Certainly, in Hebrews 2:12, the "congregation" is referring to Christ's church.

"I WILL PUT MY TRUST IN HIM" in Hebrews 2:13 is from the Septuagint version of Isaiah 8:17.

"BEHOLD, I AND THE CHILDREN WHOM GOD HAS GIVEN ME" in Hebrews 2:13 is from Isaiah 8:18 and speaking again of the church.

In all three of these Old Testament references in Hebrews 2:12-13, the one speaking in Hebrews is pictured as Christ. However, the original speakers were David in Psalm 22:22 and Isaiah in Isaiah 8:16-18. Again, we see the typology that "as it was with David and Isaiah, so it is with Christ." The types were David and Isaiah. The antitype was Christ. The comparisons were from a great king and a great prophet to the greatest King who is also the greatest Prophet. There is also the typology between the Old Testament "congregation" and the New Testament "church."

The Prince of Peace (Isaiah 9:1-7)

OT

> 1 But there will be no *more* gloom for her who was in anguish; in earlier times He treated the <u>land of Zebulun and the land of Naphtali</u> with contempt, but later on He shall make *it* glorious, by the way of the sea, on the other side of Jordan, Galilee of the Gentiles.

> ²The people who walk in darkness
> Will see a great light;
> Those who live in a dark land,
> The light will shine on them. Isaiah 9:1-2 NASB

NT

> **12** Now when Jesus heard that John had been taken into custody, He withdrew into Galilee; ¹³and leaving Nazareth, He came and settled in Capernaum, which is by the sea, in the region of Zebulun and Naphtali. ¹⁴This was to <u>fulfill what was spoken through Isaiah</u> the prophet:
>
>> ¹⁵"THE LAND OF ZEBULUN AND THE LAND OF NAPHTALI,
>> BY THE WAY OF THE SEA, BEYOND THE JORDAN, GALILEE OF THE GENTILES—
>> ¹⁶"THE PEOPLE WHO WERE SITTING IN DARKNESS SAW A GREAT LIGHT,
>> AND THOSE WHO WERE SITTING IN THE LAND AND THE SHADOW OF DEATH,
>> UPON THEM A LIGHT DAWNED." Matthew 4:12-16 NASB

Discussion: The quotation in Matthew 4:12-16 from Isaiah 9:1-2 appears to be based on the Septuagint version of the Hebrew Scriptures.

Critical scholars deny that Isaiah 9:1-2 is a prophecy of Jesus. For example, William Barclay wrote the following caustic comment concerning Matthew's use of the Old Testament:

> It was Matthew's habit to find in the Old Testament something which he could use as a prophecy about every event in Jesus' life. He finds such a prophecy in Isaiah 9:1-2. In point of fact that is another of the prophecies which Matthew tears violently from its context and uses in his own extraordinary way.[81]

However, we cannot be true to the New Testament if we hold such a destructive view. We have to choose between an inspired apostle

---

81 William Barclay, *The Gospel of Matthew, Volume 1* (Philadelphia, The Westminster Press, 1956, 1958), 68-69. (Available at the Internet Archives at http://archive.org/details/gospelofmatthewv008785mbp)

of Jesus the Christ, or an uninspired and violent critic of the New Testament.

Isaiah 9:1-7 is a very important Messianic passage because it speaks of the birth and the reign of the Messiah. Here in the first two verses, the lowly positions of Zebulum and Naphtali in the past would be reversed because of Who would live there. He would be a "great light" to those who lived in darkness. It is striking that most of the ministry and the miracles of Christ as recorded in the New Testament were in the region of the "Galilee of the Gentiles," which included those lands that were previously known as Zebulum and Naphtali. It appears that Jesus moved to Capernaum with this prophecy in mind.

Isaiah 9:3-5 portrays a future deliverance of the people in the region of Zebulum and Naphtali. This One who would bring light, and Who would be Himself a great light, will break the "rod of their oppressor" and "the yoke of their burden" and this will result in great joy.

Now if we look for a temporal fulfillment of Isaiah 9:3-5, we will not find it. In the days of Hezekiah, and as described in Isaiah chapters 36-37, the Assyrian horde came and captured all of the Northern Kingdom as well as the Southern Kingdom, with the exception of Jerusalem. God defeated the Assyrian army there. More to the point, many Israelites living in the Northern Kingdom were captured and taken back to Assyria. Therefore, this great deliverance never came in the North, and the Northern Kingdom was never again reconstituted.

However, if we look at this language as being symbolic, then Christ's ministry in the "Galilee of the Gentiles" would truly be the fulfillment in the sense that the reign of Satan, with all his terror and destruction, was defeated by Christ in His ministry there.

Isaiah 9:6-7 are truly Messianic, and the verses are the climax of this passage. It reads,

> ⁶For a child will be born to us, a son will be given to us;
> And the government will rest on His shoulders;
> And His name will be called Wonderful Counselor, Mighty God,
> Eternal Father, Prince of Peace.
> ⁷There will be no end to the increase of *His* government or of peace,
> On the throne of David and over his kingdom,

To establish it and to uphold it with justice and righteousness
From then on and forevermore.
The zeal of the LORD of hosts will accomplish this. Isaiah
9:6-7 NASB

It should be noted that Isaiah 9:6-7 was viewed as Messianic by the ancient rabbis.[82]

Critical scholars will scoff at anyone who says that Isaiah 9:6-7 is a prophecy regarding Jesus of Nazareth. They say that the names of this son were never used for Jesus of Nazareth in the New Testament and so these names cannot be applied to Him. However, it is remarkable indeed to take such a stance. We know these names had to be applied to Christ because there is no one else who could possibly be so named by God. Unlike the pagan kings, the Jews never thought of their kings as being gods. Therefore, verse six cannot be applied to anyone in the context of Isaiah's time and certainly not after the end of the Jewish kings. Who else could have ever been described by such names besides Jesus Christ? Although many of the critical scholars want to assign these names to Hezekiah so that there would be no Messianic prophecy, what we know of Hezekiah simply cannot be matched by these lofty names.

It is important that we understand these names of Christ, or descriptions of Christ, were predicted by God to Isaiah the prophet about 700 years before Christ's birth. Of the several versions of the Old Testament that I have access to, there is remarkable agreement in these names. The only major difference is that some have five names starting with "Wonderful, Counselor" (ASV, DNT, DRB, KJV, NKJV, TLB, and YLT), while the others have four names starting with "Wonderful Counselor" (CEV, ESV, GNT, GWT, HCSB, ISB, NASB, NCV, NIV, NLT, NRSV, RSV, TEV, TMSG). The first group was highly influenced by the translation of the KJV, and the others with more modern concerns. All elements of these compound names are nouns in Hebrew, so there is no differentiation based on that. Some on the basis of parallelism would unite "Wonderful" with "Counselor." It seems rather academic, so I will consider five names or characteristics of our Lord and Savior Jesus Christ.

---

82 Edersheim, *The Life and Times of Jesus the Messiah*, 993-994.

Wonderful

This is a word that describes Christ very well. His birth was wonderful because He was born of a virgin. His early years were wonderful because He was willingly obedient to Joseph and Mary though He was the Creator of the Universe. Before He took on the role of God's prophet, His daily life and His work as a carpenter were wonderful because the Son of God humbled Himself daily. He ate, He slept, He worked, He was completely human, completely incarnated. By so doing, He gave wonderful meaning to our daily lives and our daily work, regardless of how humble these might be. His baptism was wonderful because God the Father called Him His Son, and said He was well pleased with Him. His preaching was wonderful because it was God given, honest, simple, and yet profound. His miracles were wonderful because He did what no other human ever had done or could ever do. His fulfillments of Old Testament Messianic prophecies were also wonderful and brought full meaning to those Scriptures. His death on the cross was wonderful because He had the power to lay down His life at the moment of His own choosing. It was also wonderful because He willingly took our sins on Himself and bore our sins in His body on the tree–yes, He was our wonderful atoning sacrifice and He bore our sins. His shed blood was and still remains wonderful because with that blood He secured for us eternal redemption, the forgiveness of sins. On the cross Jesus was fulfilling prophecies even though the events were being accomplished unwittingly by the very people who crucified Him. His burial was wonderful because He was buried in a rich man's tomb to fulfill prophecy. His resurrection was wonderful because He was resurrected never to die again. He prophesied His own death, and He prophesied His own resurrection. His appearances after His bodily resurrection were wonderful for they give us hope beyond the veil of death. His multiple appearances after His resurrection over 40 days to more than 500 witnesses are wonderful beyond limits for we know that we will become like Him. His ascension was wonderful because He went to sit at the Father's right hand on the eternal throne of David, from which He still reigns to this very day. Yes, Jesus is wonderful!

Counselor

Jesus of Nazareth, the Son of the Living God, the One who was risen from the dead never to die again, and the prophet of His Father in heaven, gave us His counsel throughout the Gospels. The Sermon on the Mount is an excellent synopsis of His counsel. His counsel was and still remains that we turn away from our sin and love and serve God with all our hearts, souls, minds, and strengths. He counsels us to love others as we love ourselves. However, contrary to the tenets of the atheistic Enlightenment, He gives us no permission to reduce His counsel to a few things we like and then ignore the rest. It was Jesus who said,

> **46** "Why do you call Me, 'Lord, Lord,' and do not do what I say? [47]Everyone who comes to Me and hears My words and acts on them, I will show you whom he is like: [48]he is like a man building a house, who dug deep and laid a foundation on the rock; and when a flood occurred, the torrent burst against that house and could not shake it, because it had been well built. [49]But the one who has heard and has not acted *accordingly*, is like a man who built a house on the ground without any foundation; and the torrent burst against it and immediately it collapsed, and the ruin of that house was great." Luke 6:46-49 NASB

> [38]"For whoever is ashamed of Me and My words in this adulterous and sinful generation, the Son of Man will also be ashamed of him when He comes in the glory of His Father with the holy angels." Mark 8:38 NASB (see also Luke 9:26)

Mighty God

Critical theologians uniformly have a low view of Jesus. They picture Him as being flawed. They see Him as mistaken, or even as a liar over this issue of Him fulfilling Messianic prophecies. They would never agree that a description of "Mighty God" should be applied to Him. Others who have been raised in conservative churches diminish the Son of God so they will not compromise the position of the Father. However, these do not represent the biblical view of Jesus. God Himself gave Jesus the title "Mighty God" about 700 years before Jesus was born of the Virgin Mary. If the Father said His Son would

The Prince of Peace (Isaiah 9:1-7)

be called "Mighty God," we should not object, nor should we seek to repress this biblical truth.

It is true that Jesus humbled Himself in order to become our Savior by becoming our atoning sacrifice. But as Paul wrote, after this humiliation, Jesus Christ was exalted to the right hand of God:

> ⁵Have this attitude in yourselves which was also in Christ Jesus, ⁶who, although He existed in the form of God, did not regard equality with God a thing to be grasped, ⁷but emptied Himself, taking the form of a bond-servant, and *being* made in the likeness of men. ⁸Being found in appearance as a man, He humbled Himself by becoming obedient to the point of death, even death on a cross. ⁹For this reason also, God highly exalted Him, and bestowed on Him the name which is above every name, ¹⁰so that at the name of Jesus EVERY KNEE WILL BOW, of those who are in heaven and on earth and under the earth, ¹¹and that every tongue will confess that Jesus Christ is Lord, to the glory of God the Father. Philippians 2:5-11 NASB (see also Mark 14:62; 16:19; Luke 22:69; Acts 2:33; 5:31; 7:55-56 and many others)

Here we see that a title which could only be reserved for the Father is now shared by His Son Jesus Christ. Yes, Jesus is God, for John's Gospel leaves no doubt from the very beginning:

> **1** In the beginning was the Word, and the Word was with God, and the Word was God. ²He was in the beginning with God. ³All things came into being through Him, and apart from Him nothing came into being that has come into being. ⁴In Him was life, and the life was the Light of men. ⁵The Light shines in the darkness, and the darkness did not comprehend it. John 1:1-5 NASB
>
> **14** And the Word became flesh, and dwelt among us, and we saw His glory, glory as of the only begotten from the Father, full of grace and truth. John 1:14 NASB

The doubting disciple Thomas, when he saw the risen Christ's hands, feet, and side, exclaimed, "My Lord and my God!" (John 20:28) Paul called Him "...our great God and Savior Jesus Christ..." (Titus 2:13).

When we see Jesus in the Gospels, we see Him as benign. In His own words, He "...did not come to judge the world but to save the world." (John 12:47). His mighty power was not for our destruction, but for building up our faith. He did not exalt Himself. But the Father has now exalted Him, and when He comes again, it will be with His full authority, majesty, might, and power.

> [15]Then the kings of the earth and the great men and the commanders and the rich and the strong and every slave and free man hid themselves in the caves and among the rocks of the mountains; [16]and they *said to the mountains and to the rocks, "Fall on us and hide us from the presence of Him who sits on the throne, and from the wrath of the Lamb; [17]for the great day of their wrath has come, and who is able to stand?" Revelation 6:15-17 NASB

Eternal Father

Starting with Christ's baptism, we clearly see the triune nature of God, that is, the Father, the Son, and the Holy Spirit (Matthew 3:16-17). In Christ's model prayer for His disciples, He addressed the prayer to "Our Father who is in heaven" (Matthew 6:9). However, the teachings of Jesus and His apostles was that Jesus and the Father are one (John 10:30; 17:11, 22), and that Jesus and the Holy Spirit are one (2 Corinthians 3:18). Therefore, God is one (Galatians 3:20; James 2:19), and yet there are three Supreme Beings. As I have already shown repeatedly, some of the Messianic prophecies display a definite relationship between the Father and the Son. In addition, the reverence given to the Father is also given to the Son. Therefore, just as God gave this name of "Eternal Father" to His Son 700 years before He was born of the Virgin Mary, so we should not be offended at it or try to side-step it.

The ancient concept which is still alive in many people who live in Africa is that any person who helps them becomes their "father." That person may not be biologically related to the one they help, but they will still be called "father" as a term of endearment. The one who is their "father" is someone who cares for them and makes sacrifices for their good.

So as in this ancient understanding of "father," Jesus Christ has become our "father" because of His incredible love for us and His sacrificial death for us all. If we will receive it, He has promised us eternal life. He continues to watch over us with a fatherly love. He both loves and chastens us for our own benefit. He still gives gifts to us, both spiritual and physical.

Not only that, but Jesus is eternal. Our own fathers, many of whom tried their best to help us on our way, and others who may not have cared for us at all and even abandoned us—all of these were temporal and not eternal. However, Jesus is eternal. If we abide in His love by keeping His commandments, He hears our prayers and answers them (John 15:4-10).

Prince of Peace

The concept of the Messiah being a prince is consistent with His being from the ruling family of Judah, of royal descent, and the One who sits eternally on the throne of David. Clearly, at His birth He was not yet a king, but he would be given that office. At His birth, he was surely a prince!

This concept of "peace" here is prophesied elsewhere in Psalm 72:7, Isaiah 2:4 and 11:6-9. It was announced by the angels at the birth of Christ (Luke 2:10-14). Paul explicitly says that Christ is our peace by abolishing the Mosaic Law:

> [13]But now in Christ Jesus you who formerly were far off have been brought near by the blood of Christ. [14]For He Himself is our peace, who made both *groups into* one and broke down the barrier of the dividing wall, [15]by abolishing in His flesh the enmity, *which is* the Law of commandments *contained* in ordinances, so that in Himself He might make the two into one new man, *thus* establishing peace, [16]and might reconcile them both in one body to God through the cross, by it having put to death the enmity. [17]AND HE CAME AND PREACHED PEACE TO YOU WHO WERE FAR AWAY, AND PEACE TO THOSE WHO WERE NEAR; [18]for through Him we both have our access in one Spirit to the Father. Ephesians 2:13-18 NASB

Throne of David Forever

In Isaiah 9:7, another prophecy is listed, namely, that this child who would be born would have an eternal reign on the throne of David. There would be "no end" to this, and His reign would be "forevermore." This was fulfilled explicitly in Jesus according to the angel Gabriel (Luke 1:26-33).[83]

Critical theologians insist that the New Testament is wrong and deny that the passage in Isaiah refers to Christ. Instead, they assert that these prophetic terms were fulfilled in the times that the book of Isaiah was written. For example, Dr. John T. Willis insists that the son was not Jesus, but rather was Hezekiah. Dr. Willis denies that "forevermore" means "endless time."[84] He must do so to show that the angel Gabriel didn't know what he should have told Mary, or that the angel Gabriel was intentionally telling Mary a lie, or that Mary lied when she told others about her meeting with the angel Gabriel.

However, according to Swanson, the Hebrew word translated "forevermore" can mean "everlasting, forever, eternity" and was used in this manner in Genesis 3:22. According to Swanson, it also can refer to an "undetermined duration of time" that "may have limits."[85] Therefore, this passage certainly <u>can</u> mean "forevermore" just as the angel Gabriel used it in Luke 1:26-33 when he foretold these things about Jesus Christ to His mother Mary.

Evidence from Early Church History

In addition to these biblical lines of evidence, it is abundantly clear from early church history that Isaiah 9:1-2, and especially verse 6 were unashamedly claimed for Jesus Christ. As examples only, Ignatius, Justin Martyr, Irenaeus, Clement of Alexandria, and Tertullian all refer to these passages as prophecies about Christ. This is strong evidence that such a teaching regarding this passage was apostolic from the very beginning, especially regarding the names of Christ in Isaiah 9:6.

---

83 Homer Hailey, *A Commentary on Isaiah with Emphasis on the Messianic Hope* (Religious Supply, Inc., 1992), 105.
84 Willis, *Living Word Commentary: Isaiah*, 186.
85 Swanson, *Dictionary of Biblical Languages with Semantic Domains: Hebrew (Old Testament)*, 6409.

A Branch of Jesse (Isaiah 11)

First, all of Isaiah 11 was considered Messianic by ancient Jewish rabbis.[86] We find that there are two New Testament passages that refer to Isaiah 11:1, 10. Although there are no verbatim quotes in the New Testament for the rest of Isaiah 11, the descriptions Isaiah gave are clearly Messianic and therefore belong to Jesus. Therefore, we must consider the content of the whole chapter.

OT

> **1** Then a shoot will spring from the stem of Jesse,
> And a branch from his roots will bear fruit. Isaiah 11:1 NASB

NT

> [22]But when he heard that Archelaus was reigning over Judea in place of his father Herod, he was afraid to go there. Then after being warned *by God* in a dream, he left for the regions of Galilee, [23]and came and lived in a city called Nazareth. *This was* to fulfill what was spoken through the prophets: "He shall be called a Nazarene." Matthew 2:22-23 NASB

Discussion: We cannot be sure about which "prophets" Matthew was referring to in Matthew 2:23. Isaiah's prophecy concerning the "branch" may be related to Matthew's statement that the Messiah would "be called a Nazarene." Here the Hebrew word for "branch" is "nē·ṣĕr,"[87] which is similar in sound to the Hebrew pronunciation of "Nazarene." It was common among the ancient Rabbis that a sound-alike word could be important in an interpretation. Others suggest that the sound-alike of the "Nazirite" vow may also be in play.[88] However, Jesus was not a Nazirite, and this is in spite of the modern portrayals of Jesus with long hair.

In Isaiah 11:2-5, we find a striking portrayal of the Messiah for which there are no verbatim quotes in the New Testament. However, if these descriptions were given to any knowledgeable biblical

---

86 Edersheim, *The Life and Times of Jesus the Messiah*, 994.
87 Swanson, *Dictionary of Biblical Languages with Semantic Domains: Hebrew (Old Testament)*, 5916.
88 Lewis, *The Living Word Commentary: The Gospel According to Matthew, Part I*, 52.

Christian, there is no doubt that such a person would say these verses describe Christ, and only Him.

> ²The Spirit of the LORD will rest on Him,
> The spirit of wisdom and understanding,
> The spirit of counsel and strength,
> The spirit of knowledge and the fear of the LORD.
> ³And He will delight in the fear of the LORD,
> And He will not judge by what His eyes see,
> Nor make a decision by what His ears hear;
> ⁴But with righteousness He will judge the poor,
> And decide with fairness for the afflicted of the earth;
> And He will strike the earth with the rod of His mouth,
> And with the breath of His lips He will slay the wicked.
> ⁵Also righteousness will be the belt about His loins,
> And faithfulness the belt about His waist. Isaiah 11:2-5 NASB

Discussion: Several Old Testament people have been described as having the Spirit of God upon them or stirring them. This includes Moses and 70 elders (Numbers 11:17, 25), Balaam (Numbers 24:2), Joshua (Numbers 27:18), Othniel (Judges 3:10), Gideon (Judges 6:34), Jephthah (Judges 11:29), Samson (Judges 13:25; 14:6, 19; 15:14), King Saul (1 Samuel 10:6, 10; 11:6; 19:23), David (1 Samuel 16:13; 2 Samuel 23:2), the messengers of Saul (1 Samuel 19:20), Amasai (1 Chronicles 12:18), Azariah (2 Chronicles 15:1), Jahaziel (2 Chronicles 20:14), Zechariah (2 Chronicles 24:20), all the prophets (Nehemiah 9:30; Zechariah 7:12), the Messiah (Isaiah 11:2; 42:1; 48:16; 61:1), God's people (Isaiah 44:3; 59:21; Ezekiel 36:27; 37:14; 39:29; Joel 2:28-29; Haggai 2:5; Zechariah 12:10); Ezekiel (Ezekiel 2:2; 3:12, 14, 24; 11:5; 37:1), Micah (Micah 3:8), and husbands and wives (Malachi 2:15).

In Isaiah 11:2, the Spirit of the LORD brings the Messiah wisdom, understanding, counsel, strength, knowledge, and fear of the LORD. In verse 3, the Messiah delights in the fear of the LORD, and this causes Him to know fully and to judge righteously for the poor and afflicted (verse 4). Immediately, we are reminded of the coming of the Holy Spirit, descending on Jesus Christ just after His baptism, and with the mighty voice of God announcing that this same Jesus was His Son.

Righteousness and faithfulness were fully displayed in Him, and His ministry was primarily to those who were poor and afflicted.

In verse 4b, that language concerning the Messiah striking the earth with the rod of His mouth and slaying the wicked with His breath is foreign to the modern Christians who don't read their Bibles, and anathema for the post-moderns as well as the critical scholars. They insist that if there is really a heaven, then everyone, including Satan, (if there is really a Satan), will be going there. They insist that hell is contrary to the love of God and so it cannot exist. However, we need to be reminded that Jesus the Messiah will indeed kill the man of lawlessness with the breath of His mouth (2 Thessalonians 2:8). In addition, it is He who will also have a sharp two-edged sword coming forth from His mouth which He will use against disobedient Christians (Revelation 2:16). And with this same two-edged sword He will strike down the nations and "rule them with a rod of iron," and "He treads the winepress of the fierce wrath of God, the Almighty" (Revelation 19:15).

In Isaiah 11:6-9 we are given a glimpse of the people in the Messiah's kingdom. It is figurative language, but the message is clear: In His kingdom, diverse people of many temperaments will become brothers and sisters in Christ, and there will be tolerance for each other and peace that cannot be ordinarily achieved.

OT

> **10** Then in that day
> The nations will resort to the <u>root of Jesse</u>,
> Who will stand as a signal for the peoples;
> And His resting place will be glorious. Isaiah 11:10 NASB

NT

> [12]Again Isaiah says,
> "THERE SHALL COME THE ROOT OF JESSE,
> AND HE WHO ARISES TO RULE OVER THE GENTILES,
> IN HIM SHALL THE GENTILES HOPE." Romans 15:12 NASB

Discussion: Paul's quotation of Isaiah 11:10 is from the Septuagint, for there we find the Messiah ruling over the Gentiles and the Gentiles putting their hope in Him. However, Fred P. Miller's translation of the Great Isaiah Scroll has "Gentiles" here too.[89] It seems academic, though, for the "nations" obviously refer to the Gentiles.

Here is the second reference in this chapter to a future descendent of Jesse. In both instances, Jesse is mentioned instead of the unfaithful and deeply disappointing descendents of David. Therefore, this descendent would be different than the corrupt Judean kings. Not only this, but "the nations will resort to the root of Jesse...." As in the Septuagint, the Messiah would rule over the Gentiles and the Messiah would be their hope. As we consider the Judean kings following Ahaz, which is the immediate context here in Isaiah, only Hezekiah and Josiah were good kings. However, neither could be said to have the nations resorting to them with the exception of the delegation from Babylon who had heard of Hezekiah's serious illness and recovery (Isaiah 39:1-4). In no sense do we find any Judean king in those times, good or bad, ruling over the Gentiles, or having the Gentiles trust in the Judean king. Therefore, this "root of Jesse" must be Jesus Christ, for only in Him do we find that the rule over the Gentiles and the Gentiles' resort to Him and trust in Him.

In Isaiah 11:11-16, which is the remainder of this chapter, Isaiah prophesies about a "remnant" that will be restored. Yet, this is far in the future, for this restoration will be the "second" restoration. At the time Isaiah wrote this prophecy, God had not yet restored a righteous remnant. However, He would make that first restoration after the 70 years of Babylonian captivity. Then He would stir the spirit of Cyrus, king of Persia, to release the Jews from their captivity and to travel back to Palestine to "...rebuild the house of the LORD, the God of Israel...." (Ezra 1:1-4). This remnant returned with Zerubbabel in 536 BC. This was the "first" restoration of the righteous remnant. It was physical and nationalistic.

However, the "second" restoration of the righteous remnant would be led by the Messiah, Jesus of Nazareth. This is the event that Isaiah prophesied in 11:11-16. That restoration would be accomplished by the preaching of the Messiah's Gospel. His message of salvation would start in AD 30 at Jerusalem, and would reach the whole world. Peoples of all nations would come into the Messiah's kingdom. Jews and Gentiles would become one in Christ. If the success of this

---

89 Fred P. Miller, *The Translation of the Great Isaiah Scroll*, © Fred P. Miller 2001 Qumran Isaiah Scroll Translation, accessed 28 October 2013, ao.net.

restoration of the righteous remnant depended on the will and the strength of men, it could not succeed. God Himself would make it possible. Now if one is not convinced that this is the righteous remnant that Isaiah spoke of, consider what the inspired Apostle Paul wrote:

> ⁵In the same way then, there has also come to be at the present time a remnant according to *God's* gracious choice. Romans 11:5 NASB

Although the language of Isaiah 11:11-16 appears to have physical and nationalistic elements, those apparent elements never were fulfilled literally. Israel would never again reign over the Philistines, Edom, Moab, and Ammon. Therefore, the only way to view the prophecy in a biblical framework is through symbolism. Rather than an earthly rule, the Messiah overwhelmed the ruler of the world and established His own kingdom which He now rules over from heaven.

The Sun Darkened (Isaiah 13:10)

OT

> ¹⁰For the stars of heaven and their constellations
> Will not flash forth their light;
> <u>The sun will be dark when it rises</u>
> <u>And the moon will not shed its light</u>. Isaiah 13:10

> ⁴And all the host of heaven will wear away,
> And the sky will be rolled up like a scroll;
> All their hosts will also wither away
> As a leaf withers from the vine,
> Or as *one* withers from the fig tree. Isaiah 34:4

NT

> **24** "But in those days, after that tribulation, THE SUN WILL BE DARKENED AND THE MOON WILL NOT GIVE ITS LIGHT, ²⁵AND THE STARS WILL BE FALLING from heaven, and the powers that are in the heavens will be shaken." Mark 13:24-25

Discussion: See also Isaiah 24:23 and the parallel passage in Matthew 24:29. The quotation in Mark 13:25 from Isaiah 34:4 appears to be based on the Septuagint version of the Hebrew Scriptures, for there we see the vision of the stars falling.

Isaiah, in chapter 13, was foretelling the destruction of Babylon (Isaiah 13:1). In verse 10, Isaiah used hyperbolic language to describe the downfall of the Babylonian leaders. This is an example of an Old Testament prophecy being fulfilled in the Old Testament times. Just as God overthrew Sodom and Gomorrah, He would also overthrow Babylon (13:19). In Isaiah 34, the prophet was foretelling God's judgment on the nations using the same kind of hyperbole as in Isaiah 13.

In Mark 13:25 and Matthew 24:29, Jesus is prophesying of His own return. He uses the same hyperbolic language as is found in Isaiah 13 and 34. Just as surely as God had destroyed Babylon and the sinful cities of Sodom and Gomorrah in earlier times, so Christ will come and destroy the heavens and the earth (see 2 Peter 3:7, 10).

This is not the usual "Messianic" prophecy, that is, prophesying the first coming of Christ, because here Jesus is the prophet. But He was using the same kind of reasoning and language to prophesy His second coming. That is, as it was in the destruction of Babylon, Sodom, and Gomorrah, so it we be in the destruction of the heavens and earth when He comes again. Therefore, as it was for the ancient kingdoms, so it will be for the heavens and the earth. The first was terrible and with great loss of life. Yet, the second will be even more terrible and not fully comprehensible, because none of us have seen such an awful tragedy. Verily, come Lord Jesus!

Laying in Zion a Stone (Isaiah 28:16)

OT

¹⁶Therefore thus says the Lord G<small>OD</small>,
"Behold, <u>I am laying in Zion a stone</u>, a tested stone,
A costly cornerstone *for* the foundation, firmly placed.
<u>He who believes in it will not be disturbed</u>. Isaiah 28:16 NASB

NT

4 And coming to Him as to a living stone which has been rejected by men, but is choice and precious in the sight of God,

⁵you also, as living stones, are being built up as a spiritual house for a holy priesthood, to offer up spiritual sacrifices acceptable to God through Jesus Christ. ⁶For this is contained in Scripture:

> "BEHOLD, I LAY IN ZION A CHOICE STONE, A PRECIOUS CORNER *stone*,
> AND HE WHO BELIEVES IN HIM WILL NOT BE DISAPPOINTED." 1 Peter 2:4-6 NASB

⁸But what does it say? "THE WORD IS NEAR YOU, IN YOUR MOUTH AND IN YOUR HEART"—that is, the word of faith which we are preaching, ⁹that if you confess with your mouth Jesus as Lord, and believe in your heart that God raised Him from the dead, you will be saved; ¹⁰for with the heart a person believes, resulting in righteousness, and with the mouth he confesses, resulting in salvation. ¹¹For the Scripture says, "WHOEVER BELIEVES IN HIM WILL NOT BE DISAPPOINTED." Romans 10:8-11 NASB

Discussion: Isaiah 28:1-13 foretold the destruction of Ephraim because of their alcoholism. Judah was given a similar warning of destruction in Isaiah 28:14-29 because they made a covenant with death and Sheol that they might not die. In the midst of this, Isaiah quotes God regarding a "stone." God would lay the costly stone as a cornerstone for the foundation. In the context of Isaiah 28, this stone appears to be for the purpose of faith, for God says that if they believe "in it," they will "not be disturbed."

Jacob called God "the Shepherd, the Stone of Israel" in Genesis 49:24. Moses called God the "Rock" in Deuteronomy 32:4, and it is clear that "Rock" was a name for God. David called God "my God, my rock" in 2 Samuel 22:2-3. However, in Isaiah 28:16, it was God who was laying a stone for "the foundation." The Temple had already been in existence for centuries, so the "foundation" was not for that purpose. Therefore, God was not the stone spoken of in Isaiah 28:16 since He was the One who would lay the stone for the foundation.

Both the apostles Peter and Paul appear to be quoting from the Septuagint version of the Old Testament, which is our oldest version. The "stone" is called "it" in the version we have in our Old Testament. However, in the Septuagint it is called αὐτός (autos), and this meant a definite person or thing.[90] Obviously, both Peter and Paul thought the "stone" meant Jesus the Messiah. Paul also called Jesus the "foundation" (1 Corinthians 3:11) and the "cornerstone" (Ephesians 2:20) using the same Greek words as is found in the Septuagint.

Now as to the meaning of this passage for the Jews of Isaiah's time, it is not clear from the context how they understood this "stone." However, it is of interest that Edersheim found that Isaiah 28:16 was considered Messianic in the Targum, and the oral version of the Targum existed before the birth of Christ. Later even Rashi considered this verse Messianic.[91] Therefore, it is clear that the Jews in the first century AD considered Isaiah 28:16 Messianic just as the apostles did.

Healings & the Gospel (Isaiah 35:5-6)

OT

> [5]Then the eyes of the blind will be opened
> And the ears of the deaf will be unstopped.
> [6]Then the lame will leap like a deer,
> And the tongue of the mute will shout for joy. Isaiah 35:5-6a NASB

> **1** The Spirit of the Lord God is upon me,
> Because the Lord has anointed me
> To bring good news to the afflicted;
> He has sent me to bind up the brokenhearted,
> To proclaim liberty to captives
> And freedom to prisoners; Isaiah 61:1 NASB

NT

> **2** Now when John, while imprisoned, heard of the works of Christ, he sent *word* by his disciples [3]and said to Him, "Are You the Expected One, or shall we look for someone else?" [4]Jesus answered and said to them, "Go and report to John what you hear and see: [5]*the* BLIND RECEIVE SIGHT and *the* lame walk, *the* lepers are cleansed *and* the deaf hear, *the* dead are raised

---

90 Swanson, *Dictionary of Biblical Languages with Semantic Domains: Hebrew (Old Testament)*, definition 899.
91 Edersheim, *The Life and Times of Jesus the Messiah*, 995.

up, and *the* POOR HAVE THE GOSPEL PREACHED TO THEM. ⁶And blessed is he who does not take offense at Me." Matthew 11:2-6 NASB

Discussion: Isaiah 35 described a happy future for Judah. In verse 5, Isaiah's prophecy described miraculous healings for those who were blind, deaf, lame, or mute. He went on to speak of water becoming abundant in the desert. He also spoke of a highway, but not an ordinary one. Only the redeemed could walk on that highway. The unclean, the fools, and the vicious beasts would not be found on this highway. This would allow the ransomed of the Lord to return to Zion with gladness.

Isaiah 61 also spoke of the exaltation of the afflicted. In verse 1, the "good news" would be brought to the afflicted. The Septuagint used the Greek word εὐαγγελίζω (euangelizō) which meant "good news," and it was used in the New Testament to mean "proclaim good news" or "preach the gospel."[92] The Hebrew word for "afflicted" encompassed the concept of being oppressed, needy, or poor.[93] Jesus quoted Isaiah 61:1-2 in Luke 4:17-21, saying that this scripture was fulfilled in their hearing.

In Matthew 11:2-3, Jesus received a question from the imprisoned John the Baptist regarding whether or not Jesus was "the Expected One." Clearly, John was asking Jesus if He was the Messiah. Jesus replied in verses 4-6 with the real evidence of miraculous healings found in Isaiah 35:5. In addition, Jesus gave the evidence of Isaiah 61:1 that the gospel was preached to the poor. See Luke 7:18-23 for the parallel account.

In responding to John, Jesus did not mention "fulfillment" or any similar word. However, it was clear to Jesus that He was indeed fulfilling both Isaiah 35:5-6a and 61:1, and John the Baptist would have clearly understood that too.

We should consider who, besides our Lord Jesus Christ, could have fulfilled these prophecies in Isaiah. Is there anyone from Isaiah onward in history, even to this day, who could claim such a fulfillment? Who opened the eyes of the blind, who caused the deaf

---

92 Swanson, *Dictionary of Biblical Languages with Semantic Domains: Hebrew (Old Testament),* definition 2294.
93 Swanson, *Dictionary of Biblical Languages with Semantic Domains: Hebrew (Old Testament),* definition 6705.

to hear, who healed the lame, and who caused the mute to speak? Who, since the beginning of history, can claim to have performed such miracles? This Scripture can only be fulfilled in Jesus the Messiah. This should be more than sufficient evidence for anyone who respects the biblical record. However, if people do not believe the biblical record, they can believe whatever they choose. This is why the liberal, critical biblical scholars do not believe that Jesus fulfilled Messianic prophecies—they don't believe the biblical record.

It should be noted that Isaiah 35:5-6 was repeatedly applied to Messianic times according to Edersheim.[94] Thus, the use of this passage by Matthew would have certainly resonated as being Messianic with the Jews in the first century AD and beyond.

Voice in the Wilderness (Isaiah 40:3-5)

OT

3 A voice is calling,
"Clear the way for the Lord in the wilderness;
Make smooth in the desert a highway for our God.
⁴"Let every valley be lifted up,
And every mountain and hill be made low;
And let the rough ground become a plain,
And the rugged terrain a broad valley;
⁵Then the glory of the Lord will be revealed,
And all flesh will see *it* together;
For the mouth of the Lord has spoken." Isaiah 40:3-5 NASB

NT

1 Now in the fifteenth year of the reign of Tiberius Caesar, when Pontius Pilate was governor of Judea, and Herod was tetrarch of Galilee, and his brother Philip was tetrarch of the region of Ituraea and Trachonitis, and Lysanias was tetrarch of Abilene, ²in the high priesthood of Annas and Caiaphas, the word of God came to John, the son of Zacharias, in the wilderness. ³And he came into all the district around the Jordan, preaching a baptism of repentance for the forgiveness

---

94 Edersheim, *The Life and Times of Jesus the Messiah,* 996.

of sins; ⁴as it is written in the book of the words of Isaiah the prophet,

> "THE VOICE OF ONE CRYING IN THE WILDERNESS,
> 'MAKE READY THE WAY OF THE LORD,
> MAKE HIS PATHS STRAIGHT.
> ⁵'EVERY RAVINE WILL BE FILLED,
> AND EVERY MOUNTAIN AND HILL WILL BE BROUGHT LOW;
> THE CROOKED WILL BECOME STRAIGHT,
> AND THE ROUGH ROADS SMOOTH;
> ⁶AND ALL FLESH WILL SEE THE SALVATION OF GOD.' " Luke 3:1-6 NASB

Discussion: The passage in Luke is the longest quotation of Isaiah 40:3-5. Matthew 3:3; Mark 1:2-3; and John 1:23 are parallel passages. Mark starts with quoting Malachi 3:1 and then Isaiah 40:3. All of the New Testament passages are from the Septuagint. As is frequently the case, the Septuagint translation is somewhat different from the much later Masoretic Text. It should be noted that the "THE VOICE OF ONE CRYING IN THE WILDERNESS" in Luke 3:4 is very similar to Miller's translation of the *Great Isaiah Scroll* which is "A voice of one crying in the wilderness...."[95] However, the Dead Sea Scrolls Bible translates the same passage as "A voice cries out, 'In the wilderness prepare the way of the Lord....'."[96]

Isaiah 40 is a chapter of comfort and of the knowledge of the greatness and sovereignty of God. It contains a warning about the foolishness of idolatry and an admonition to "wait for the LORD." Amid this is a prophecy about a prophet whose work would be to announce and "clear the way of the LORD in the wilderness." Here the "LORD" is the Hebrew YHWH or "Yahweh."

The liberal, critical scholars insist that this passage was fulfilled in the time of Isaiah, and it meant nothing more than building a nice road for a king. However, their application of this passage to the times of Isaiah is theoretical, since they have no recorded biblical narrative to confirm such a claim. Rather, we find that the ancient rabbis considered these verses to be Messianic.[97] Certainly, the synoptic gospel writers

---

95 Fred P. Miller, *The Translation of the Great Isaiah Scroll*, © 2001, accessed 28 October 2013, http://www.ao.net/~fmoeller/qa-tran.htm#c6 .
96 *The Dead Sea Scrolls Bible,* Abegg, Flint, & Ulrich (Trs, commentary).
97 Edersheim, *The Life and Times of Jesus the Messiah,* 996.

assign this to John the Baptist. The apostle John testified that John the Baptist said this himself. Therefore, there is a uniform judgment in the Gospels that this prophecy was fulfilled in John the Baptist as a forerunner for our Lord Jesus Christ.

Which prophet living at the time of Isaiah or later could have fulfilled this passage? Isaiah lived in Jerusalem. There is no evidence that Isaiah went out in the wilderness to make a way for the LORD or even to make a nice road for a king. No other Jewish prophet living after Isaiah went into the wilderness to make "a highway for God" with the exception of John the Baptist. Which documented prophet am I overlooking? Who went into the wilderness to preach the message of God except for John the Baptist? The critical scholars cannot point to any narrative that shows this fulfillment in the times of Isaiah or in the times of any other Old Testament prophet. Rather than trust the New Testament, they invent possibilities and speak of fictitious prophets.

There is no one else who could have fulfilled this prophecy except for the God-inspired fulfillment in John the Baptist.

Behold, My Servant (Isaiah 42:1-4)

OT

1 "Behold, My Servant, whom I uphold;
My chosen one *in whom* My soul delights.
I have put My Spirit upon Him;
He will bring forth justice to the nations.
²"He will not cry out or raise *His voice*,
Nor make His voice heard in the street.
³"A bruised reed He will not break
And a dimly burning wick He will not extinguish;
He will faithfully bring forth justice.
⁴"He will not be disheartened or crushed
Until He has established justice in the earth;
And the coastlands will wait expectantly for His law." Isaiah 42:1-4 NASB

NT

15 But Jesus, aware of *this*, withdrew from there. Many followed Him, and He healed them all, ¹⁶and warned them not to tell who He was. ¹⁷*This was* to fulfill what was spoken through Isaiah the prophet:

¹⁸"BEHOLD, MY SERVANT WHOM I HAVE CHOSEN;
MY BELOVED IN WHOM MY SOUL IS WELL-PLEASED;
I WILL PUT MY SPIRIT UPON HIM,
AND HE SHALL PROCLAIM JUSTICE TO THE GENTILES.
¹⁹"HE WILL NOT QUARREL, NOR CRY OUT;
NOR WILL ANYONE HEAR HIS VOICE IN THE STREETS.
²⁰"A BATTERED REED HE WILL NOT BREAK OFF,
AND A SMOLDERING WICK HE WILL NOT PUT OUT,
UNTIL HE LEADS JUSTICE TO VICTORY.
²¹"AND IN HIS NAME THE GENTILES WILL HOPE." Matthew 12:15-21 NASB

Discussion: In Isaiah 41:28-29, God wanted to give His people "a messenger of good news." However, when he looked upon them, He found no counselor among them who could do the job. Rather they were all false and were idolaters. In contrast to this, God speaks of "My Servant" in Isaiah 42:1 who would accomplish what God wants. The critical question is, who is this "Servant" that God identifies?

It is clear that the ancient rabbis viewed the Servant of Isaiah 42:1 as the Messiah according to Edersheim.⁹⁸ Certainly, early Christian writers such as Justin Martyr, Tertullian, and Origen identified this Servant as our Lord Jesus Christ. The liberal, critical scholars will never admit that the Servant is our Lord Jesus Christ, but instead, they give a list of many other people, especially Israel, who should be identified as the Servant.

It is not without some reason that these unbelievers deny that Jesus is the Servant in this passage and in passages to come in Isaiah. In Isaiah, God calls the following people "My servant":

1. Isaiah—Isaiah went about naked and barefoot for three years as a sign against Egypt and Cush (Isaiah 20:3).
2. Eliakim—a judgment against Shebna, that Eliakim would take his place to rule (Isaiah 22:20).

---
98 Edersheim, *The Life and Times of Jesus the Messiah*, 996.

3. David—God would defend and save Jerusalem for David's sake (Isaiah 37:35).
4. Israel—also called "Jacob," and a descendent of Abraham—God will uphold Israel in the face of many dangers against Israel (Isaiah 41:8ff).
5. Unnamed servant—the unnamed servant of Isaiah 42:1-7 whom we are considering in this passage.
6. Probably contrasting Isaiah with Israel—God says His servant must be like the deaf and blind in order to be His messenger. But (presumed Israel) would never understand God's message (Isaiah 42:19-20).
7. Israel—Israel is called "My witnesses" and "My servant" who can testify that God can predict the future and idols cannot. Israel also can testify that He is the only God (Isaiah 43:8-13).
8. Israel—God will pour out blessing on Israel (Isaiah 44:1-6).
9. Israel—Israel must remember that God formed them, forgave them, and redeemed them (Isaiah 44:21-23).
10. God's prophets—God's prophets for whom He confirmed His word and performed the purpose of His messengers (Isaiah 44:24-26).
11. Israel—God foretells that He will use Cyrus to bless Israel (Isaiah 45:1-7).
12. Israel—God foretells that He will use Cyrus to liberate His people from Babylonian captivity (Isaiah 48:20).
13. Israel as an individual—God commissions this individual to bring back Israel to Him (Isaiah 49:1-13).
14. The Suffering Servant—This individual would carry our sins, die for us, and justify us (Isaiah 52:13-53:12).

Also, in Jeremiah, God called the following "My servant": Nebuchadnezzar (25:9; 27:6; 43:10), Jacob (30:10; 46:27-28), and David (33:21-22, 26). In Ezekiel, God called the following "My servant": Jacob (28:25; 37:25) and David (34:23-24; 37:24).

Six times in the above list from Isaiah, the servant is not called Israel. Four of these called "servant" cannot be Israel. Two are unnamed. In our present text, "Isaiah" 42:1-7, God does not designate a specific name for "My Servant." However, the job description in Isaiah 42:1-7 clearly shows that the only One who could fulfill this ministry is our Lord Jesus Christ.

I have put my Spirit upon Him (Isaiah 42:1)

Although there are many examples in the Old Testament of the Spirit coming upon certain people (see Discussion on Isaiah 11), there is nothing in Scripture that can compare to the Spirit coming upon Christ (Matthew 3:16-17; Mark 1:10; Luke 3:22; John 1:32).

He brings justice to the nations (Isaiah 42:1)

Jesus is the only Jew who ever brought forth justice for the nations. There was no such concern for the Gentiles among any of the other Jews in the Old Testament. Therefore, Israel could never have been the Servant of Isaiah 42:1. Only our Lord Jesus Christ could have ever fulfilled this prophecy.

He will not cry out (Isaiah 42:2)

The way Jesus conducted His ministry was different from any other leader in the history of Judaism. Jesus was a calm teacher from God. He was not a rebel rouser. He did not wear a sword nor rattle the sword. He told the truth to bring the people back to God.

A bruised reed He will not break (Isaiah 42:3)

Jesus was compassionate, helped the suffering, and lifted up the fallen. He was full of mercy and compassion. His healings were beyond counting. No other Jew of any time can match the mercy and compassion of Christ.

He leads justice to victory (Isaiah 42:4)

The Hebrew word translated "justice" means "a state or condition of fairness in disputes."[99] A magnificent example of His divine justice was Christ giving Himself as an offering and a sacrifice for our sins (Ephesians 5:2). He bore our sins in His body on the tree (1 Peter 2:24). By His shed blood He purchased for us eternal redemption (Hebrews 9:12). In addition, by His atoning death, He justifies us before the Father (Romans 3:21-24, 28-30; 4:25; 5:16, 18; Galatians 3:8). This means we have the ultimate victory in our Lord Jesus Christ! What a wonderful and divine concept of justice! Yet, it meant

---

[99] Swanson, *Dictionary of Biblical Languages with Semantic Domains : Hebrew (Old Testament)*, definition 5477.

the ultimate injustice to Him so that we could be justified before God. What king besides Jesus was so concerned about this kind of justice?

In His name the Gentiles will hope (Isaiah 42:4)

Here the Septuagint translated "Gentiles" and the Masoretic Text "coastlands." In verse 1, the Masoretic Text translated "nations" and the Septuagint "Gentiles." Regardless, it is clear that Isaiah 42:1-7 speaks of the Messiah being the hope of the Gentiles. Other than our Lord Jesus Christ, what other Jew did the Gentiles look to for their hope? Simply put, there is none of any significance. Even if one would strain to find some Jew that fits this prophecy, no one can match the Lord Jesus Christ in this matter.

Although Matthew did not quote further from this passage in Isaiah, he certainly opened the window for this prophecy regarding our Lord. So we must continue in Isaiah 42:5-9 to show how Christ fulfilled these as well.

> 5 Thus says God the LORD,
> Who created the heavens and stretched them out,
> Who spread out the earth and its offspring,
> Who gives breath to the people on it
> And spirit to those who walk in it,
> 6"I am the LORD, I have called You in righteousness,
> I will also hold You by the hand and watch over You,
> And I will appoint You as a covenant to the people,
> As a light to the nations,
> 7To open blind eyes,
> To bring out prisoners from the dungeon
> And those who dwell in darkness from the prison.
> 8"I am the LORD, that is My name;
> I will not give My glory to another,
> Nor My praise to graven images.
> 9"Behold, the former things have come to pass,
> Now I declare new things;
> Before they spring forth I proclaim *them* to you." Isaiah 42:5-9 NASB

I called...I hold...I watch over You (Isaiah 42:6)

This isolated quote does not clearly define the recipient of the LORD's loving attention. However, the person was greatly beloved by God. The phrase "called You in righteousness" foretold the righteousness of our Lord Jesus Christ. As a part of Isaiah 42:1-7, it is obvious that the recipient is Jesus.

I appoint You as a covenant (Isaiah 42:6)

This prophecy implies there was another covenant other than the Mosaic Covenant that God would make, and it would be centered in a person (see also Isaiah 49:8; Jeremiah 31:31). Some would argue that this Servant is the nation of Israel and point to Isaiah 49:3. Yet, how can a degenerate Israel become the righteous Servant Israel and be a covenant to all the peoples on the earth? That never happened. Rather, this would be the "second Moses," the Lord Jesus Christ. The Lord Jesus Christ was the true fulfillment because only in Him was light given to the nations. This "new covenant" was confirmed in Luke 22:20; 1 Corinthians 11:25; 2 Corinthians 3:6; Hebrews 8:7-8, 13; 9:15; 12:24. So Jesus is the branch of Jesse, the embodiment of Israel, and the Servant Messiah.

To open blind eyes...release prisoners (Isaiah 42:7)

How many blind people in the Old Testament were healed of their blindness by the Jews? Did the nation of Israel ever find a cure for blindness? It was only Jesus Christ who showed that the blind could be healed and only by miraculous healings (Matthew 9:27-31; 11:5; 12:22; 15:30-31; 20:30-34; 21:14; Mark 8:22-25; 10:46-52; Luke 7:21-22; 18:35-43; John 9:1-7).

Jesus Christ showed in a very literal fashion His release of His apostles from prison in Acts 5:17-20. He again showed it literally for Peter in Acts 12:1-11. In a like manner, He has released millions and millions of prisoners from the grasp of Satan. Before Jesus, all of humanity was in darkness. Even to this day Jesus brings spiritual deliverance and light to whomever will come to Him in faith and obedience.

Every Knee Bows (Isaiah 45:22-23)

OT

²²"Turn to Me and be saved, all the ends of the earth;
For I am God, and there is no other.
²³"I have sworn by Myself,
The word has gone forth from My mouth in righteousness
And will not turn back,
That to Me <u>every knee will bow</u>, every tongue will swear *allegiance*. Isaiah 45:22-23 NASB

NT

⁵Have this attitude in yourselves which was also in Christ Jesus, ⁶who, although He existed in the form of God, did not regard equality with God a thing to be grasped, ⁷but emptied Himself, taking the form of a bond-servant, *and* being made in the likeness of men. ⁸Being found in appearance as a man, He humbled Himself by becoming obedient to the point of death, even death on a cross. ⁹For this reason also, God highly exalted Him, and bestowed on Him the name which is above every name, ¹⁰so that at the name of Jesus EVERY KNEE WILL BOW, of those who are in heaven and on earth and under the earth, ¹¹and that every tongue will confess that Jesus Christ is Lord, to the glory of God the Father. Philippians 2:5-11 NASB

Discussion: The immediate context of Isaiah 45:23 was God's rebuke of idolatry in the Israelites and how useless the idols were. He demanded that the idols do as He did, such as predicting the future. Of course, the idols couldn't make a sound. In the midst of this He prophecies that "every knee shall bow."

It should be noted that Edersheim found that Isaiah 45:22 was considered Messianic by the ancient rabbis.[100]

Paul refers to Isaiah 45:23 in Philippians 2:10. This is in the midst of one of the most beautiful statements regarding Christ's death, burial, and resurrection. It stresses the humility and the exaltation of Christ. Paul applies these principles to the Philippians in their own situation.

---

100 Edersheim, *The Life and Times of Jesus the Messiah*, 996.

When Jesus comes again, "every knee shall bow" and "every tongue will confess that Jesus Christ is Lord."

Isaiah 45:22-23 is an excellent display of "as with the Father, so with the Son." As Christians, we believe in the Father, the Son, and the Holy Spirit (Matthew 3:16-17). The Father has given the Son all authority in heaven and on earth (Matthew 28:18). Therefore, we must show our Lord Jesus Christ both our worship and confession of faith, for this is the Father's will, and it is to the Father's glory.

Light for the Gentiles (Isaiah 49:1-13)

OT

> ⁶He says, "It is too small a thing that You should be My Servant
> To raise up the tribes of Jacob and to restore the preserved ones of Israel;
> I will also make You <u>a light of the nations</u>
> So that My salvation may reach to the end of the earth." Isaiah 49:6 NASB

NT

> **44** The next Sabbath nearly the whole city assembled to hear the word of the Lord. ⁴⁵But when the Jews saw the crowds, they were filled with jealousy and began contradicting the things spoken by Paul, and were blaspheming. ⁴⁶Paul and Barnabas spoke out boldly and said, "It was necessary that the word of God be spoken to you first; since you repudiate it and judge yourselves unworthy of eternal life, behold, we are turning to the Gentiles. ⁴⁷For so the Lord has commanded us,
>
> > 'I HAVE PLACED YOU AS A LIGHT FOR THE GENTILES,
> > THAT YOU MAY BRING SALVATION TO THE END OF THE EARTH.'"
> > Acts 13:44-47 NASB

Discussion: In Isaiah 49:1-13, we find another "My Servant" prophecy. Here the servant is called "Israel" in 49:3. However, the servant is clearly an individual and speaks as an individual. The charge from the LORD to His Servant was to restore Israel back to Him (Isaiah 49:5). The LORD gave the Servant an additional objective which was being a "light to the nations." As that light, God's salvation would "reach to the end of the earth" (Isaiah 49:6). The Servant would be despised and abhorred by Israel, but kings would see Him, then arise, and bow down (Isaiah 49:7). God promised to keep and help the Servant, but He also would "give You for a covenant of the people" (Isaiah 49:8—see also Isaiah 42:6). Because of these things, there would be great blessings and happiness from God (Isaiah 49:8-13).

Clearly, Paul and Barnabas, during the first missionary journey at Pisidian Antioch, used this Old Testament passage in Acts 13:47 to show that it was the command of the Lord that they preach the gospel to the Gentiles. They viewed this passage as the justification for this action. By so doing, Paul and Barnabas honored Christ's example in this matter (Matthew 15:21-28; Mark 7:24-30) as well as His command to take the Gospel to all nations (Matthew 28:19). By our Master's example and command, Gentiles were, and still are, saved by the millions.

Edersheim records that Isaiah 49:8-10 and verse 12 were considered Messianic by the ancient rabbis.[101]

However, the liberal, critical theologians would never allow any Messianic prophecy to be admitted as such. Rather, they attack the New Testament so that the sacred Scriptures would carry no credibility or authority for Christianity. They insist that this Servant must be Israel and not Christ. It is somewhat difficult to conceptualize how Israel could bring Israel back to God. Perhaps they identify "good Israel" as the righteous remnant and the "bad Israel" as the rest. These theologians wish to attribute the verses to undocumented Jewish evangelists who supposedly preached to Jews and convinced them to give up their idols. Perhaps that sounds reasonable, even if it is without documentation. However, we must require answers to three questions:

1. Give us the name of the Jew, other than Jesus Christ, who was "a light to the Gentiles."
2. Give us the name of the Jew, other than Jesus Christ, who caused God's salvation to reach all nations, including the Gentiles.
3. Give us the name of the Jew, other than Jesus Christ, who became a covenant for all people, including the Gentiles.

---

101 Edersheim, *The Life and Times of Jesus the Messiah,* 996.

Such evidence must be real and not fictitious. Something this big must have been documented. Where are the documents?

Until the liberal, critical theologians present evidence to the contrary, Jesus Christ is the only person who fulfills this prophecy.

The Suffering Servant (Isaiah 52:13 through 53:12)

Isaiah 52:13 through 53:12 is the flagship concerning Messianic prophecies. This passage has converted many Jews to Christianity. For the believers in Christ, this passage touches our souls and brings tears to our eyes when we read it or hear it read. We know that this passage cannot refer to anyone except our Lord Jesus Christ.

Edersheim showed that the ancient rabbis understood that Isaiah 52:13, 53:5, and 53:10 were all considered Messianic. In fact, the Messianic name "Leprous" was based on Isaiah 53.[102]

Because of the length of this Old Testament passage as well as the multiple New Testament passages that will be cited, Isaiah 52:13 through 53:12 will be cited in its entirety. Then the passage will be discussed in several sections with the New Testament passages.

OT

> 13 Behold, My servant will prosper,
> He will be high and lifted up and greatly exalted.
> ¹⁴Just as many were astonished at you, *My people,*
> So His appearance was marred more than any man
> And His form more than the sons of men.
> ¹⁵Thus He will sprinkle many nations,
> Kings will shut their mouths on account of Him;
> For what had not been told them they will see,
> And what they had not heard they will understand. Isaiah 52:13-15 NASB
>
> 1 Who has believed our message?
> And to whom has the arm of the LORD been revealed?
> ²For He grew up before Him like a tender shoot,

---

[102] Edersheim, *The Life and Times of Jesus the Messiah*, 997-998.

And like a root out of parched ground;
He has no *stately* form or majesty
That we should look upon Him,
Nor appearance that we should be attracted to Him.
³He was despised and forsaken of men,
A man of sorrows and acquainted with grief;
And like one from whom men hide their face
He was despised, and we did not esteem Him.
4 Surely our griefs He Himself bore,
And our sorrows He carried;
Yet we ourselves esteemed Him stricken,
Smitten of God, and afflicted.
⁵But He was pierced through for our transgressions,
He was crushed for our iniquities;
The chastening for our well-being *fell* upon Him,
And by His scourging we are healed.
⁶All of us like sheep have gone astray,
Each of us has turned to his own way;
But the LORD has caused the iniquity of us all
To fall on Him.
7 He was oppressed and He was afflicted,
Yet He did not open His mouth;
Like a lamb that is led to slaughter,
And like a sheep that is silent before its shearers,
So He did not open His mouth.
⁸By oppression and judgment He was taken away;
And as for His generation, who considered
That He was cut off out of the land of the living
For the transgression of my people, to whom the stroke *was
    due*?
⁹His grave was assigned with wicked men,
Yet He was with a rich man in His death,
Because He had done no violence,
Nor was there any deceit in His mouth.
10 But the LORD was pleased
To crush Him, putting *Him* to grief;
If He would render Himself *as* a guilt offering,
He will see *His* offspring,

He will prolong *His* days,
And the good pleasure of the Lord will prosper in His hand.
¹¹As a result of the anguish of His soul,
He will *see it* and be satisfied;
By His knowledge the Righteous One,
My Servant, will justify the many,
As He will bear their iniquities.
¹²Therefore, I will allot Him a portion with the great,
And He will divide the booty with the strong;
Because He poured out Himself to death,
And was numbered with the transgressors;
Yet He Himself bore the sin of many,
And interceded for the transgressors. Isaiah 53:1-12 NASB

My Servant Exalted, then Marred

OT

13 Behold, My servant will prosper,
He will be high and lifted up and greatly exalted.
¹⁴Just as many were astonished at you, *My people,*
So His appearance was marred more than any man
And His form more than the sons of men. Isaiah 52:13-14
    NASB

Discussion: At the very beginning of this lengthy passage, we read in Isaiah 52:13 that "My servant" will be exalted. As with some of the other "servant" passages, the servant is not identified by Isaiah.[103] In Isaiah 52:13 through 53:12, "My servant" is clearly an individual and not a group of people.

However, after this introduction of exaltation for "My servant," this servant was "marred more than any man." The Hebrew word translated "marred" refers to the servant being mutilated to the point of being repugnant.[104] This should remind us of the trauma sustained by our Lord Jesus Christ. He was beaten and struck by the Jews (Luke 22:63-64). The soldiers of the governor twisted together a crown of thorns and then struck him on the head with a reed (Matthew 27:27-

---

103 See the list of these "servant" passages in the discussion of Isaiah 42:1-4.
104 Swanson, *Dictionary of Biblical Languages with Semantic Domains : Hebrew (Old Testament)*, definition 5425.

31). He was scourged (Mark 15:15; John 19:1). He was crucified (Matthew 27:35; Mark 15:15; Luke 23:33; John 19:18).

The Gentiles Will Believe in Him

OT

> [15]Thus He will sprinkle many nations,
> Kings will shut their mouths on account of Him;
> For what had not been told them they will see,
> And what they had not heard they will understand. Isaiah 52:15 NASB

NT

> [20]And thus I aspired to preach the gospel, not where Christ was *already* named, so that I would not build on another man's foundation; [21]but as it is written,
>
> > "THEY WHO HAD NO NEWS OF HIM SHALL SEE,
> > AND THEY WHO HAVE NOT HEARD SHALL UNDERSTAND."
> > Romans 15:20-21 NASB

> [4]By referring to this, when you read you can understand my insight into the mystery of Christ, [5]which in other generations was not made known to the sons of men, as it has now been revealed to His holy apostles and prophets in the Spirit; [6]*to be specific,* that the Gentiles are fellow heirs and fellow members of the body, and fellow partakers of the promise in Christ Jesus through the gospel, [7]of which I was made a minister, according to the gift of God's grace which was given to me according to the working of His power. Ephesians 3:4-7 NASB

Discussion: The Hebrew word translated "sprinkle" in the NASB is also translated as "startle."[105] "Startle" would fit the context of the remainder of the verse, so it seems to be the logical translation. Historically, the Gentiles, and even their kings, were "startled" by the Gospel. As a general measure, the Gentiles understood and accepted the Gospel better than the Jews did. The inclusion of the "nations," or the Gentiles, into God's salvation in Christ is clearly a fulfillment of Isaiah 52:15.

---

[105] Swanson, *Dictionary of Biblical Languages with Semantic Domains : Hebrew (Old Testament)*, definition 5684, 5685.

The Suffering Servant (Isaiah 52:13 through 53:12)

He Was Unrecognized by the Jews

OT

1 <u>Who has believed our message?</u>
And to whom has the arm of the LORD been revealed?
²For He grew up before Him like a tender shoot,
And like a root out of parched ground;
He has no *stately* form or majesty
That we should look upon Him,
Nor appearance that we should be attracted to Him. Isaiah 53:1-2 NASB

NT

(**36b**) These things Jesus spoke, and He went away and hid Himself from them. ³⁷But though He had performed so many signs before them, yet they were not believing in Him. ³⁸*This was* to fulfill the word of Isaiah the prophet which he spoke: "LORD, WHO HAS BELIEVED OUR REPORT? AND TO WHOM HAS THE ARM OF THE LORD BEEN REVEALED?" ³⁹For this reason they could not believe, for Isaiah said again, ⁴⁰"HE HAS BLINDED THEIR EYES AND HE HARDENED THEIR HEART, SO THAT THEY WOULD NOT SEE WITH THEIR EYES AND PERCEIVE WITH THEIR HEART, AND BE CONVERTED AND I HEAL THEM." ⁴¹<u>These things Isaiah said because he saw His glory, and he spoke of Him</u>. ⁴²Nevertheless many even of the rulers believed in Him, but because of the Pharisees they were not confessing *Him*, for fear that they would be put out of the synagogue; ⁴³for they loved the approval of men rather than the approval of God. John 12:36b-43 NASB

16 However, they did not all heed the good news; for Isaiah says, "LORD, WHO HAS BELIEVED OUR REPORT?" ¹⁷So faith comes from hearing, and hearing by the word of Christ. Romans 10:16-17 NASB

Discussion: Isaiah foretold that the Messiah would not be recognized by His own people. This was, and still is, a sad situation. When the Messiah came, the Jews were waiting for a mighty leader who would free them from the Roman oppressors. They certainly didn't suspect that a poor and lowly carpenter from Galilee could fill the role. He didn't teach like a rebel who stood against the Roman Empire. Where was His sword, where was the battle cry? When He died on the cross, He was finished in their minds. Therefore, the majority of the Jews never considered that Jesus was the chosen One because He did not fit their preconceived image. They did not understand what the Gentiles would immediately apprehend when the Gospel was given to them.

We should note that John said, "These things Isaiah said because he saw His glory, and he spoke of Him." Isaiah saw Christ, and Isaiah knew that his people would not recognize Him.

John 12:36b-43 quotes both Isaiah 53:1 and Isaiah 6:10. Isaiah 6:10 was considered previously.

He Was Despised

OT

> ³He was despised and forsaken of men,
> A man of sorrows and acquainted with grief;
> And like one from whom men hide their face
> He was despised, and we did not esteem Him.   Isaiah 53:3
>   NASB

Discussion: Truly Christ was despised. "¹¹He came to His own, and those who were His own did not receive Him" (John 1:11 NASB). Herod the Great deeply wanted to kill the baby Jesus (Matthew 2:16). The people of His own town Nazareth wanted to throw Him down a cliff (Luke 4:28-30). A later Herod also wanted to kill Him (Luke 13:31). Twice the Jews in Jerusalem were determined to stone Him to death (John 8:57-59; 10:31-33). At His crucifixion, everyone, including the chief priests, scribes, elders, those passing by, and even the two criminals who were crucified with Him insulted Him as He hung on the cross (Matthew 27:41-44). Yes, He was despised and forsaken. He was a man of sorrows.

He Bore Our Griefs and Sorrows

OT

> 4 Surely our griefs He Himself bore,
> And our sorrows He carried;

Yet we ourselves esteemed Him <u>stricken,</u>
<u>Smitten</u> of God, and <u>afflicted</u>. Isaiah 53:4 NASB

NT

14 When Jesus came into Peter's home, He saw his mother-in-law lying sick in bed with a fever. [15] He touched her hand, and the fever left her; and she got up and waited on Him. [16] When evening came, they brought to Him many who were demon-possessed; and He cast out the spirits with a word, and healed all who were ill. [17] *This was* to fulfill what was spoken through Isaiah the prophet: "HE HIMSELF TOOK OUR INFIRMITIES AND CARRIED AWAY OUR DISEASES." Matthew 8:14-17 NASB

Discussion: The Hebrew word in Isaiah 53:4 that is translated "griefs" from the Masoretic Text can be translated "illness," "wound," or "affliction."[106] The Dead Sea Scrolls Bible translated this same word as "sufferings." The word translated "sorrows" by both the Masoretic Text and Dead Sea Scrolls Bible can be translated as "pain" or "anguish."[107] The Masoretic Text appeared to emphasize the burden of emotional pain, but the ancient Septuagint version that was available to the New Testament writers may have emphasized the physical suffering from disease because that is what Matthew saw and recorded. That kind of healing was exactly what Jesus did in His ministry. What is recorded in His ministry makes modern medicine with all its amazing machinery look like a small candle waving in the night breeze. But His is like the blazing summer sun as He touched, or simply spoke—and they were healed.

He Was Stricken, Smitten, & Afflicted

NT

[7] The Jews answered him, "We have a law, and by that law He ought to die because He made Himself out *to be* the Son of God." John 19:7 NASB

Discussion: Isaiah's statements that the Messiah would be stricken, smitten, and afflicted are easily perceived in Christ's ministry.

---

106 Swanson, *Dictionary of Biblical Languages with Semantic Domains : Hebrew (Old Testament)*, definition 2716.
107 Swanson, *Dictionary of Biblical Languages with Semantic Domains : Hebrew (Old Testament)*, definition 4799.

Here, we should explore some of the weighty reasons why Jesus was persecuted, robbed of a legal trial before the Jews, brutally scourged, and unjustly crucified by the Roman authority.

The Christ—Messiah

"Messiah" is a Hebrew word meaning the "anointed one." "Christ" is the Greek translation of that Hebrew word. The words refer to the same person in two different languages, and were identified with Christ very early in His ministry (see John 1:41; 4:25-26).

The Hebrew word for "Messiah" was used in the Old Testament 39 times to designate a person who was anointed. Its most ancient use was concerning the anointed priest (Leviticus 4:3, 5, 16, 26; 6:22). In 1 Samuel as well as the rest of the Old Testament, the Jewish king became "His anointed" (1 Samuel 2:10, 35; 12:3-5; 16:6; 24:6, 10; 26:9, 16, 23; 2 Samuel 1:14, 16; 19:21; 22:51; 23:1; 2 Chronicles 6:42; Psalm 2:2; 18:50; 20:6; 28:8; 84:9; 89:38, 51; 132:10, 17; Lamentations 4:20; Habakkuk 3:13). The same word describes a special prince or official in Daniel 9:25-26. It appears that the same word was also used figuratively to describe His prophets and perhaps Israel in 1 Chronicles 16:22 and Psalm 105:15. Lastly, the same word was used figuratively to describe Cyrus in Isaiah 45:1.

Given the wide usage of "Messiah" in the Old Testament, one could wonder why the Jewish officials were so upset with Jesus being identified as the "Christ" or the "Messiah." However, the issue was political and not religious. The Jewish leaders were very concerned that an individual identified as the "Messiah" or the "Christ" would result in severe repercussions on Israel from the Roman Empire:

> **47** Therefore the chief priests and the Pharisees convened a council, and were saying, "What are we doing? For this man is performing many signs. [48]If we let Him *go on* like this, all men will believe in Him, and the Romans will come and take away both our place and our nation." [49]But one of them, Caiaphas, who was high priest that year, said to them, "You know nothing at all, [50]nor do you take into account that it is expedient for you that one man die for the people, and that the whole nation not perish." [51]Now he did not say this on his own initiative, but being high priest that year, he prophesied that Jesus was going to die for the nation, [52]and not for the

nation only, but in order that He might also gather together into one the children of God who are scattered abroad. ⁵³So from that day on they planned together to kill Him. John 11:47-53 NASB

So it was expedient, according to Caiaphas the high priest, for Jesus Christ to be executed in order to save Israel from a possible brutal Roman backlash.

The Son of God

As with the word "Messiah," the phrase "son of God" is also found in the Old Testament. This phrase was applied to a number of different entities. In Job 2:1, the phrase was used to describe the spiritual beings. It is used to describe Israel in Exodus 4:22. In 2 Samuel 7:14, this phrase is used to describe Solomon and the other kings in David's lineage. In Psalm 2:2, 7, 12, the phrase is used to describe the anointed Judean king, and is clearly Messianic in nature (see discussion on Psalms 2). It is used to describe Adam in Luke 3:38. It is used to describe all Christians in John 1:12-13. Lastly, this phrase is used repeatedly to describe our Lord Jesus Christ.

The first to apply the phrase "Son of God" to Jesus was the angel Gabriel who informed the Virgin Mary that she would be with child by the Holy Spirit. He said that Jesus would "be called the Son of the Most High" (Luke 1:32). He again said "the holy Child shall be called the Son of God" (Luke 1:35).

God reaffirmed this title regarding His Son Jesus Christ after His baptism:

> ¹⁶After being baptized, Jesus came up immediately from the water; and behold, the heavens were opened, and he saw the Spirit of God descending as a dove *and* lighting on Him, ¹⁷and behold, a voice out of the heavens said, "This is My beloved Son, in whom I am well-pleased." Matthew 3:16-17 NASB (see Luke 3:22 also)

John the Baptist baptized Jesus, and gave witness to what he saw and heard after that, saying,

> **29** The next day he *saw Jesus coming to him and *said, "Behold, the Lamb of God who takes away the sin of the world! ³⁰This is He on behalf of whom I said, 'After me comes

a Man who has a higher rank than I, for He existed before me.' ³¹I did not recognize Him, but so that He might be manifested to Israel, I came baptizing in water." ³²John testified saying, "I have seen the Spirit descending as a dove out of heaven, and He remained upon Him. ³³I did not recognize Him, but He who sent me to baptize in water said to me, 'He upon whom you see the Spirit descending and remaining upon Him, this is the One who baptizes in the Holy Spirit.' ³⁴I myself have seen, and have testified that this is the Son of God." John 1:29-34 NASB

The next entity who applied this title to Jesus addressed Him in hopes of creating doubt in Him. It was the devil himself. Twice Satan began his challenge to Christ by saying, "If You are the Son of God..." (Matthew 4:3 and 4:6). The replies of Jesus clearly showed that He loved the Word of God and replied using that same Word of God. Furthermore, Jesus refused to become the imperial ruler of earth in Satan's domain and refused to trust Satan rather than His Father in heaven. Adam and Eve trusted Satan rather than God. But Jesus trusted the Word of God over Satan's lies. Jesus won.

Following this Nathanael was the next to call Jesus the "Son of God" (John 1:49). When Jesus Christ was near people who had demon possession, the demons cried out in fear and called Jesus the "Son of God" (Matthew 8:29; Mark 3:11; Luke 4:41). Martha also confessed that Jesus was the Son of God (John 11:27).

Jesus Himself taught that He was the Son of God (John 3:18; 5:25; 10:36; 11:4). When He was on trial before the Council of the elders, they asked Him, "Are you the Son of God, then?" He answered, "Yes I am" (Luke 22:70). The centurion who was at the cross when Jesus died remarked that Jesus was the "Son of God" (Matthew 27:54; Mark 15:39).

Shortly after Paul's conversion, he started his ministry by affirming that Jesus was the Son of God (Acts 9:20). When Mark wrote his gospel, the first sentence included his confession that Jesus was indeed the Son of God (Mark 1:1). This same confession is found in Romans, 2 Corinthians, Galatians, Ephesians, Hebrews, 1 John, and Revelation. When the apostle John wrote a summary of his gospel, he included this same title of Jesus Christ (John 20:31).

Therefore, we find that the phrase "son of God" was used in the Old Testament to describe several entities, including the Messiah in Psalms 2. In the New Testament, the phrase was reserved for Jesus Christ. As with the title "Christ" or "Messiah," the title "Son of God" was politically charged, and the Jewish leadership deeply desired to kill Jesus in order to make those titles go away. They were afraid that the Romans would come and take everything away if the titles made it to the ear of the Emperor. In their minds, it was better that "one man die for the people, and that the whole nation not perish."

I and The Father are One

22 At that time the Feast of the Dedication took place at Jerusalem; [23]it was winter, and Jesus was walking in the temple in the portico of Solomon. [24]The Jews then gathered around Him, and were saying to Him, "How long will You keep us in suspense? If You are the Christ, tell us plainly." [25]Jesus answered them, "I told you, and you do not believe; the works that I do in My Father's name, these testify of Me. [26]But you do not believe because you are not of My sheep. [27]My sheep hear My voice, and I know them, and they follow Me; [28]and I give eternal life to them, and they will never perish; and no one will snatch them out of My hand. [29]My Father, who has given *them* to Me, is greater than all; and no one is able to snatch *them* out of the Father's hand. [30]I and the Father are one." John 10:22-30 NASB

22 The glory which You have given Me I have given to them, that they may be one, just as We are one; [23]I in them and You in Me, that they may be perfected in unity, so that the world may know that You sent Me, and loved them, even as You have loved Me. John 17:22-23 NASB

One can clearly see the response to Christ's comment in John 10:30—the Jews were immediate in their decision to stone Him. Since this was an offensive statement, Jesus continued to defend His claim to be Deity by citing Psalm 82 in John 10:34 as follows:

[6]I said, "You are gods,
And all of you are sons of the Most High." Psalm 82:6 NASB

Jesus continued His argument that He was in the Father, and the Father was in Him (John 10:38). However, the Jews were again determined to stone Him, but Jesus "eluded their grasp."

Jesus' claim to Deity was actually a much more powerful claim than being the Christ (Messiah) or the Son of God. The two titles were worn by others in the Old Testament, albeit infinitely lesser when compared to Jesus. But, no Jew in the Old Testament ever claimed to be Deity.

In summary, the titles of Christ (Messiah), Son of God, and Jesus' claim to be Deity were more than enough for the Jews to exercise "righteous" wrath and to make Jesus stricken, smitten, and afflicted.

Pierced, Crushed, Chastened, Scourged

OT

⁵But He was pierced through for our transgressions,
He was crushed for our iniquities;
The chastening for our well-being *fell* upon Him,
And by His scourging we are healed. Isaiah 53:5 NASB

There are four words in this verse that are shocking in their description. These are pierced, crushed, chastened, and scourged. In these we find the four-fold description of Christ's unjust punishments.

Pierced

NT

31 Then the Jews, because it was the day of preparation, so that the bodies would not remain on the cross on the Sabbath (for that Sabbath was a high day), asked Pilate that their legs might be broken, and *that* they might be taken away. ³²So the soldiers came, and broke the legs of the first man and of the other who was crucified with Him; ³³but coming to Jesus, when they saw that He was already dead, they did not break His legs. ³⁴But one of the soldiers pierced His side with a spear, and immediately blood and water came out. ³⁵And he who has seen has testified, and his testimony is true; and he knows that he is telling the truth, so that you also may believe. ³⁶For these things came to pass to fulfill the Scripture, "NOT A BONE OF HIM SHALL BE BROKEN." ³⁷And again another Scripture

says, "THEY SHALL LOOK ON HIM WHOM THEY PIERCED." John 19:31-37 NASB (Old Testament citations: Psalm 34:20 and Zechariah 12:10)

4 John to the seven churches that are in Asia: Grace to you and peace, from Him who is and who was and who is to come, and from the seven Spirits who are before His throne, ⁵and from Jesus Christ, the faithful witness, the firstborn of the dead, and the ruler of the kings of the earth. To Him who loves us and released us from our sins by His blood— ⁶and He has made us *to be* a kingdom, priests to His God and Father—to Him *be* the glory and the dominion forever and ever. Amen. ⁷BEHOLD, HE IS COMING WITH THE CLOUDS, and every eye will see Him, even those who pierced Him; and all the tribes of the earth will mourn over Him. So it is to be. Amen. Revelation 1:4-7 NASB (Old Testament citation: Daniel 7:13)

The Hebrew word in Isaiah 53:5 which is translated "pierced" in the NASB is translated in this manner in the distinguished Hebrew lexicons written by Swanson, Brown-Driver-Briggs, as well as Gesenius & Tregelles. The English versions that follow the preferred translation of Isaiah 53:5 include the HCSB, NAB, NASB, NIV, NLT, and YLT. However, most English versions translate it as "wounded" following the Authorized Version (i.e., KJV) as found in the ASV, CEV, DNT, DRB, ESV, GWT, ICB, KJV, NCV, NKJV, NRSV, RSV, TEV, and TLB.

The piercing of Jesus by the soldier occurred after Jesus had died. It was to make sure that Jesus was dead. The soldiers had broken the legs of the other two men who were crucified with Jesus in order to hasten their deaths. John saw the soldier and saw the sudden gush of blood and water from Jesus' side. Undoubtedly, the soldier, in his expertise of killing, knew how to aim the fatal pierce of the spear through the lung and into the heart thus explaining the sudden gush of blood. Undoubtedly, a pleural effusion caused by His hanging on the cross was present. This, too, was drained with the same pierce from the soldier's spear.

The crucifixion of Christ is difficult for us to grasp today. The cross was a way to kill someone who was despised. It was designed to kill the victim slowly and with extraordinary suffering. The longer they stayed on the cross, the more horrifying they became to those who saw them. The cross was the ultimate machine of torture and death. The cross was the ultimate machine to warn others that they must not transgress Roman law. The cross has been sanitized in art and in thought, especially in the Modern Era. But it was brutal and horrifying. We should understand fully the sufferings of our Savior that we might have an even greater appreciation of what He voluntarily took upon Himself for our sake.

The hammering of nails into His wrists and feet to secure Jesus on the cross is not referred to as being a piercing phenomenon in the New Testament. However, it was an incredibly painful piercing, and it caused unimaginable pain while Jesus hung on the cross. He experienced excruciating pain in His feet when He pushed up His body so He could breathe and horrific pain in His wrists when He let His body down to relieve the incredible pain in His feet.

According to Isaiah, the piercing of Jesus was "for our transgressions." It was like the death of the sacrificial lamb who bore the sins of the worshipper. Even so, Christ bore in His body on the cross the sins of every person who has lived or will ever live (Hebrews 9:28; 1 Peter 2:24).

Crushed

The Messiah would be "crushed." According to Swanson, this Hebrew word means a wound from a violent pressing force.[108] Certainly, Christ was beaten by both the Jews and the Romans and was also scourged. However, the nature of those injuries would have been different than what we would think of when we hear the word "crushed." There was a definite scenario that would fit this prophecy:

> **17** They took Jesus, therefore, and He went out, bearing His own cross, to the place called the Place of a Skull, which is called in Hebrew, Golgotha. John 19:17 NASB

The apostle John does not mention any help Jesus received in carrying the cross. This is explained by Matthew as follows:

> **27** Then the soldiers of the governor took Jesus into the Praetorium and gathered the whole *Roman* cohort around

---

108 Swanson, *Dictionary of Biblical Languages with Semantic Domains : Hebrew (Old Testament)*, definition 1917.

The Suffering Servant (Isaiah 52:13 through 53:12)

Him. ²⁸They stripped Him and put a scarlet robe on Him. ²⁹And after twisting together a crown of thorns, they put it on His head, and a reed in His right hand; and they knelt down before Him and mocked Him, saying, "Hail, King of the Jews!" ³⁰They spat on Him, and took the reed and *began* to beat Him on the head. ³¹After they had mocked Him, they took the *scarlet* robe off Him and put His *own* garments back on Him, and led Him away to crucify Him.

32 As they were coming out, they found a man of Cyrene named Simon, whom they pressed into service to bear His cross. Matthew 27:27-31 NASB

The weight of the cross would vary from cross to cross. If Jesus was carrying only the patibulum (cross-piece), the weight could have been from 75-125 pounds.[109] If He was carrying the entire cross (patibulum and stipes), the weight could easily have been 300 pounds or more.

It is clear that Christ bore His own cross for some distance before they pressed Simon of Cyrene to bear the cross. Although the text does not say, many assume that Jesus fell under the crushing load of the cross and simply could not carry it. This is a believable scenario since Jesus had been beaten and scourged and was probably in hypotensive shock from blood loss. Under these circumstances, the weight of the cross would have been crushing, and that crushing weight would have harmed Jesus even more.

Chastened

The Messiah would be chastened. The Hebrew word indicates a legal punishment.[110] The judicial penalty for Jesus the Christ—the Messiah—the Son of God—and the "I and the Father are one" claimer—was death by the most horrific means possible.

65 Then the high priest tore his robes and said, "He has blasphemed! What further need do we have of witnesses? Behold, you have now heard the blasphemy; ⁶⁶what do you

---

109 William D. Edwards, MD, Wesley J Gabel, MDiv, Floyd E Hosmer, MS, AMT, "Study On The Physical Death Of Christ," *JAMA* 1986; 255:1455-1463 (available online at http://www.frugalsites.net/jesus/crucifixion.htm)
110 Swanson, *Dictionary of Biblical Languages with Semantic Domains : Hebrew (Old Testament)*, definition 4592.

think?" They answered, "He deserves death!" Matthew 26:65-66 NASB

As mentioned before, under the Law of Moses, anyone who blasphemed the name of God was to be killed (Leviticus 24:16). Unfortunately for those Jews, Christ's claims were true, and He had not blasphemed the name of God.

Scourged

The Messiah would be scourged. The Hebrew word means a wound from a damaging blow.[111] The scourging of Christ is difficult for us to grasp today because we have never seen such a brutal instrument designed specifically for such severe humiliation and bodily punishment before death. The Roman scourge had a handle to which was affixed several cords or leather thongs. These cords or thongs were weighted with jagged pieces of metal and bone in order to viciously pound human flesh and rip human flesh to pieces. The scourging usually was given to the back and loins, but the face and the abdomen were often targets as well. The scourging alone often killed the victim.[112] Christ was truly "marred more than any man" (Isaiah 52:14).

The picture of Isaiah 53:5 is that of substitution. Christ takes the penalty for our sins, and we receive well-being and healing. The substitution becomes even more clear in Isaiah 53:6.

All Of Us Like Sheep Have Gone Astray

OT

> ⁶All of us like sheep have gone astray,
> Each of us has turned to his own way;
> But the LORD has caused the iniquity of us all
> To fall on Him. Isaiah 53:6 NASB

---

111 Swanson, *Dictionary of Biblical Languages with Semantic Domains : Hebrew (Old Testament)*, definition 2467.
112 Henry E. Dosker, "Scourge," in *The International Standard Bible Encyclopaedia*, Volume IV (James Orr, John L Nuelsen, Edgar Y. Mullins, Morris O. Evans, Melvin Grove Kyle, editors) (Grand Rapids, Michigan: WM. B. Eerdmans Publishing CO., 1939, 1956), 2704.

NT

> **21** For you have been called for this purpose, since Christ also suffered for you, leaving you an example for you to follow in His steps, ²²WHO COMMITTED NO SIN, NOR WAS ANY DECEIT FOUND IN HIS MOUTH; ²³and while being reviled, He did not revile in return; while suffering, He uttered no threats, but kept entrusting *Himself* to Him who judges righteously; ²⁴and He Himself bore our sins in His body on the cross, so that we might die to sin and live to righteousness; for by His wounds you were healed. ²⁵For you were continually straying like sheep, but now you have returned to the Shepherd and Guardian of your souls. 1 Peter 2:21-25 NASB

Discussion: Because we are sinners, we deserve to receive all of the evil that Christ received. However, He took our sins and our convictions and our penalties and bore these in His body on the cross, even to the point of His death. It was our transgressions and our iniquities that killed Jesus Christ, our precious Lord and Savior. Instead of death, we receive life. We received well-being and healing because of His vicarious death. For us, this is the unexpected gift that God the Father has given to us in our Lord Jesus Christ.

He Did Not Open His Mouth

OT

> **7** He was oppressed and He was afflicted,
> Yet He did not open His mouth;
> Like a lamb that is led to slaughter,
> And <u>like a sheep that is silent</u> before its shearers,
> So He did not open His mouth. Isaiah 53:7 NASB

NT

> (Before the Council) ⁶³But Jesus kept silent. Matthew 26:63 NASB

> (Before Pilate) ¹⁴And He did not answer him with regard to even a *single* charge, so the governor was quite amazed. Matthew 27:14 NASB

> (Before the Council) ⁶¹But He kept silent and did not answer. Mark 14:61 NASB

(Before Pilate) ⁵But Jesus made no further answer; so Pilate was amazed. Mark 15:5 NASB

(Before Herod) ⁹And he questioned Him at some length; but He answered him nothing. Luke 23:9 NASB

(Before Pilate) ⁸Therefore when Pilate heard this statement, he was even more afraid; ⁹and he entered into the Praetorium again and *said to Jesus, "Where are You from?" But Jesus gave him no answer. John 19:8-9 NASB.

³⁰Philip ran up and heard him reading Isaiah the prophet, and said, "Do you understand what you are reading?" ³¹And he said, "Well, how could I, unless someone guides me?" And he invited Philip to come up and sit with him. ³²Now the passage of Scripture which he was reading was this:

> "HE WAS LED AS A SHEEP TO THE SLAUGHTER;
> AND AS A LAMB BEFORE ITS SHEARER IS SILENT,
> SO HE DOES NOT OPEN HIS MOUTH.
> ³³"IN HUMILIATION HIS JUDGMENT WAS TAKEN AWAY;
> WHO WILL RELATE HIS GENERATION?
> FOR HIS LIFE IS REMOVED FROM THE EARTH."

³⁴The eunuch answered Philip and said, "Please tell me, of whom does the prophet say this? Of himself or of someone else?" ³⁵Then Philip opened his mouth, and beginning from this Scripture he preached Jesus to him. Acts 8:30-35 NASB

Discussion: One of the more extraordinary things was that Jesus did not try to defend Himself against the charges brought against Him before the Jewish Council, Pilate, or Herod. All four of the gospel writers mentioned this. The Ethiopian eunuch was amazed about this silence when he was reading Isaiah 53 while riding in his chariot. Philip used this passage to preach Jesus to the Ethiopian. The Ethiopian believed in Jesus, and the Ethiopian was baptized. Countless millions after the Ethiopian also heard the message about our Lord Jesus Christ in Isaiah 53, they believed Isaiah's prophetic message about the Messiah, and they were baptized into Christ.

The Suffering Servant (Isaiah 52:13 through 53:12)

By Oppression and Judgment

OT

⁸By oppression and judgment He was taken away;
And as for His generation, who considered
That He was cut off out of the land of the living
For the transgression of my people, to whom the stroke *was due*? Isaiah 53:8 NASB

NT

(See the quotation of Isaiah 53:8 from the Septuagint on the previous page—it is in Acts 8:33)

Discussion: Jesus was oppressed by the Jews and the Romans. Judgment was rendered against Him, and that judgment was death on a cross. Yet His death was not in vain, for He died bearing the sins of those who judicially murdered Him. They deserved God's judgment and punishment. But He took their transgressions on Himself and paid the debt that no ordinary human being could ever pay.

His Grave...with Wicked...with A Rich Man

OT

⁹His grave was assigned with wicked men,
Yet He was with a rich man in His death,
Because He had done no violence,
Nor was there any deceit in His mouth. Isaiah 53:9 NASB

NT

38 At that time two robbers *were crucified with Him, one on the right and one on the left. Matthew 27:38 NASB

57 When it was evening, there came a rich man from Arimathea, named Joseph, who himself had also become a disciple of Jesus. ⁵⁸This man went to Pilate and asked for the body of Jesus. Then Pilate ordered it to be given *to him*. ⁵⁹And Joseph took the body and wrapped it in a clean linen cloth, ⁶⁰and laid it in his own new tomb, which he had hewn out in the rock; and he rolled a large stone against the entrance of the tomb and went away. ⁶¹And Mary Magdalene was there, and the other Mary, sitting opposite the grave. Matthew 27:57-61 NASB

²¹For you have been called for this purpose, since Christ also suffered for you, leaving you an example for you to follow in His steps, ²²WHO COMMITTED NO SIN, NOR WAS ANY DECEIT FOUND IN HIS MOUTH; ²³and while being reviled, He did not revile in return; while suffering, He uttered no threats, but kept entrusting *Himself* to Him who judges righteously; ²⁴and He Himself bore our sins in His body on the cross, so that we might die to sin and live to righteousness; for by His wounds you were healed. ²⁵For you were continually straying like sheep, but now you have returned to the Shepherd and Guardian of your souls. 1 Peter 2:21-25 NASB

Discussion: Jesus was crucified between two men, and Matthew identified these men as robbers. Therefore, Jesus was treated as a common criminal in spite of His righteous life.

Where would the Jews have buried Jesus if Joseph of Arimathea had not come forward? We can be sure that the Jews would have wanted Him buried in dishonor among wicked men, just as the two robbers were buried. But Joseph, who was a rich man, and a disciple of Jesus, came forward and asked Pilate for His body. Pilate gave Jesus' body to Joseph, and Joseph then buried Jesus in his own new tomb, one that had never been defiled by a dead person. Why? Because Jesus had done no violence, and no deceit was found in His mouth as Peter so elegantly described.

The LORD Was Pleased to Crush Him

OT

10 But the LORD was pleased
To crush Him, putting *Him* to grief;
If He would render Himself *as* a guilt offering,
He will see *His* offspring,
He will prolong *His* days,
And the good pleasure of the LORD will prosper in His hand.
Isaiah 53:10 NASB

NT

29 The next day he *saw Jesus coming to him and *said, "Behold, the Lamb of God who takes away the sin of the world! John 1:29 NASB

35 Again the next day John was standing with two of his disciples, ³⁶and he looked at Jesus as He walked, and *said, "Behold, the Lamb of God!" John 1:35-36 NASB

Discussion: See the discussion at Isaiah 53:5 regarding Jesus being "crushed."

In Isaiah 53:7, Isaiah described the Messiah as "...like a lamb that is led to the slaughter...." He bore our griefs and carried our sorrows. Our iniquities and our punishments were placed on Him. He was killed for our transgressions.

The Messiah's offering was for "guilt" according to the NASB. This is variously translated in the English versions as "for sin" (ASV, CEV, DNT, DRB, ESV, KJV, NAB, NKJV, NLT, REV, NRSV, TLB, TMSG), a "guilt offering" (NASB, NIV, YLT), a "penalty offering" (ISB, NCV), "for wrong doings" (GWT), "restitution" (HCSB), and "to bring forgiveness" (TEV). It is translated "offering for sin" in the Dead Sea Scrolls Bible and the Septuagint.

However, it appears to be with good reason that the NASB chose this wording because the Hebrew word used here is exactly the same as the word describing the trespass or guilt offerings described in Leviticus in multiple places. In this offering, no blood was applied to the horns of the altar. Instead, the guilt was expiated by "compensation to the wronged person or his representative." Brown-Driver-Briggs explain this clearly as follows:

> The Messianic servant offers himself as an מָשָׁא in compensation for the sins of the people, interposing for them as their substitute Is 53:10 (incorrectly offering for sin AV RV).[113]

Because the Messiah rendered Himself as a guilt offering and died in our place, Isaiah wrote that "He will see *His* offspring" (Isaiah 53:10). How can this happen unless there is a resurrection from

---

113 F. Brown, S. R. Driver, & C. A. Briggs, *Enhanced Brown-Driver-Briggs Hebrew and English Lexicon* (Oak Harbor, WA: Logos Research Systems, 2000), definition of מָשָׁא.

the dead? God will prolong His days, and the Messiah will prosper because of the good pleasure of the LORD. No wonder Christ knew that He would resurrect from the dead!

He Will See It and Be Satisfied

OT

>[11]As a result of the anguish of His soul,
>He will see *it* and be satisfied;
>By His knowledge the Righteous One,
>My Servant, will justify the many,
>As He will bear their iniquities. Isaiah 53:11 NASB

NT

>"[14]I am the good shepherd, and I know My own and My own know Me, [15]even as the Father knows Me and I know the Father; and I lay down My life for the sheep. [16]I have other sheep, which are not of this fold; I must bring them also, and they will hear My voice; and they will become one flock *with* one shepherd. [17]For this reason the Father loves Me, because I lay down My life so that I may take it again. [18]No one has taken it away from Me, but I lay it down on My own initiative. I have authority to lay it down, and I have authority to take it up again. This commandment I received from My Father." John 10:14-18 NASB

>**18** So then as through one transgression there resulted condemnation to all men, even so through one act of righteousness there resulted justification of life to all men. [19]For as through the one man's disobedience the many were made sinners, even so through the obedience of the One the many will be made righteous. Romans 5:18-19 NASB.

Discussion: The Father saw the Messiah's anguish on the cross and He was satisfied. Through this full act of substitution, Christ was punished for the sins of all people, and His Father accepted that and was satisfied.

As illustrated from Jesus' comments in John 10:14-18, He had great understanding regarding what would happen to Himself and how those things would be the basis for our salvation. Indeed, He has justified us. This means that He has made us righteous, He has vindicated us, and we are innocent of all charges against us.[114] He bore our iniquities. Yes, He bore them away (see also Isaiah 53:5-6).

Because He Poured Out Himself To Death
OT

> [12]Therefore, I will allot Him a portion with the great,
> And He will divide the booty with the strong;
> Because He poured out Himself to death,
> And was numbered with the transgressors;
> Yet He Himself bore the sin of many,
> And interceded for the transgressors. Isaiah 53:12 NASB

NT

> [9]For this reason also, God highly exalted Him, and bestowed on Him the name which is above every name, [10]so that at the name of Jesus EVERY KNEE WILL BOW, of those who are in heaven and on earth and under the earth, [11]and that every tongue will confess that Jesus Christ is Lord, to the glory of God the Father. Philippians 2:9-11 NASB

> "[37]For I tell you that this which is written must be fulfilled in Me, 'AND HE WAS NUMBERED WITH TRANSGRESSORS'; for that which refers to Me has *its* fulfillment." Luke 22:37 NASB

Discussion: Our Lord Jesus Christ has indeed been exalted and given a name that is above every name. He is seated at the right hand of the Father. The reason for this is that He poured out Himself even to death on the cross. Indeed, He was numbered with the transgressors. Thank God that He bore our sins and interceded for us, the transgressors!

On reflection of Isaiah 52:13 through 53:12, it should be obvious that the New Testament writers quoted more from this passage than any other passage in the Old Testament. Just as the Ethiopian eunuch was touched deeply and converted to Christ because of this passage, so many others have been similarly touched and converted. We see this passage fulfilled in our Lord Jesus Christ. May it ever be that

---

114 Swanson, *Dictionary of Biblical Languages with Semantic Domains : Hebrew (Old Testament)*, definition 7405.

Bible-believing Christians will always cherish this passage in Isaiah as a true prophecy about God's Messiah, our Lord Jesus Christ, the Son of the Living God.

The Jews, the people of Islam, and the liberal, critical theologians insist that Jesus cannot be the one who fulfilled this passage in Isaiah. The Jews and the liberal, critical theologians insist that this passage was speaking of Israel and not of Jesus Christ. You must make your own decision by carefully reading the passage. You must decide to follow the unbelievers, or to follow Christ.

All Be Taught of God (Isaiah 54:13)

OT

> [13]"All your sons will be taught of the LORD;
> And the well-being of your sons will be great. Isaiah 54:13 NASB

NT

> **41** Therefore the Jews were grumbling about Him, because He said, "I am the bread that came down out of heaven." [42]They were saying, "Is not this Jesus, the son of Joseph, whose father and mother we know? How does He now say, 'I have come down out of heaven'?" [43]Jesus answered and said to them, "Do not grumble among yourselves. [44]No one can come to Me unless the Father who sent Me draws him; and I will raise him up on the last day. [45]It is written in the prophets, 'AND THEY SHALL BE TAUGHT OF GOD.' Everyone who has heard and learned from the Father, comes to Me. [46]Not that anyone has seen the Father, except the One who is from God; He has seen the Father. [47]Truly, truly, I say to you, he who believes has eternal life. [48]I am the bread of life. [49]Your fathers ate the manna in the wilderness, and they died. [50]This is the bread which comes down out of heaven, so that one may eat of it and not die. [51]I am the living bread that came down out of heaven; if anyone eats of this bread, he will live forever; and the bread also which I will give for the life of the world is My flesh." John 6:41-51 NASB

Discussion: Isaiah 54 is a chapter of good news because God told the Jews that there would be a time when they would have His compassion and they would flourish again. God would again establish and protect them. Isaiah 54:13 promised that their sons would be taught of the LORD, and because of this, their well-being would be great. Isaiah 54:2, 5, 11, 13, 15 were all considered Messianic according to the ancient rabbis.[115]

When Jesus said that He was the bread that came down from heaven, they disbelieved Him because they knew Joseph and Mary. Speaking to their unbelief, Jesus used this Old Testament passage to show that those who have been taught by God would come to Him. The negative is implied, that is, if they were not taught by God, they would not come to Him.

Have you been taught by God or by unbelievers? God's instruction for us today is found in the New Testament.

Covenant with David (Isaiah 55:3)

OT

> ³"Incline your ear and come to Me.
> Listen, that you may live;
> And I will make an everlasting covenant with you,
> *According to* the faithful mercies shown to David. Isaiah 55:3 NASB

NT

> ³⁴*As for the fact* that He raised Him up from the dead, no longer to return to decay, He has spoken in this way: 'I WILL GIVE YOU THE HOLY *and* SURE *blessings* OF DAVID.' Acts 13:34 NASB

Discussion: Isaiah 55 described the blessing that will come to the Jewish people if they will truly listen to God's voice. The "everlasting covenant" and the "faithful mercies shown to David" are found in 2 Samuel 7:16 as follows:

---

115 Edersheim, *The Life and Times of Jesus the Messiah*, 998.

"¹⁶Your house and your kingdom shall endure before Me forever; your throne shall be established forever." 2 Samuel 7:16 NASB

Paul in Acts 13:13ff was in Pisidian Antioch preaching on the Sabbath day to the Jews in a synagogue. This sermon had several references to the fulfillment of Old Testament Messianic prophecies in Jesus Christ. In this specific instance, Paul was teaching the necessity of the resurrection of Jesus Christ. Only in this way could Jesus Christ reign forever on the throne of David. This was the same promise given to Mary by the angel Gabriel:

> ³⁰The angel said to her, "Do not be afraid, Mary; for you have found favor with God. ³¹And behold, you will conceive in your womb and bear a son, and you shall name Him Jesus. ³²He will be great and will be called the Son of the Most High; and the Lord God will give Him the throne of His father David; ³³and He will reign over the house of Jacob forever, and His kingdom will have no end." Luke 1:30-33 NASB

Therefore, God's promise to David necessitated the resurrection of Jesus Christ from the dead.[116] Jesus Christ fulfilled the promise God made with David and with Israel, and He Himself is the covenant.

A House For All Nations (Isaiah 56:6-8)

OT

> **6** "Also the foreigners who join themselves to the LORD,
> To minister to Him, and to love the name of the LORD,
> To be His servants, every one who keeps from profaning the sabbath
> And holds fast My covenant;
> ⁷Even those I will bring to My holy mountain
> And make them joyful in My house of prayer.
> Their burnt offerings and their sacrifices will be acceptable on My altar;

---

116 Richard Oster, *The Acts of the Apostles Part II 13:1-28:31*, in *The Living Word Commentary*, Everett Ferguson, editor (Abilene, TX: ACU Press, 1979, 1984), 17-18.

A House For All Nations (Isaiah 56:6-8)

For My house will be called a house of prayer for all the peoples."
⁸The Lord GOD, who gathers the dispersed of Israel, declares, "Yet *others* I will gather to them, to those *already* gathered."
Isaiah 56:6-8 NASB

NT

15 Then they *came to Jerusalem. And He entered the temple and began to drive out those who were buying and selling in the temple, and overturned the tables of the money changers and the seats of those who were selling doves; ¹⁶and He would not permit anyone to carry merchandise through the temple. ¹⁷And He *began* to teach and say to them, "Is it not written, 'MY HOUSE SHALL BE CALLED A HOUSE OF PRAYER FOR ALL THE NATIONS'? But you have made it a ROBBERS' DEN." ¹⁸The chief priests and the scribes heard *this,* and *began* seeking how to destroy Him; for they were afraid of Him, for the whole crowd was astonished at His teaching. Mark 11:15-18 NASB (See also Matthew 21:12-13; Luke 19:45-46)

Discussion: God has always been concerned about all the people of the earth. Unfortunately, the majority of people have had little interest in a God that they cannot hear or see. In more recent times, atheism has become popular, especially in Europe. This position completely denies that there is any god of any kind. However, God is love (1 John 4:8, 16), and He has always been, and He always will be concerned about all His children.

Certainly, this concept is seen clearly in the Old Testament. God chose Abraham and made a covenant with him and his descendents. God's promises to Abraham included a son, uncountable descendents, the land of Canaan, and that <u>all the peoples of the earth would be blessed in Abraham</u> (Genesis 12:3; 13:14-18; 15:4, 7, 18; 17:6-8, 18-21; 18:17-18; 22:18). Regarding this blessing for all the peoples of the earth being our Lord Jesus Christ, see the discussion on Genesis 22:18.

Even though God especially chose Abraham and his descendents, God continued in His concern for the foreigners in the Old Testament. Many of the Egyptians left with Moses in the Exodus from Egypt (Exodus 12:38). Some of the foreigners were married to Jews

(Leviticus 24:10). At times these foreigners caused problems during the wilderness wanderings (Numbers 11:4). However, God's Law that was given to the Jews through Moses at Mount Sinai protected the foreigners. God commanded the Jews to love the sojourners since they themselves had been sojourners in Egypt (Deuteronomy 10:19). The foreigners were given the same protection as the Jews in the cities of refuge (Numbers 35:15). The foreigners who were hired servants had to be treated just like a Jewish hired servant and could not be oppressed or have their daily wage withheld (Deuteronomy 24:14-15). They could even inherit land in the nation of Israel (Ezekiel 47:21-23).[117] At the dedication of the first Temple, Solomon specifically prayed for those foreigners who sought the one and only true God (1 Kings 8:41, 43; 2 Chronicles 6:32-33).

However, the 70 years of Babylonian captivity drastically changed that relationship between Jews and foreigners. Undoubtedly the Jews were treated with malignant malice in every aspect of their lives in Babylonian captivity. They appeared to lose the sense of being a fellow sojourner in this life with others. Therefore, after returning from Babylonian captivity, the Jews separated from Israel all those of foreign descent (Nehemiah 13:3). It would be hard to picture Nehemiah tolerating any foreigner coming near the second Temple.

There appeared to be some change in this by the time Herod the Great built the Jews a magnificent Temple in Jerusalem. We find from Josephus that there were four courts in this Temple, and into the first court even foreigners could come.[118] This was later called "the Court of the Gentiles."[119] We also find out that this same court was used for trading and commerce rather than giving the foreigners a place to pray and praise the one and only true God. This evil practice was completely unacceptable to our Lord Jesus Christ. Twice He drove the business people out of that court. The first episode was near the

---

[117] H. Porter, "Gentiles,"in *The International Standard Bible Encyclopaedia*, Volume II (James Orr, John L Nuelsen, Edgar Y. Mullins, Morris O. Evans, Melvin Grove Kyle, editors) (Grand Rapids, Michigan: WM. B. Eerdmans Publishing CO., 1939, 1956), 1215

[118] Flavius Josephus, *Against Apion*, Book II, Paragraph 8 (available on the Internet at http://www.ccel.org/j/josephus/works/apion-2.htm).

[119] W. Shaw Caldecott and James Orr, "Temple,"in *The International Standard Bible Encyclopaedia*, Volume IV (James Orr, John L Nuelsen, Edgar Y. Mullins, Morris O. Evans, Melvin Grove Kyle, editors) (Grand Rapids, Michigan: WM. B. Eerdmans Publishing CO., 1939, 1956), 2937.

beginning of His ministry (John 2:13-16). The second episode was near the end of His ministry, and this is cited with the quotation of Mark 11:15-18 above. Jesus had the same expectation as His Father, and that was to make His house a house of prayer for all the peoples and nations.

How was this statement in Isaiah 56:7 fulfilled? Certainly Christ's rejection of the Jewish practice of using the Court of the Gentiles as a business and a market did not stop with Christ's rebukes. It was not Israel that cared for the nations and all the foreigners who sought after the only true and living God. Within 40 years of Jesus' ministry, the Romans came and destroyed Jerusalem and its magnificent Temple. Never since AD 70 has there been another Jewish Temple to which we can look toward and find God's house as a place of prayer for the nations.

We can see this very phenomenon in the church of the New Testament. It was in the church that God's house became a place of prayer for the nations. The writer of Hebrews said it well:

> [5]Now Moses was faithful in all His house as a servant, for a testimony of those things which were to be spoken later; [6]but Christ *was faithful* as a Son over His house—whose house we are, if we hold fast our confidence and the boast of our hope firm until the end. Hebrews 3:5-6 NASB

We should note that Isaiah 56:7 was considered Messianic by the ancient rabbis according to Edersheim.[120]

A New Covenant (Jeremiah 31:31-34)

OT

> **31** "Behold, days are coming," declares the LORD, "when I will make a new covenant with the house of Israel and with the house of Judah, [32]not like the covenant which I made with their fathers in the day I took them by the hand to bring them out of the land of Egypt, My covenant which they broke, although I was a husband to them," declares the LORD. [33]"But this is the covenant which I will make with the house of Israel

---

120 Edersheim, *The Life and Times of Jesus the Messiah,* 998.

after those days," declares the Lord, "I will put My law within them and on their heart I will write it; and I will be their God, and they shall be My people. ³⁴They will not teach again, each man his neighbor and each man his brother, saying, 'Know the Lord,' for they will all know Me, from the least of them to the greatest of them," declares the Lord, "for I will forgive their iniquity, and their sin I will remember no more." Jeremiah 31:31-34 NASB

NT

⁷For if that first *covenant* had been faultless, there would have been no occasion sought for a second. ⁸For finding fault with them, He says,

> "Behold, days are coming, says the Lord,
> When I will effect a new covenant
> With the house of Israel and with the house of Judah;
> ⁹Not like the covenant which I made with their fathers
> On the day when I took them by the hand
> To lead them out of the land of Egypt;
> For they did not continue in My covenant,
> And I did not care for them, says the Lord.
> ¹⁰"For this is the covenant that I will make with the house of Israel
> After those days, says the Lord:
> I will put My laws into their minds,
> And I will write them on their hearts.
> And I will be their God,
> And they shall be My people.
> ¹¹"And they shall not teach everyone his fellow citizen,
> And everyone his brother, saying, 'Know the Lord,'
> For all will know Me,
> From the least to the greatest of them.
> ¹²"For I will be merciful to their iniquities,
> And I will remember their sins no more."

¹³When He said, "A new *covenant*," He has made the first obsolete. But whatever is becoming obsolete and growing old is ready to disappear. Hebrews 8:7-12 NASB

Discussion: This concept of a "New Covenant" and it being brought by Jesus Christ was discussed thoroughly in Deuteronomy 18:15, 18. Simply put, there was no one else except Christ who could bring about this New Covenant. Therefore, the prophecy about this New Covenant in Jeremiah 31:31-34 was a Messianic prophecy and it was fulfilled by our Lord Jesus Christ.

Edersheim confirmed that Jeremiah 31:31, 33, 34 were considered to be Messianic by ancient rabbis.[121]

The Son of Man (Daniel 7:13-14)

OT

13 "I kept looking in the night visions,
And behold, with the clouds of heaven
One like a Son of Man was coming,
And He came up to the Ancient of Days
And was presented before Him.
14 "And to Him was given dominion,
Glory and a kingdom,
That all the peoples, nations and *men of every* language
Might serve Him.
His dominion is an everlasting dominion
Which will not pass away;
And His kingdom is one
Which will not be destroyed. Daniel 7:13-14 NASB

NT

29 "But immediately after the tribulation of those days THE SUN WILL BE DARKENED, AND THE MOON WILL NOT GIVE ITS LIGHT, AND THE STARS WILL FALL from the sky, and the powers of the heavens will be shaken. 30 And then the sign of the Son of Man will appear in the sky, and then all the tribes of the earth will mourn, and they will see the SON OF MAN COMING ON THE CLOUDS OF THE SKY with power and great glory. 31 And He will send forth His angels with A GREAT TRUMPET and THEY WILL GATHER TOGETHER His elect from the four winds, from one end

---

121 Edersheim, *The Life and Times of Jesus the Messiah,* 1003.

of the sky to the other. Matthew 24:29-31 NASB (see also Mark 13:24-27; 14:62; Luke 21:25-28; Revelation 1:7, 13)

15 Then the seventh angel sounded; and there were loud voices in heaven, saying,
"The kingdom of the world has become *the kingdom* of our Lord and of His Christ; and He will reign forever and ever." Revelation 11:15 NASB

[30]The angel said to her, "Do not be afraid, Mary; for you have found favor with God. [31]And behold, you will conceive in your womb and bear a son, and you shall name Him Jesus. [32]He will be great and will be called the Son of the Most High; and the Lord God will give Him the throne of His father David; [33]and <u>He will reign over the house of Jacob forever, and His kingdom will have no end</u>." Luke 1:30-33 NASB

[28]Therefore, since we receive <u>a kingdom which cannot be shaken,</u> let us show gratitude, by which we may offer to God an acceptable service with reverence and awe; [29]for our God is a consuming fire. Hebrews 12:28-29 NASB

Discussion: The most striking thing about this passage in Daniel is that our Lord Jesus Christ used the term "Son of Man" to describe Himself approximately 80 times in the New Testament. He thereby showed that this passage in Daniel 7 referred to Him and to His kingdom.

The Son of Man coming on "the clouds of heaven" in Daniel 7:13 was repeatedly related to the second coming of Christ in the New Testament. In like manner, the "kingdom" received by the Son of Man was clearly the kingdom already received by Jesus Christ and by His church. Part of this passage in Daniel has already been fulfilled in Christ's kingdom, but the second coming of Christ is still in the future.

Edersheim confirmed that Daniel 7:13 was considered Messianic by ancient rabbis.[122]

---

122 Edersheim, *The Life and Times of Jesus the Messiah,* 1004.

70 Weeks & Messiah (Daniel 9:24-27)

OT

24 "Seventy weeks have been decreed for your people and your holy city, to finish the transgression, to make an end of sin, to make atonement for iniquity, to bring in everlasting righteousness, to seal up vision and prophecy and to anoint the most holy *place*. ²⁵So you are to know and discern *that* from the issuing of a decree to restore and rebuild Jerusalem until Messiah the Prince *there will be* seven weeks and sixty-two weeks; it will be built again, with plaza and moat, even in times of distress. ²⁶Then after the sixty-two weeks the Messiah will be cut off and have nothing, and the people of the prince who is to come will destroy the city and the sanctuary. And its end *will come* with a flood; even to the end there will be war; <u>desolations</u> are determined. ²⁷And he will make a firm covenant with the many for one week, but in the middle of the week he will put a stop to sacrifice and grain offering; and <u>on the wing of abominations</u> *will come* one who makes desolate, even until a complete destruction, one that is decreed, is poured out on the one who makes desolate." Daniel 9:24-27 NASB

NT

15 "Therefore when you see the ABOMINATION OF DESOLATION which was spoken of through Daniel the prophet, standing in the holy place (let the reader understand), ¹⁶then those who are in Judea must flee to the mountains. ¹⁷Whoever is on the housetop must not go down to get the things out that are in his house. ¹⁸Whoever is in the field must not turn back to get his cloak. Matthew 24:15-18 NASB

20 "But when you see Jerusalem surrounded by armies, then recognize that her desolation is near. ²¹Then those who are in Judea must flee to the mountains, and those who are in the midst of the city must leave, and those who are in the country must not enter the city; ²²because these are days of vengeance, so that all things which are written will be fulfilled. ²³Woe to those who are pregnant and to those who are nursing babies in those days; for there will be great distress upon the land and wrath to this people; ²⁴and they will fall by the edge of the sword, and will be led captive into all the nations; and Jerusalem will be trampled under foot by the Gentiles until the times of the Gentiles are fulfilled. Luke 21:20-24 NASB

Discussion: The phrase that Jesus spoke, "abomination of desolation" in Matthew, is from the Septuagint. The English translation of the Septuagint by Brenton is as follows:

> **24** Seventy weeks have been determined upon thy people, and upon the holy city, for sin to be ended, and to seal up transgressions, and to blot out the iniquities, and to make atonement for iniquities, and to bring in everlasting righteousness, and to seal the vision and the prophet, and to anoint the Most Holy. ²⁵And thou shalt know and understand, that from the going forth of the command for the answer and for the building of Jerusalem until <u>Christ</u> the prince *there shall be* seven weeks, and sixty-two weeks; and then *the time* shall return, and the street shall be built, and the wall, and the times shall be exhausted. ²⁶And after the sixty-two weeks, the anointed one shall be destroyed, and there is no judgment in him: and he shall destroy the city and the sanctuary with the prince that is coming: they shall be cut off with a flood, and to the end of the war which is rapidly completed he shall appoint *the city* to desolations. ²⁷And one week shall establish the covenant with many: and in the midst of the week my sacrifice and drink-offering shall be taken away: and on the temple *shall be* the <u>abomination of desolations</u>; and at the end of the time an end shall be put to the desolation. Daniel 9:24-27 Septuagint[123]

This passage speaks of "seventy weeks" from the time of the decree to "restore and rebuild Jerusalem" (verse 25) until the destruction of Jerusalem (verses 26-27). At the mark of the 69th week, the "anointed one" ("Messiah" NASB; "Christ" Septuagint) would be destroyed. The destruction of Jerusalem will occur at the end of the "seventy weeks."

---

123 Brenton, *The Septuagint with Apocrypha: Greek and English*, 1065.

The first thing we should realize is that "seventy weeks" cannot be a literal term, but rather a symbolic term. Otherwise, from the decree to rebuild the temple until the destruction of Jerusalem would be only 1.34 years, or just 490 days, which is a historical impossibility. In fact, the Hebrew word translated "week" in this passage is used often to describe a literal week in the Old Testament, but that literal approach does not resolve the problem.

Some people attempt to correct this literal "error" by saying that "seventy weeks" means 490 years rather than 490 days. However, that would be introducing something into the passage that never was there. If one insists on this "correction" of God's word, he would continue to be in a dilemma. From the decree of **Cyrus** in 536 BC for the Jews to return to Jerusalem and rebuild the "house of the LORD" (Ezra 1:3), until the destruction of Jerusalem in AD 70, would be 606 years. If one tries to solve the problem by using **Darius**' edict to finish rebuilding the Temple in about 520 BC (Ezra 6:1-12), that would still involve 590 years until the destruction of Jerusalem, and that would be 100 years too much. Then one might choose the edict of **Artaxerxes** to Ezra in 458 BC (Ezra 7:11-26) to take offerings to the Temple in Jerusalem. However, this would entail 528 years, and this would still be off by 38 years. Therefore, changing the 490 days to 490 years won't solve the dilemma.

However, one can view the "seventy weeks" as symbolic language. The Jews frequently used certain numbers to invoke symbolic meanings, and these numbers were 3, 4, 7 and its multiples, 10, and 12. By far the most prominent of the symbolic numbers was 7 and its multiples, and they occurred nearly 600 times in the Bible. The symbolic nature of these numbers reach back deep into antiquity. The number 7 suggested "completeness." Seven multiplied by 10 was regarded as an intensified 7. Seventy times 7 meant a very forceful "always," and this is the way Jesus used it in His reply to Peter regarding how many times Peter should forgive another person (Matthew 8:22).[124]

Undoubtedly, that was the way the number "seventy weeks" (which is equivalent to 7 x 10 x 7, or 490 days) was meant to be

---

124 William Taylor Smith, "Number," in *The International Standard Bible Encyclopaedia*, Volume III (James Orr, John L Nuelsen, Edgar Y. Mullins, Morris O. Evans, Melvin Grove Kyle, editors) (Grand Rapids, Michigan: WM. B. Eerdmans Publishing CO., 1939, 1956), 2157-2163.

understood in Daniel 9:24. Symbolically, God forcefully announced a completeness concerning the Jews and the destruction of Jerusalem; an utter completeness that He would not revoke. He did it using the symbolic phrase, "seventy weeks."

The fact that Jesus quoted from Daniel 9:27 means that He fully understood the prophecy meant that He would come in the 69th "week," and He would be "cut off and have nothing." He also knew from this chapter in Daniel that relatively soon Jerusalem would be destroyed by the Romans. The sign would be the "abomination of desolations" standing in the "holy place."

Now this sign about the "abomination of desolation" standing in the "holy place" is somewhat cryptic. Obviously, this was written in such a way so that the enemies of Christianity couldn't understand it. The Romans at that time were pagan idolators and were an abomination who caused desolation whenever they attacked any country or city. The "holy place" in Matthew's account evidently represented Jerusalem.

It is clear from Josephus[125] that the Roman leader Cestius, at the beginning of the Roman war against the Jews, surrounded and attempted to take Jerusalem, but gave up without a sufficient reason and retreated with his troops. Then the Jews attacked the Romans as they retreated and inflicted serious losses. This event would have reminded the Christians in Jerusalem about the need to immediately flee. When Titus returned to Jerusalem with the Roman legions, there was no longer any chance for anyone to escape. Perhaps it was in that hiatus between the two Roman armies when the Jewish Christians took the opportunity to escape and flee to safety at Pella.[126]

Now the liberal, critical theologians insist that the book of Daniel was not written by Daniel, but by an unknown Jew in the second century BC. None of the events in Daniel were true in an historical sense. Some would say that the "anointed one" was not Jesus, but was Onias III in 171 BC (2 Maccabees 4:23-28).[127] Others would say that this passage in Daniel was fulfilled when Antiochus Epiphanes

---

125 Flavius Josephus, *Wars*, Book II, ch XIX, section 6, 7.
126 Eusebius Pamphilus, *Ecclesiastical History*, Book III, Chapter V, (Grand Rapids: Baker Books House), 86.
127 Mark W. Hamilton, "Daniel," in *The Transforming Word*, (Editors: Hamilton, Mark W., Cukrowski, Kenneth L., Shankle, Nancy W., Thompson, James, and Willis, John T.), (Abilene: Abilene Christian University Press, 2009), 662.

demanded the Jews sacrifice an abominable offering (2 Maccabees 6:1-11). The liberal, critical theologians would never allow Jesus to interpret the Old Testament Scriptures.

However, if this passage in Daniel can be applied <u>partially</u> to such situations, it is certainly fulfilled in its completeness from the lips of our Lord Jesus Christ. Aside from Jerusalem being destroyed by Babylon in 586 BC, Jerusalem was not entirely destroyed again until AD 70. Therefore, Jesus was the only Person who could be referred to by Daniel as the Anointed One, the Christ, the Messiah.

Out of Egypt (Hosea 11:1)

OT

> **1** When Israel *was* a youth I loved him,
> And out of Egypt I called My son. Hosea 11:1 NASB

NT

> **13** Now when they had gone, behold, an angel of the Lord *appeared to Joseph in a dream and said, "Get up! Take the Child and His mother and flee to Egypt, and remain there until I tell you; for Herod is going to search for the Child to destroy Him."
> **14** So Joseph got up and took the Child and His mother while it was still night, and left for Egypt. ¹⁵He remained there until the death of Herod. This was to fulfill what had been spoken by the Lord through the prophet: "OUT OF EGYPT I CALLED MY SON." Matthew 2:13-15 NASB

Discussion: The "son" in Hosea 11:1 was the nation of Israel. The fulfillment in Matthew 2:15 is a type fulfillment. As it was with Israel, so it was with the ideal Israelite, Jesus.[128] This illustrates the lesser to the greater, from Israel to Christ.

---

[128] Lewis, *The Living Word Commentary: The Gospel According to Matthew, Part I*, 49.

3 Days & 3 Nights (Jonah 1:17)

OT

> 17 And the LORD appointed a great fish to swallow Jonah, and Jonah was in the stomach of the fish three days and three nights. Jonah 1:17 NASB

NT

> 38 Then some of the scribes and Pharisees said to Him, "Teacher, we want to see a sign from You." ³⁹But He answered and said to them, "An evil and adulterous generation craves for a sign; and *yet* no sign will be given to it but the sign of Jonah the prophet; ⁴⁰for just as JONAH WAS THREE DAYS AND THREE NIGHTS IN THE BELLY OF THE SEA MONSTER, so will the Son of Man be three days and three nights in the heart of the earth. ⁴¹The men of Nineveh will stand up with this generation at the judgment, and will condemn it because they repented at the preaching of Jonah; and behold, something greater than Jonah is here. ⁴²*The* Queen of *the* South will rise up with this generation at the judgment and will condemn it, because she came from the ends of the earth to hear the wisdom of Solomon; and behold, something greater than Solomon is here. Matthew 12:38-42 NASB

Discussion: Once again, this is a type fulfillment. It shows that Jonah was important, but Jesus was and remains infinitely more important than Jonah. In the same passage, Solomon was important, but Jesus was and is infinitely more important than Solomon. The three days and three nights were very significant for Jonah as well as the people of Nineveh. However, the death, burial, and resurrection of Jesus Christ holds the ultimate significance for every human being on earth from the beginning of time to the end of time.

Bethlehem Ephrathah (Micah 5:2)

OT

²"But as for you, Bethlehem Ephrathah,
Too little to be among the clans of Judah,
From you One will go forth for Me to be ruler in Israel.
His goings forth are from long ago,
From the days of eternity." Micah 5:2 NASB

NT

1 Now after Jesus was born in Bethlehem of Judea in the days of Herod the king, magi from the east arrived in Jerusalem, saying, ²"Where is He who has been born King of the Jews? For we saw His star in the east and have come to worship Him." ³When Herod the king heard this, he was troubled, and all Jerusalem with him. ⁴Gathering together all the chief priests and scribes of the people, he inquired of them where the Messiah was to be born. ⁵They said to him, "In Bethlehem of Judea; for this is what has been written by the prophet:

⁶'AND YOU, BETHLEHEM, LAND OF JUDAH,
ARE BY NO MEANS LEAST AMONG THE LEADERS OF JUDAH;
FOR OUT OF YOU SHALL COME FORTH A RULER
WHO WILL SHEPHERD MY PEOPLE ISRAEL.' " Matthew 2:1-6 NASB

Discussion: This is solid evidence that the Jews at the time of Jesus certainly held some of their Scriptures to contain Messianic prophecies. This is a prophecy that a Jewish King would be born in Bethlehem. He had to be born in Bethlehem since that was the city of David (1 Samuel 17:12). This was the information Herod demanded of the chief priests and the scribes. They wisely did not quote to him the next sentence which indicates that this king was special, for He existed "from the days of eternity." The Septuagint says, "and his goings forth were from the beginning, even from eternity."[129]

---

129 Brenton, *The Septuagint with Apocrypha: Greek and English* (Hendrickson Publishers), 1100.

The description of this unique Jewish King shows that He existed "from the days of eternity." Therefore, this unique Jewish King cannot be any of the kings of Israel or Judah that we read about in the Old Testament. Rather, this description can only be fulfilled in our Lord Jesus Christ, because only He is from the beginning, even to eternity.

Edersheim confirmed that Micah 5:2 was Messianic according to the ancient rabbis.[130]

Mounted on a Donkey (Zechariah 9:9)

OT

⁹Rejoice greatly, O daughter of Zion!
Shout in *triumph*, O daughter of Jerusalem!
Behold, your king is coming to you;
He is just and endowed with salvation,
Humble, and mounted on a donkey,
Even on a colt, the foal of a donkey.
¹⁰I will cut off the chariot from Ephraim
And the horse from Jerusalem;
And the bow of war will be cut off.
And He will speak peace to the nations;
And His dominion will be from sea to sea,
And from the River to the ends of the earth. Zechariah 9:9-10 NASB

NT

1 When they had approached Jerusalem and had come to Bethphage, at the Mount of Olives, then Jesus sent two disciples, ²saying to them, "Go into the village opposite you, and immediately you will find a donkey tied *there* and a colt with her; untie them and bring them to Me. ³If anyone says anything to you, you shall say, 'The Lord has need of them,' and immediately he will send them." ⁴This took place to fulfill what was spoken through the prophet:

⁵"SAY TO THE DAUGHTER OF ZION,
   'BEHOLD YOUR KING IS COMING TO YOU,

---

130 Edersheim, *The Life and Times of Jesus the Messiah*, 1005.

GENTLE, AND MOUNTED ON A DONKEY,
EVEN ON A COLT, THE FOAL OF A BEAST OF BURDEN.' " Matthew 21:1-5 NASB (see also John 12:15)

Discussion: The setting of Zechariah was in the time after the Babylonian captivity when the Jews had returned to Jerusalem and started building the temple in about 536 BC. The Jews met much resistance from the people living in that area and were forced to cease the construction. Zechariah started his ministry as a prophet in about 520 BC. Haggai and Zechariah worked together to strengthen the resolve of the Jews to rebuild the Temple and the prophets succeeded in their goal.[131]

The passage in Zechariah 9:9-10 is at the end of a section (9:1-10) that contains prophecies against neighboring nations. Verses 9 and 10 are an abrupt change, and they address Jerusalem instead. It is obviously prophetic in nature and speaks about a king who will enter Jerusalem on a donkey. This king would be just and "endowed with salvation." In a time of relative peace, this divine King will speak peace to the nations, and His domain will be the entire earth.

Jesus obviously had this prophecy in mind when He requested the donkey and the colt to be brought to Him. His entrance into Jerusalem was accompanied by the people shouting that He was the Son of David, because they understood that He was the Messianic King who was prophesied by Zechariah. Indeed, He had to be such a king, for His dominion was the entire earth. As such, there is no person who could fulfill this prophecy except our Lord Jesus Christ.

Edersheim confirmed that Zechariah 9:9-10 was widely recognized as a Messianic prophecy according to the ancient rabbis.[132]

Whom They Pierced (Zechariah 12:10)

OT

10 "I will pour out on the house of David and on the inhabitants of Jerusalem, the Spirit of grace and of supplication, so that they will look on <u>Me</u> whom they have pierced;

---

131 Rubel Shelly, *A Book-By-Book Study of the Old Testament* (Nashville: 20th Century Christian Foundation, 1982), 115.
132 Edersheim, *The Life and Times of Jesus the Messiah,* 985, 1006.

and they will mourn for Him, as one mourns for an only son, and they will weep bitterly over Him like the bitter weeping over a firstborn. Zechariah 12:10 NASB

NT

31 Then the Jews, because it was the day of preparation, so that the bodies would not remain on the cross on the Sabbath (for that Sabbath was a high day), asked Pilate that their legs might be broken, and *that* they might be taken away. ³²So the soldiers came, and broke the legs of the first man and of the other who was crucified with Him; ³³but coming to Jesus, when they saw that He was already dead, they did not break His legs. ³⁴But one of the soldiers pierced His side with a spear, and immediately blood and water came out. ³⁵And he who has seen has testified, and his testimony is true; and he knows that he is telling the truth, so that you also may believe. ³⁶For these things came to pass to fulfill the Scripture, "NOT A BONE OF HIM SHALL BE BROKEN." ³⁷And again another Scripture says, "THEY SHALL LOOK ON HIM WHOM THEY PIERCED." John 19:31-37 NASB

Discussion: The piercing of the Messiah is clearly reflected in Zechariah 12:10. It is interesting that piercing the Messiah in this passage is the same as piercing God (Me...Him...Him). The mourning for Him would be very great.

The piercing of Jesus on the cross was after He died. It was done to make sure He was really dead. It was also a substitute for breaking his legs so as to hasten His death. Blood and water came out when the spear was pulled out of Jesus. This is evidence that His heart and lungs were pierced—a lethal wound by itself if He had still been alive. Those who claim that Jesus didn't die but just swooned on the cross and later awoke in the tomb are completely unrealistic and without any reasonable medical knowledge regarding how lethal this kind of wound was.

Could this passage in Zechariah be fulfilled in anyone besides Jesus? Certainly no one comes to mind. Zechariah was written after the Jews returned from Babylonian captivity and there were no more Jewish kings. In fact, there is no one in history after Zechariah that could fit this description except our Lord Jesus Christ. His divine nature is surely implied in Zechariah 12:10 (Me...Him...Him). Surely this was for Christ alone.

The discussion regarding "not a bone of Him shall be broken" (Psalm 34:20) is found in the discussion of Psalm 22.

Edersheim confirmed that Zechariah 12:10 was considered Messianic in the Talmud.[133]

Prepare Your Way (Malachi 3:1)

OT

1 "Behold, I am going to send My messenger, and he will clear the way before Me. And the Lord, whom you seek, will suddenly come to His temple; and the messenger of the covenant, in whom you delight, behold, He is coming," Malachi 3:1 NASB

NT

7 As these men were going *away*, Jesus began to speak to the crowds about John, "What did you go out into the wilderness to see? A reed shaken by the wind? ⁸But what did you go out to see? A man dressed in soft *clothing*? Those who wear soft *clothing* are in kings' palaces! ⁹But what did you go out to see? A prophet? Yes, I tell you, and one who is more than a prophet. ¹⁰This is the one about whom it is written,

'BEHOLD, I SEND MY MESSENGER AHEAD OF YOU,
WHO WILL PREPARE YOUR WAY BEFORE YOU.'

¹¹Truly I say to you, among those born of women there has not arisen *anyone* greater than John the Baptist! Yet the one who is least in the kingdom of heaven is greater than he. ¹²From the days of John the Baptist until now the kingdom of heaven suffers violence, and violent men take it by force. ¹³For all the prophets and the Law prophesied until John. ¹⁴And if you are willing to accept *it*, John himself is Elijah who was to come. ¹⁵He who has ears to hear, let him hear. Matthew 11:7-15 NASB (see also Mark 1:2; Luke 1:76; 7:27)

---

133 Edersheim, *The Life and Times of Jesus the Messiah*, 1006.

Discussion: In Malachi 3:1, God prophesied that He would send a messenger to clear His way. Then the Lord would come to His temple. God then speaks of "the messenger of the covenant" who is coming also. Per Edersheim, ancient Jewish comments on this passage identified Elijah as the forerunner of the Messiah since he was promised to return (Malachi 4:5).[134]

In the New Testament, an angel informed the aged Zacharias that his barren and aged wife Elizabeth would bear him a son, and that this son would be the forerunner of Christ. Specifically, the angel told Zacharias the following:

> [13]But the angel said to him, "Do not be afraid, Zacharias, for your petition has been heard, and your wife Elizabeth will bear you a son, and you will give him the name John. [14]You will have joy and gladness, and many will rejoice at his birth. [15]For he will be great in the sight of the Lord; and he will drink no wine or liquor, and he will be filled with the Holy Spirit while yet in his mother's womb. [16]And he will turn many of the sons of Israel back to the Lord their God." Luke 1:13-16 NASB

The disciples of Christ did not understand fully the prophecies regarding John the Baptist. Specifically, they did not understand that John the Baptist would come in the spirit and power of Elijah. Jesus helped them understand as follows:

> **9** As they were coming down from the mountain, Jesus commanded them, saying, "Tell the vision to no one until the Son of Man has risen from the dead." [10]And His disciples asked Him, "Why then do the scribes say that Elijah must come first?" [11]And He answered and said, "Elijah is coming and will restore all things; [12]but I say to you that Elijah already came, and they did not recognize him, but did to him whatever they wished. So also the Son of Man is going to suffer at their hands." [13]Then the disciples understood that He had spoken to them about John the Baptist. Matthew 17:9-13 NASB (see also Mark 9:11-13)

---

134 Edersheim, *The Life and Times of Jesus the Messiah,* 1007.

Malachi 3:1 is truly a prophecy of John the Baptist as well as Jesus the Messiah. John was to "clear the way" for the Messiah. The Messiah would "suddenly come to His Temple", and this was fulfilled when Jesus cleansed the Temple (John 2:13-17).

Turn Hearts of Fathers (Malachi 4:6)

OT

> 5 "Behold, I am going to send you Elijah the prophet before the coming of the great and terrible day of the LORD. ⁶He will restore the hearts of the fathers to *their* children and the hearts of the children to their fathers, so that I will not come and smite the land with a curse." Malachi 4:5-6 NASB

NT

> ¹⁷"It is he who will go *as a forerunner* before Him in the spirit and power of Elijah, TO TURN THE HEARTS OF THE FATHERS BACK TO THE CHILDREN, and the disobedient to the attitude of the righteous, so as to make ready a people prepared for the Lord." Luke 1:17 NASB

Discussion: It is interesting that the spiritual awakening of the Jewish people in the days of John the Baptist included a restoring of the hearts of the fathers to their children and restoring of the hearts of the children to their fathers. This spiritual awakening changed the disobedient to the attitude of the righteous. This was the goal of John the Baptist, and he successfully prepared the people for our Lord Jesus Christ.

It should be noted that Malachi 4:5 was widely deemed to represent the forerunner of the Messiah according to the ancient rabbis.[135]

---

135 Edersheim, *The Life and Times of Jesus the Messiah,* 1007.

Conclusion

I would like to thank all the readers who have evaluated carefully all the 58 pieces of evidence that I have assembled and discussed in this book. It is my hope that you have been touched by this Scriptural evidence and that you now believe, or you now are more confident in your belief, that our Lord Jesus Christ fulfilled and still fulfills Messianic Prophecies found in the Old Testament.

If this is now your position, then you are a real believer in Christ because He very clearly claimed that certain prophecies in the Old Testament were written specifically about Him and fulfilled by Him. If this is now your position, then you are also a real believer in the writings of the apostles and prophets of our Lord Jesus Christ who wrote the New Testament for our learning and salvation. Take care to build up your faith continually by regularly reading and studying the Scriptures.

However, if this is not now your position, I hope you will continue to study this issue. Please understand that if this is not your position, then you have not believed what our Lord Jesus Christ taught, nor what His apostles and prophets wrote and taught in the New Testament. This is a precarious position because how can you be Christ's disciple and enjoy His promises if you do not believe what He spoke? Don't allow a liberal, critical biblical scholar to destroy your faith and your hope in eternal life.

Please remember that this is not an exhaustive study of all the Old Testament prophecies that were fulfilled in the Old Testament times or in the New Testament times. Nor is this an exhaustive study of all the potential Messianic Prophecies that were fulfilled in Christ. However, I consider this evidence is more than enough to convince a reasonable person that Jesus was indeed telling the truth, and we can trust what He said.

If you would like to read other presentations on this topic that affirm the ancient Christian understanding of Messianic Prophecies, I would certainly encourage you to do so. The book on this subject by Edward Dewart is excellent, and I recommend it. It is available in paperback and e-books. You can find the details of this book in the Bibliography. In addition, the book entitled *"It Is Written"* by Richard Hodgson is available in e-book format. It is excellent in that Hodgson also presents a wonderful view of Old Testament prophecies that were fulfilled in the Old Testament times. You can get further information on these two books at desertwillowpublishingonline.com.

You might also like to read the book by Michael Rydelnik entitled *The Messianic Hope: Is the Hebrew Bible Really Messianic?* This is available as a hardback and is an excellent resource.

Bibliography

Angus, S. "Vulgate," in James Orr, John L. Nuelsen, Edgar Y. Mullins, Morris O. Evans, and Melvin Grove Kyle (editors), *The International Standard Bible Encyclopaedia, Volume IV.* Grand Rapids, Mich.: Wm. B. Eerdmans Publishing Co., 1939, 1956.

Anonymous, *Wikipedia*, "Taylor and Sennacherib Prisms," http://en.wikipedia.org/wiki/Sennacherib%27s_Prism, accessed 01/01/2013.

Ash, Anthony L., and Miller, Clyde M. *Living Word Commentary on the Old Testament: Psalms.* (Editor John T. Willis) Abilene: ACU Press, 1980, 1984. (This commentary does not acknowledge that Jesus fulfilled messianic prophecies.)

Augustine of Hippo, "Expositions on the Book of Psalms" (A. C. Coxe, Trans.), in *A Select Library of the Nicene and Post-Nicene Fathers of the Christian Church, First Series, Volume VIII: Saint Augustine: Expositions on the Book of Psalms* (P. Schaff, Ed.) (New York: Christian Literature Company, 1888. (The many books in this set are available at the Internet Archive at http://archive.org/details/texts.)

Barclay, William, *The Gospel of Matthew, Volume 1* (Philadelphia, The Westminister Press, 1956, 1958). (Available at the Internet Archives at http://archive.org/details/gospelofmatthewv008785mbp)

Barnes, Albert. *Barnes' Notes on the New Testament*, http://www.studylight.org/com/bnn/view.cgi?book=heb&chapter=001

Barraclough, Henry. "My Lord Has Garments," in *Great Songs of the Church*, Number Two. Chicago: Great Songs Press, 1972.

Bauer, Walter; Danker, Frederick W.; Arndt, William F.; Gingrich, F. Wilbur (BDAG). *A Greek-English Lexicon of the New Testament and Other Early Christian Literature*, second edition. Chicago: The University of Chicago Press, 1957, 1979.

Brenton, Sir Lancelot C. L. *The Septuagint with Apocrypha: Greek and English.* Hendrickson Publishers. (This book is still in print. The English only translation of the *Septuagint* by Brenton is available at the Internet Archive at http://archive.org/details/septuagintversio00bren.)

Brown, F., S., Driver, S. R., & Briggs, C. A. *Enhanced Brown-Driver-Briggs Hebrew and English Lexicon.* Oak Harbor, WA: Logos Research Systems, 2000.

Caldecott, W. Shaw and Orr, James. "Temple,"in *The International Standard Bible Encyclopaedia*, Volume IV (James Orr, John L Nuelsen, Edgar Y. Mullins, Morris O. Evans, Melvin Grove Kyle, editors). Grand Rapids, Michigan: WM. B. Eerdmans Publishing CO., 1939, 1956.

Clarke, Adam. *The Adam Clark Commentary*, Psalm XCVII, http://www.studylight.org/com.

Coffman, Burton. *Coffman Commentaries on the Old and New Testaments.* (Coffman Commentaries are available to freely view on the Internet at: http://www.studylight.org/com. Dr. Coffman lived 1905-2006 and his printed commentaries on the whole Bible are still in print. He strongly believed that Jesus Christ was the Messiah and that He fulfilled messianic prophecies in the Old Testament.)

Dewart, Edward Hartley. *Jesus the Messiah in Prophecy and Fulfilment: A Review and Refutation of the Negative Theory of Messianic Prophecy.* Toronto: William Briggs, 1891. (This public domain book is available in OCR reprints at internet vendors and also can be read at the Internet Archives at http://archive.org/details/jesusthemessiah00dewauoft. Since I could not find a quality e-book in EPUB or Mobipocket formats, I produced one, the details of which can be viewed at http://www.desertwillowpublishingonline.com. His book epitomizes the wide gulf between liberal theologians who deny messianic prophecies and those who believe in messianic prophecies which were fulfilled by Jesus Christ.)

Dosker, Henry E. "Scourge," in *The International Standard Bible Encyclopaedia*, Volume IV (James Orr, John L Nuelsen, Edgar Y. Mullins, Morris O. Evans, Melvin Grove Kyle, editors) (Grand Rapids, Michigan: WM. B. Eerdmans Publishing CO, 1939, 1956.

Edersheim, Alfred. *The Life and Times of Jesus the Messiah* (New Updated Edition, Complete and Unabridged in One Volume). Hendrickson Publishers, Inc., 1993. (Edersheim lived 1825-1889, was born a Jew and was converted to Christianity. He was an excellent conservative scholar. Volumes 1 and 2 of this title can be found at the Internet Archive at http://archive.org/details/texts [simply type in the title into the "Search" box]. The one-volume version of this book is still in print by Hendrickson Publishers.)

Edwards, William D., MD, Gabel, Westley J, MDiv, Hosmer, Floyd E, MS, AMT, "Study On The Physical Death Of Christ," *JAMA* 1986; 255:1455-1463 (available online at http://www.frugalsites.net/jesus/crucifixion.htm)

Ferguson, Everett. *A Cappella Music in the Public Worship of the Church*, fourth edition. Abilene: Desert Willow Publishing, 2013. (This is the best objective treatise on this subject that I know.)

Hailey, Homer. *A Commentary on Isaiah with Emphasis on the Messianic Hope*. Religious Supply, Inc., 1992.

Hamilton, Mark W. "Daniel," in *The Transforming Word*, (Editors: Hamilton, Mark W., Cukrowski, Kenneth L., Shankle, Nancy W., Thompson, James, and Willis, John T.). Abilene: Abilene Christian University Press, 2009.

Josephus, Falvius. *Against Apion*, Book II, Paragraph 8. (available on the Internet at http://www.ccel.org/j/josephus/works/apion-2.htm).

Josephus, Falvius. *Wars*, Book II, ch XIX, section 6, 7. (available on the Internet at http://www.ccel.org/j/josephus/works/apion-2.htm)

Irenaeus of Lyons. "Irenæus against Heresies," in A. Roberts, J. Donaldson & A. C. Coxe (Eds.), *The Ante-Nicene Fathers, Volume I: The Apostolic Fathers with Justin Martyr and Irenaeus* (A. Roberts, J. Donaldson & A. C. Coxe, Ed.). Buffalo, NY: Christian Literature Company, 1885. (The many books in this set are available at the Internet Archive at http://archive.org/details/texts.)

Levertoff, Paul. "Synagogue," in *The International Standard Bible Encyclopaedia*, Volume IV (James Orr, John L Nuelsen, Edgar Y. Mullins, Morris O. Evans, Melvin Grove Kyle, editors). Grand Rapids, Michigan: WM. B. Eerdmans Publishing CO., 1939, 1956. (All volumes of *The International Standard Bible Encyclopaedia* with James Orr as chief editor are available at the Internet Archives at http://archive.org/details/texts.)

Lewis, Jack P. *The Living Word Commentary: The Gospel According to Matthew, Part I*. Abilene: ACU Press, 1976.

Lewis, Jack P. *The Living Word Commentary: The Gospel According to Matthew, Part II*. Abilene: ACU Press, 1976, 1984.

Lightfoot, Neil R. *How We Got the Bible*, second edition. Grand Rapids, Michigan: Baker Book House, 1963, 1988.

Louw, J. P., & Nida, E. A., *Vol. 1: Greek-English lexicon of the New Testament: Based on semantic domains* (electronic ed. of the 2nd edition). New York: United Bible Societies, 1996.

Miller, Fred P. *The Translation of the Great Isaiah Scroll*, © 2001, accessed 28 October 2013, http://www.ao.net/~fmoeller/qa-tran.htm#c6

Miller, James. "Music," in *The International Standard Bible Encyclopaedia* (Editors; James Orr, John L. Nuelsen, Edgar Y. Mullins, Morris O. Evans, Melvin Grove Kyle), Volume III. Grand Rapids: WM. B. Eerdmands Publishing Company, 1939, 1956. (All volumes of *The International Standard Bible Encyclopaedia* with James Orr as chief editor are available at the Internet Archives at http://archive.org/details/texts.)

Mohler, R. Albert. "Air Conditioning Hell: How Liberalism Happens." In *IX Marks Ministries eJournal* (January/February 2010). (can be read online at http://www.albertmohler.com/2010/01/26/air-conditioning-hell-how-liberalism-happens/).

Monks at Decani Monastery in Kosovo. *The Doctrine of the Orthodox Church: Worship & Sacraments*, http://orthodoxinfo.com/general/doctrine3.aspx.

Pamphilus, Eusebius. *Ecclesiastical History*, Book III, Chapter V. Grand Rapids, MI: Baker Book House.

Oster, Richard. *The Acts of the Apostles Part II 13:1-28:31*, in *The Living Word Commentary*, Everett Ferguson, editor. Abilene, TX: ACU Press, 1979, 1984.

Porter, H. "Gentiles," in *The International Standard Bible Encyclopaedia*, Volume II (James Orr, John L Nuelsen, Edgar Y. Mullins, Morris O. Evans, Melvin Grove Kyle, editors). Grand Rapids, Michigan: WM. B. Eerdmans Publishing CO., 1939, 1956.

Rydelnik, Michael, *The Messianic Hope: Is the Hebrew Bible Really Messianic?* B&H Publishing Group, 2010. (This is an excellent book by a Jewish Christian scholar whose primary thesis is that the Hebrew Scriptures are themselves messianic in nature.)

Sampey, John Richard. "Book of Psalms," in *The International Standard Bible Encyclopaedia* (Editors: James Orr, John L. Nuelsen, Edgar Y. Mullins, Morris O. Evans, Melvin Grove Kyle), Volume IV. Grand Rapids: WM. B. Eerdmands Publishing Company, 1939, 1956. (All volumes of *The International Standard Bible Encyclopaedia* with James

Orr as chief editor are available at the Internet Archives at http://archive.org/details/texts.)

Schaff, Philip. *History of the Christian Church, Volume 3.* Peabody: Hendrickson Publishers, Inc., 1867. (All of the volumes of Schaff's *History of the Christian Church* as well as many of his other books are available at the Internet Archive and can be viewed without charge at http://archive.org/details/texts. In additional, his *History of the Christian Church* is still in print.)

Schwartzkopff, Paul. *The Prophecies of Jesus Christ Relating to His Death, Resurrection, and Second Coming, and Their Fulfilment*, (translated by Neil Buchanan). Edinburgh: T. & T. Clark, 1897. (This book is available at the Internet Archive and can be viewed free of charge at http://archive.org/details/propheciesofjesu00schwuoft. (This book was written by a liberal German theologian who thought Jesus was not divine and rather imperfect and flawed in His thoughts and reasonings.)

Shelly, Rubel. *A Book-By-Book Study of the Old Testament.* Nashville: 20th Century Christian Foundation, 1982. (This book is an excellent resource, but is out of print and ridiculously expensive now.)

Smith, William Taylor. "Number,"in *The International Standard Bible Encyclopaedia*, Volume III (James Orr, John L Nuelsen, Edgar Y. Mullins, Morris O. Evans, Melvin Grove Kyle, editors). Grand Rapids, Michigan: WM. B. Eerdmans Publishing CO., 1939, 1956.

Stevens, William Arnold and Burton, Ernest De Witt. *A Harmony of the Gospels for Historical Study.* New York: Charles Scribner's Sons, 1932. (This book is available as a free EPUB e-book download from Barnes and Noble. It is also available at the Internet Archive at http://archive.org/details/aharmonygospels03burtgoog.)

Swanson, James A. *Dictionary of Biblical Languages with Semantic Domains: Hebrew (Old Testament)* (electronic ed.). Oak Harbor: Logos Research Systems, Inc., 1997.

Thackeray, H. St. J. "Septuagint," in James Orr, John L. Nuelsen, Edgar Y. Mullins, Morris O. Evans, and Melvin Grove Kyle (editors), *The International Standard Bible Encyclopaedia, Volume IV.* Grand Rapids, Mich.: Wm. B. Eerdmans Publishing Co., 1939, 1956.

The Dead Sea Scrolls Bible: The Oldest Known Bible Translated for the First Time into English. Translated by and with Commentary by Martin Abegg, Jr., Peter Flint, and Eugene Ulrich. HarperCollins, 1999 (paperback) and 2012 (e-book).

The Digital Dead Sea Scrolls, Great Isaiah Scroll, http://dss.collections.imj.org.il/chapters_pg, © The Israel Museum, Jerusalem, 1995-2012.

Vadney, Victor. *The Arrogant Journey: Hermeneutics and Church History.* Abilene, Texas: Desert Willow Publishing, 2012. (For more information, see http://www.desertwillowpublishingonline.com.)

Vadney, Victor. *God's Covenants and Restorations.* Abilene: Desert Willow Publishing, 2011. (For more information, see http://www.desertwillowpublishingonline.com.)

Vine, W. E. *An Expository Dictionary of New Testament Word with their Precise Meanings for English Readers*, Volume III (Old Tappan: Fleming H. Revell Company), 56. (This can be accessed at http://www2.mf.no/bibel/vines.html.)

Willis, John T. "Old Testament Prophecy," in *The Transforming Word* (Editors: Hamilton, Mark W., Cukrowski, Kenneth L., Shankle, Nancy W., Thompson, James, and Willis, John T.). Abilene: Abilene Christian University Press, 2009. (This is a one-volume commentary on the entire Bible. Dr. Willis denied that any Old Testament Prophecy was fulfilled in Jesus or the church.)

Willis, John T. *Living Word Commentary: Isaiah.* Austin: Sweet Publishing Company, 1980. (At the time of this writing, Dr. Willis freely admitted that the messianic prophecy of Isaiah 52:13-52:13 could be fulfilled only by Jesus Christ [pp. 417-427]. However, it was clear also that he had serious concerns about other messianic prophecies.)

Index of Biblical Passages

OLD TESTAMENT

Genesis
1:1	34
1:1-2	33
2:24	34, 35
3:15	35, 36, 37
3:22	128
4:4	66
8:20-21	66
12:3	37, 175
12:7-8	66
13:4	66
13:14-18	175
15:4	175
15:7	175
15:18	175
17:6-8	175
17:18-21	175
18:17-18	175
20:6	48
22:5	66
22:9	66
22:18	37, 175
24:43	115
26:25	66
31:10-11	48
33:20	66
35:3	66
35:7	66
46:2	48
49:9-10	38, 39
49:24	135

Exodus
1:5	16
2:8	115
4:1-9	43
4:22	157
7:14ff	43
8:1ff	43
8:16ff	43
8:20ff	43
9:1ff	43
9:8ff	43
9:18ff	43
10:1ff	43
10:21ff	43
12:38	175
12:46	63
13:15-16	43
13:21-22	49
14:13ff	43
14:13-14	79
14:26-29	43
15:22ff	43
16:1ff	43
17:1ff	43
17:6	56, 57
17:15	66
20:24-26	66
21:24	46

(Exodus continued)
24:4-6 66
27:1-8 66
33:11 47
40:34ff 43

Leviticus
1 102
1:7 103
2 102
3 102
3:13 103
4:1-5:13 103
4:3 156
4:5 156
4:16 156
4:26 156
5:14-6:7 103
6:18 103
6:22 156
7:10 103
7:33 103
15:16 35
17:1-9 66
19:12 46
21:1 103
24:10 176
24:16 164
24:20 46

Numbers
9:12 63
11:4 176
11:17 130
11:25 130
12:1-8 .... 47, 48
12:3 80
16 42
21:4-9 57
24:2 130
24:17 .... 39, 40, 41
24:18 40
27:18 130

30:2 46
35:15 176

Deuteronomy
10:19 176
12:13-14 66
17:14-20 41
18:15 .... 41, 42, 50, 179
18:18 .... 41, 42, 50, 179
18:19 41
18:21-22 9
19:21 46
21:22-23 50
21:23 .... 50, 51
23:3-6 47
23:21 46
24:14-15 176
25:17-19 47
32:4 135
32:43 96
34:9-12 42
34:10 47

Judges
3:10 130
6:34 130
11:29 130
13:25 130
14:6 130
14:19 130
15:14 130

1 Samuel
1:3 66
1:9 67
2:10 156
2:35 156
4:3 67
10:6 130
10:8 103
10:10 130
11:6 130
12:3-5 156

13:8-13	103
16:6	156
16:13	130
16:23	83
17:12	187
19:20	130
19:23	130
21:1-9	90
22:6-23	90
24:6	156
24:10	156
26:9	156
26:16	156
26:23	156

2 Samuel
1:14	156
1:16	156
6:12	67
6:13-15	102, 103
7	52
7:12-16	51, 107
7:14	157
7:16	173, 174
15	75
19:21	156
22:2-3	135
22:51	156
23:1	156
23:2	130

1 Kings
3:5	48
8:41	176
8:43	176
8:62	102, 103
9:25	102, 103
22:39	83

1 Chronicles
12:18	130
15:16	83
15:28	83
16	67
16:22	156
16:42	83
17:4	67
21:18	67
22:1-19	67

2 Chronicles
3-4	67
6:32-33	176
6:42	156
9:17	83
15:1	130
20:14	130
24:20	130
26:16-21	103
29:25	83
34:12	83
36:22	69

Ezra
1:1-4	132
1:1-8	69
1:3	183
3:7	69
6:1-12	183
7:11-26	69, 183

Nehemiah
9:30	130
13:3	176

Job
2:1	157
33:15	48
38:1	48

Psalms
1-41	30
2	54, 157, 159
2:1-3	53
2:2	53, 156, 157
2:7	55, 157
2:8	54, 55

(Psalms continued)
2:12 157
8:1-2 .... 55, 97, 98
8:2 56
16:8-10 .... 57, 108
16:8-11 28
16:9 58
16:10 108
18:50 156
20:6 156
21:6 78
21(22):22 LXX 66
22 ...... 58, 59, 61, 62, 64, 119, 191
22:1 .... 59, 60
22:6-8 60
22:7 59
22:8 59
22:11-13 60
22:14 .... 62, 63
22:14-18 .... 61, 62
22:15 .... 59, 63
22:17 63
22:18 .... 59, 64
22:19-21 64
22:21 65
22:22 .... 59, 65, 66, 119
22:22-25 65
22:26 69
22:26-31 69
22:27-28 69
22:29 69
23 77
28:8 156
31:5 65
34:20 .... 63, 161, 191
35 .... 70, 74
35:19 .... 70, 88
40 73
40:6-8 71
40:7 73
40:12 73
40:14-15 74

41 75
41:9 75
42-72 30
45 .... 77, 88
45:1 .... 77, 87
45:2 78
45:2a 77
45:2b 78
45:3 78
45:4 .... 79, 80, 81
45:6 .... 82, 83
45:6-7 .... 76, 83
45:7 82
45:8 83
45:8b 84
45:9-15 85
45:10-11 86
45:16 87
45:17 87
68:25 116
69 .... 70, 74, 88, 99
69:1-21 93
69:4 .... 70, 88
69:9 .... 88, 89, 90
69:21 .... 63, 88, 91, 92
69:22-28 93
69:25 .... 88, 92, 93, 99
69:28 93
69:29 93
69:30-36 93
72:7 127
73-89 30
78 94
78:2 94
82 159
82:6 159
84:9 156
89:3-4 107
89:38 156
89:51 156
90-106 30
93-101 97

Index of Biblical Passages—Proverbs

97 .... 96, 97	6:1-7 109
97:7 96	6:5b 109
102 98	6:8-10 110
102:25-27 98	6:8-13 109
105:15 156	6:9-10 .... 95, 111, 112
107-150 30	6:10 154
109 .... 74, 99	7 113
109:1-31 47	7:10-16 112
109:8 .... 93, 99	7:14 .... 36, 112, 114, 115, 116
110 .... 19, 100, 101	8:6-8 114
110:1 .... 28, 100, 101	8:8 114
110:4 .... 46, 101, 103	8:10 114
118 .... 104, 105, 106	8:13 118
118:22 118	8:13-15 .... 117, 118
118:22-23 .... 104, 105, 106	8:14 117
118:26 106	8:16-18 .... 118, 119
132 107	8:17 119
132:10 156	8:18 119
132:11 .... 28, 107, 108	9:1-2 .... 120, 128
132:11-12 107	9:1-7 .... 119, 121
132:17 156	9:3-5 121
135:9 43	9:6 128
136:15 .... 43, 79	9:6-7 .... 121, 122
137:7-9 47	9:7 127
139:19-24 47	11 .... 129, 143
150 .... 83, 84	11:1 129
	11:2 130

Proverbs

30:19 116	11:2-5 .... 129, 130
	11:3 130

Ecclesiastes

5:4 46	11:4 .... 130, 131
	11:6-9 .... 127, 131
	11:10 .... 129, 131

Song of Solomon

1:3 116	11:11-16 .... 132, 133
6:8 116	13 134
	13:1 134
	13:10 .... 133, 134

Isaiah

2:2 87	13:19 134
2:4 127	20:3 141
6 109	22:20 141
6:1 56	24:23 133
6:1-3 .... 108, 109	28 135
	28:1-13 135

207

(Isaiah continued)
28:14-29 135
28:16 .... 118, 134, 135, 136
34 134
34:4 133
35 137
35:5 137
35:5-6 .... 136, 137, 138
36 113
36-37 121
37 113
37:35 142
39:1-4 132
40 139
40:3 139
40:3-5 .... 138, 139
41:8ff 142
41:21-26 10
41:28-29 141
42:1 .... 130, 141, 143, 144
42:2 143
42:1-4 140
42:1-7 .... 142, 144, 145
42:2 143
42:3 143
42:4 .... 143, 144
42:5-9 144
42:6 .... 145, 148
42:7 145
42:19-20 142
43:8-13 142
44:1-6 142
44:3 130
44:21-23 142
44:24-26 142
45:1 156
45:1-4 69
45:1-7 142
45:22 146
45:22-23 .... 146, 147
45:23 146
46:8-11 10

48:16 130
48:20 142
49:1-13 .... 142, 147
49:3 .... 145, 147
49:5 147
49:6 .... 147, 148
49:7 148
49:8 .... 145, 148
49:8-10 148
49:8-13 148
49:12 148
52:13 .... 149, 151
52:13-14 151
52:13-15 149
52:13-53:12 ....
    25, 142, 149, 150, 151, 171
52:14 164
52:15 152
53 .... 17, 149, 166
53:1 154
53:1-2 153
53:1-12 151
53:3 154
53:4 .... 154, 155
53:5 .. 73, 149, 160, 161, 164, 169
53:5-6 171
53:6 164
53:7 .... 165, 169
53:8 167
53:9 167
53:10 .... 149, 168, 169
53:11 .... 73, 170
53:12 171
54 173
54:2 173
54:5 173
54:11 173
54:13 .... 172, 173
54:15 173
55 173
55:3 173
56:6-8 .... 174, 175

56:7 .... 88, 177
59:21 130
61 137
61:1 .... 130, 136, 137
61:1-2 137

Jeremiah
25:9 142
27:6 142
30:10 142
31:31 145
31:31-34 .... 45, 177, 178, 179
33:21-22 142
33:26 142
43:10 142
46:27-28 142

Lamentations
4:20 156

Ezekiel
1:1 48
2:2 130
3:12 130
3:14 130
3:24 130
11:5 130
28:25 142
34:23-24 142
36:27 130
37:1 130
37:14 130
37:24 142
37:25 142
39:29 130
47:21-23 176

Daniel
1:1-4:37 69
6:1-28 69
6:28 69
7 180
7:13 .... 161, 180

7:13-14 179
7:16 11
8:2 48
8:15-16 11
8:27 11
9:24 184
9:24-27 181
9:24-27 LXX 182
9:25 182
9:25-26 156
9:26-27 182
9:27 184
10:8 48
10:16 48

Hosea
11:1 185

Joel
2:28-29 130
2:28-32 28

Amos
3:15 83

Jonah
1:17 .... 27, 186

Micah
3:8 130
5:2 .... 22, 187, 188

Habakkuk
3:13 156

Haggai
2:5 130

Zechariah
1:19 11
7:12 130
8:22 88
9:1-10 189
9:9-10 .... 188, 189

Jesus Christ *Fulfills* Messianic Prophecies

(Zechariah continued)
12:10 ...... 130, 161, 189, 190, 191

Malachi
2:15 130
3:1 .... 139, 191, 192, 193
4:5 .... 192, 193
4:5-6 193

NEW TESTAMENT

Matthew
1:1 52
1:1-17 39
1:18-25 113
1:20 48
1:22-23 .... 35, 36
2:1-2 39
2:1-6 .... 22, 187
2:13-15 185
2:15 185
2:16 154
2:22-23 129
2:23 129
3:3 139
3:15 81
3:16-17 ..... 82, 126, 143, 147, 157
4:1-11 36
4:3 158
4:6 158
4:12-16 120
5:1-7:28 46
5:5 80
5:6 81
5:10 81
5:17 46
5:20 81
5:21-26 46
5:22 99
5:27-30 46
5:29 99
5:30 99
5:31-32 46
5:33-37 46
5:43-48 46
6:1f 81
6:9 126
8:14-17 155
8:22 183
8:29 158
9:27-31 145
10:37 87
11:2-3 137
11:2-6 137
11:4-6 137
11:5 145
11:7-15 191
11:29 80
12:15-21 141
12:22 145
12:38-42 .... 27, 186
13 95
13:3-9 95
13:10-17 .... 95, 111
13:18-23 95
13:24-30 95
13:31-32 95
13:33 95
13:34-35 .... 94, 95
13:36-43 95
13:44 95
13:45-46 95
13:47-50 95
14:13-21 69
15:21-28 148
15:30-31 145
15:32-38 69
17:5 95
17:9-13 192
20:30-34 145
21:1-5 .... 188, 189
21:12-13 175
21:14 145
21:15-16 56
21:16 57

210

Index of Biblical Passages—Mark

21:23 104
21:32 81
21:42 104
21:42-44 104
22:41-45 100
22:44 100
23:37-39 106
23:39 106
24:15-18 181
24:29 .... 133, 134
24:29-31 .... 179, 180
26:23 75
26:24 100
26:63 165
26:64 100
26:65-66 .... 163, 164
26:67 60
27:14 165
27:22-23 70
27:27-31 .... 151, 152, 163
27:32 62
27:34 92
27:35 152
27:38 167
27:39-44 .... 60, 61
27:41-44 154
27:46 59
27:48 92
27:54 158
27:57-61 .... 167, 168
28:18 147
28:19 .... 88, 148
28:20 45

Mark
1:1 158
1:2 191
1:2-3 139
1:10 143
3:11 158
4:12 111
6:33-44 69

7:24-30 148
8:1-10 69
8:22-25 145
8:38 124
9:7 95
9:11-13 192
10:45 77
10:46-52 145
11:15-18 .... 175, 177
12:10 105
12:36 100
13:24-25 133
13:24-27 180
13:25 .... 133, 134
14:61 165
14:62 .... 100, 125, 180
15:5 166
15:13-14 70
15:15 152
15:21 62
15:23 92
15:29-32 61
15:34 59
15:36 92
15:39 158
16:19 125

Luke
1:11 48
1:13-16 192
1:17 193
1:22 48
1:26-33 128
1:27 39
1:30-33 .... 174, 180
1:32 .... 52, 78, 157
1:32-33 40
1:35 157
1:69 52
1:75 81
1:76 191
2:10-14 127

211

(Luke continued)
2:51 81
3:1-6 139
3:4 139
3:21-22 82
3:22 143
3:38 157
4:17-21 137
4:28-30 154
4:41 158
6:46-49 124
7:18-23 137
7:21-22 145
7:27 191
8:10 111
9:12-17 69
9:26 124
9:35 96
13:25 134
13:31 154
13:35 106
14:26 87
14:27 82
16:13 87
18:35-43 145
19:38 107
19:45-46 175
20:17 105
20:42-43 100
21:20-24 .... 78, 181, 182
21:25-28 180
22:20 145
22:21 75
22:37 171
22:63-64 151
22:69 .... 78, 100, 125
22:70 158
23:9 166
23:11 60
23:21 70
23:26 62
23:33 152

23:35-37 61
23:36 92
23:46 65
24:25-27 21
24:27 25
24:44 25
24:44-49 21

John
1:1-4 56
1:1-5 .... 25, 26, 33, 125
1:11 154
1:12-13 157
1:14 .... 33, 77, 79, 125
1:16 77
1:17 .... 45, 79
1:23 139
1:29 169
1:29-34 .... 82, 158
1:32 143
1:35-36 169
1:41 156
1:45 21
1:49 158
2:1-11 44
2:13-16 177
2:13-17 .... 90, 193
2:17 90
3:13-14 57
3:18 158
3:25-30 85
4:25-26 156
4:34 48
5:19 .... 26, 56
5:21-23 26
5:25 158
5:30 48
5:39 21
5:46 .... 21, 24, 25
6:1-15 69
6:38 48
6:41-51 172

8:28	48
8:31-32	79
8:45	79
8:46	73
8:57-59	154
9:1-7	145
10:14-18	170
10:17-18	62, 63, 108
10:22-30	159
10:30	26, 48, 56, 126, 159
10:31-33	154
10:34	159
10:36	158
10:38	160
11:4	158
11:25-26	50
11:27	158
11:39-44	50
11:47-53	157
12:13	107
12:15	189
12:25-26	87
12:36b-43	153, 154
12:37-41	111
12:40-41	109
12:41	56, 109
12:47	126
13:18-19	75
14:6	45, 79
14:9	26
14:10	48, 56
14:28	26
14:30	73
15:4-10	127
15:20	45
15:22-25	70
16:12-15	26
16:13	26
16:13-14	45
17:11	48, 56, 126
17:22	48, 56, 126
17:22-23	159
19:1	152
19:6	70
19:7	155
19:8-9	166
19:15	70
19:17	62, 162
19:18	152
19:23-24	61, 64
19:28	63
19:28-30	92
19:30	65
19:31-37	160, 161, 190
19:36	63
19:39-40	83
20:28	125
20:31	158

Acts

1:3	36
1:15	111
1:15-20	93
1:20	93, 99
2	28, 58, 105
2:17-21	105
2:22-28	58
2:25-28	58, 105
2:29-31	107
2:30	52, 105, 108
2:31	28, 29, 58, 108
2:33	125
2:34	100
2:34-35	105
3:22	41
3:25	37
3:26	37
4:11	105
4:23-26	53
4:26	53
5:17-20	145
5:31	125
7:14	16
7:37	41

(Acts continued)
7:55-56 125
8:26-38 25
8:30-35 166
8:33 167
9:20 158
10:11 48
10:35 81
12:1-11 145
13 58
13:33 55
13:13ff 174
13:34 173
13:35 58
13:44-47 147
13:47 148
15:1-35 47
15:11 77
17:31 81
22:17 48
24:25 81

Romans
1:17 81
3:21 81
3:21-24 143
3:22 81
3:24 .... 45, 77
3:25 81
3:26 81
3:28-30 143
4:3 81
4:5 81
4:9 81
4:11 81
4:13 81
4:22 81
4:25 143
5:15 77
5:16 143
5:17 81
5:18 143

5:18-19 170
6:13 81
6:16 81
6:18 81
8:10 81
8:17 87
9:30 81
10:4 81
10:8-11 135
10:16-17 153
11:5 133
14:17 81
15:1-3 90
15:12 .... 38, 131
15:20-21 152

1 Corinthians
1:4 77
1:30 81
3:11 136
5:7 63
10:1-4 57
10:9 57
11:25 145
15:6 36

2 Corinthians
3:6 145
3:17-18 34
3:18 126
4:4 26
5:21 73
6:7 81
6:14 81
8:9 .... 77, 81
10:1 80

Galatians
1:6 77
3:6 81
3:8 143
3:10-14 50
3:20 126

5:5 81

Ephesians
1:6 78
1:7 45
1:21 82
2:8 78
2:13-18 127
2:20 136
3:4-7 152
4:24 81
5:2 143
5:9 81
5:22-33 28
5:25-32 86
5:31-32 34
6:17 79

Philippians
2:5-8 80
2:5-11 .... 125, 146
2:9-11 171
2:10 146
3:6 81

Colossians
1:14 45
1:15 26
3:1 78

2 Thessalonians
1:6-9 94
2:8 131

1 Timothy
6:11 81

2 Timothy
2:22 81
3:16 .... 11, 77, 81
3:16-17 11
4:8 81

Titus
2:13 125
3:7 77

Hebrews
1 .... 52, 96
1:5 .... 52, 55
1:5b 52
1:6 96
1:8-9 76
1:9 .... 81, 82
1:10-12 98
2:10-13 119
2:12 .... 65, 66, 119
2:12-13 119
2:13 119
2:14-15 37
2:15 50
3:5-6 177
4:12 79
4:15 73
5:5 55
5:6 .... 46, 101
5:10 46
6:20 46
7:11 46
7:12 .... 46, 102, 103
7:14 38
7:17 .... 46, 101
7:21 101
7:25 102
7:26 73
8:1 78
8:7-8 145
8:7-12 178
8:13 145
9:12 .... 45, 143
9:15 145
9:28 .... 73, 162
10:1-10 72
10:12-13 100
11:7 81

(Hebrews continued)
11:26 57
11:33 81
12:2 78
12:11 81
12:24 145
12:28-29 180

James
1:20 81
2:19 126
2:22-23 81

1 Peter
1:10 78
1:10-12 .... 11, 24
2:4-8 .... 117, 118
2:7 105
2:9 46
2:21-25 .... 165, 168
2:22 73
2:24 .... 45, 59, 73, 81, 143, 162
3:14 81

2 Peter
1:1 81
1:19 40
1:20-21 11
2:5 81
2:21 81
3:7 134
3:10 134
3:13 81

1 John
2:29 81
3:5 73
3:7 81
3:10 81
4:8 175
4:16 175

Revelation
1:4-7 161
1:6 46
1:7 180
1:13 180
1:16 79
2:16 .... 79, 131
3:7 52
5:4-5 38
5:8 84
5:10 46
6:15-17 126
11:15 180
12:12 37
14:2-3 84
15:2 84
17:14 .... 40, 82, 105
19:7-9 86
19:11 81
19:15 .... 79, 131
19:16 .... 40, 82, 105
20:6 46
21:2 86
21:9-10 86
22:1 78
22:3 78
22:11 81
22:16 .... 38, 40
22:17 86

www.ingramcontent.com/pod-product-compliance
Lightning Source LLC
LaVergne TN
LVHW051048080426
835508LV00019B/1773